Hard as Nails!

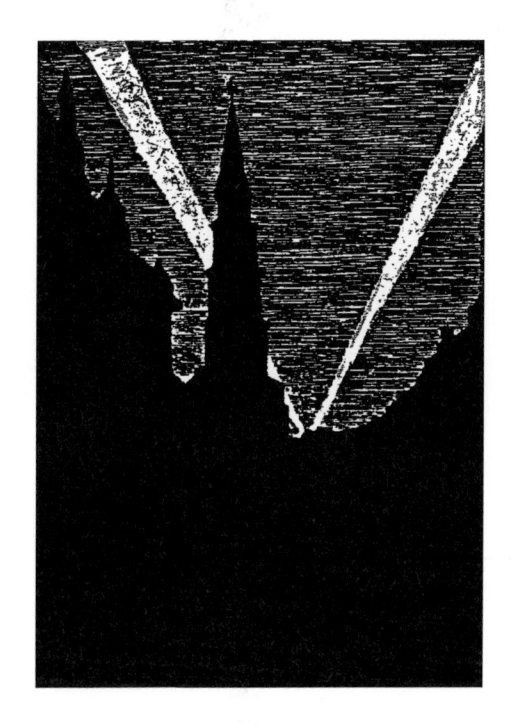

**THE HOME GUARD
IN FALKIRK DISTRICT**

Hard as Nails!

THE HOME GUARD
IN FALKIRK DISTRICT

Geoff B Bailey

FALKIRK LOCAL HISTORY SOCIETY

Hard as Nails! published 2008 by

Falkirk Local History Society
11 Neilson Street,
Falkirk,
FK1 5AQ

©Geoff B Bailey 2008

The Society is very grateful to Falkirk Council for financial support from the Falkirk Common Good Fund and also to Andrew Bain for his generous contribution to the production costs.

All rights reserved. No part of this publication may be reproduced, or transmitted in any form, without the permission of Falkirk Local History Society. Contact via the society website www.falkirklocalhistorysocety.co.uk

ISBN 978 0 9560480 0 4

The cover photograph is of the ICI Home Guard in the grounds of Kerse House in June 1941.

Cover Design by James Hutcheson

Printed and bound in Scotland by Bell & Bain Limited

Contents

PREFACE

1.	*Introduction*	1
2.	*First Steps*	27
3.	*Weapons*	57
4.	*On Guard*	89
5.	*More Weapons*	129
6.	*Training and Exercise*	167
7.	*Defence in Deapth*	195
8.	*The End*	233
APPENDIX 1	*Structure of Local Units*	241
APPENDIX 2	*Home Guard Platoons*	253
APPENDIX 3	*Exercise Reports*	275
APPENDIX 4	*Social Events*	283
Index		291
Abbreviations		295

Preface

There were many unsung heroes in the Falkirk district in the Second World War. The men and women who left their communities to serve in the armed forces, the workers on 12-hour shifts in the local industries, the farmers producing extra food under difficult conditions and the parents dealing with rationing to name just a few. Yet, it is a group of people who fulfilled these roles and then gave freely of their 'spare' time to defend their homes throughout the Falkirk district that are seen to epitomise the spirit of the country. Everyone has heard of the Home Guard.

From Castlecary in the west to Bo'ness in the east, and from Airth in the north to Slamannan in the south, they came forth in good measure at Britain's most desperate hour to lay their lives on the line. Like the Bo'ness man who said his last goodbye to his young son as he left the house to face the ruthless and efficient invader that he believed was at his door. These men stood shoulder to shoulder with their friends and family. At first they were ill-equipped and knives tied to broom handles actually appeared in Bonnybridge, which failed even to impress the small boys there. Nor did they have any preparation and the regular army was too busy to help. The one thing they had in abundance was enthusiasm and this brought with it hope, made tangible by improvisation. In 1940 they watched and waited for an enemy that was expected with the next tide. In 1941 they equipped and waited as Britain was defeated almost everywhere. In 1942 they trained and waited as the German war machine was halted in its tracks. They waited in 1943, gaining in experience and improving tactics. For four and a half years they prepared and the enemy never came.

The situation in each part of Britain was unique and the Home Guard reflected this. Platoons arose spontaneously from the communities, so that even small villages such as Avonbridge had its own unit. Often these settlements were close together, as at Shieldhill and California, resulting in great rivalry. The story of a machine gun being delivered to one section and the ammunition for it to the other – not to be united until the invasion occurred – is worthy of the writers of Dad's Army. It is such tales that bring the story of the Home Guard in the Falkirk area to life and I would like to thank the guardsmen and their relatives who have generously shared them with me so that they can be passed on to you. These people are too numerous to list here, but they appear throughout the text. Their names are preserved in these pages as a tribute to their contribution to our present day liberties. Unfortunately, several have died since I had the opportunity to meet them. This is true also of my friend Andrew Arthur, who kindly encouraged this work at its beginning. Andrew left school and worked at the Dock Pit in Bo'ness during the war. He worked alongside the men who formed the core of the Home Guard there and even then appreciated how great an effort it required. He knew that they were made of stern stuff – "hard as nails", he said. Hard they were, but it is their humour and comradeship that shines through the decades since the war.

Another Andrew, Andrew Bain, discovered that this book was being considered and provided the necessary stimulus to complete it. His helpful suggestions have been incorporated and the present format has resulted.

This book is a history, both social and event-based, of the Home Guard in the Falkirk district. It is not a general account of the Home Guard in Britain and it is the detail of the area that makes it a unique study. A history of the airfield at Grangemouth has already been published by Airfield Focus and a third book on the war in the area is under preparation. It will examine the maritime contribution of the area and so will concentrate on Grangemouth and Bo'ness. These later volumes are to be published by the Falkirk Local History Society to who great credit is due. Having already produced over twenty journals of authoritative research, that now form the prime source of the area's history, the Society is to be commended on its achievements. I would particularly like to thank Ian Scott for the hard work and time that he has put into these publications. His passion for the history of the area is our good fortune, as is that of the Grangemouth Heritage Trust, which has, once again, generously provided photographs and encouragement. The area is well served by these two voluntary bodies.

Above all I would like to thank the people of the Falkirk district who have taken me into their homes and plied me with tea and stories. This book is dedicated to that wartime generation.

Geoff Bailey
September 2008.

CHAPTER ONE

Introduction

Formation

On the afternoon of Tuesday 14th May 1940 the following telegram was received at the headquarters of the Stirling County Constabulary from the Secretary of State:

> Broadcast will be made at 9.10 pm today inviting male British subjects between 17 and 65 to register for Local Defence Volunteers Corps against enemy landings by parachute or otherwise. Registration will be at any Police Station. Circular follows. In meantime, please ensure forthwith that all stations are prepared to receive registrations.

The hurried nature of the appeal was readily apparent by the short notice and lack of practical detail. In the event, not all of the police offices in Stirlingshire and West Lothian were notified before the broadcast and many of the police were unaware of the urgency of the project. The main police stations in Falkirk and Bo'ness were, naturally, amongst the first to be handed the information and were told to take the name of each individual with their address, age, whether familiar with firearms, present occupation, any previous military experience and whether they were prepared to serve away from home (though this last was thought to be rather academic). At Falkirk the police duly commenced the process of making up forms that could be filled in as the volunteers trickled in the next day. At this stage it was far from clear who would use the information on this register, though the police had been told that they would not be concerned with the running or administration of the new force.

Anthony Eden made his Tuesday night broadcast as scheduled:

> I want to speak to you tonight about the form of warfare which the Germans have been deploying so extensively against Holland and Belgium – namely the dropping of troops by parachute behind the main defensive lines. Let me say at once that the

danger to us from this particular menace, although it undoubtedly exists, should not be exaggerated. We have made preparations to meet it already.

Let me describe to you the system under which these parachute raids are carried out. The troops arrive by aeroplane – but let it be remembered that any such aeroplane seeking to penetrate here would have to do so in the teeth of the anti-aircraft defences of this country. If such penetration is effected, the parachutists are then dropped, it may be by day, it may be by night. These troops are specially armed, equipped and some of them have undergone specialised training. Their function is to seize important points, such as aerodromes, power stations, villages, railway junctions, and telephone exchanges, either for the purpose of destroying them at once, or of holding them until the arrival of reinforcements. The purpose of the parachute attack is to disorganise and confuse, as a preparation for the landing of troops by aircraft.

The success of such an attack depends on speed. Consequently, the measures to defeat such an attack must be prompt and rapid. It is upon this basis that our plans have been laid. You will not expect me to tell you, or the enemy, what our plans are, but we are confident that they will be effective. However, in order to leave nothing to chance and to supplement, from sources as yet untapped, the means of defence already arranged, we are going to ask you to help us, in a manner which I know will be welcome to thousands of you. Since the war began the Government have received countless inquiries from all over the Kingdom from men of all ages who are for one reason or another not at present engaged in military service, and who wish to do something for the defence of the country.

Now is your opportunity. We want large numbers of such men in Great Britain who are British subjects, between the ages of 17 and 65 to come forward now and offer their service in order to make assurance doubly sure. The name of the new force which is now to be raised will be the "Local Defence Volunteers". This name, Local Defence Volunteers, describes its duties in three words. It must be understood that this is, so to speak, a spare-time job, so there will be no need for any volunteer to abandon his present occupation.

Part-time members of existing civil defence organisations should ask their officers' advice before registering under the scheme. Men who ultimately become due for calling up under the National Service (Armed Forces) Act may join temporarily, and will be released to join the Army when they are required to serve. Now, a word to those who propose to volunteer. When on duty you will form part of the Armed Forces, and your period of service will be for the duration of the war. You will not be paid, but you will receive uniform and will be armed. You will be entrusted with certain vital duties, for which reasonable fitness and a knowledge of firearms are necessary. These duties will not require you to live away from your homes. In order to volunteer, what you have to do is to give in your name at your local police station; and then, as and when we want you, we will let you know.

Introduction

Within a matter of a few minutes men began to appear at Falkirk Police Station on the corner of West Bridge Street and Hope Street and their names were duly noted. At Bo'ness the arrival of volunteers at that late hour took the police by surprise and scraps of paper had to be used to improvise a register. The men who came forward so eagerly knew that they were making history and their spirits were not dampened when they were told that they would be contacted in due course. Most of the enthusiasts who had heard the speech did wait until the next day and called into the various police offices on their way to or from work. By Wednesday evening the Falkirk police office had 60 names of intending recruits. Two days later the number was up to 200, with applications still coming in. In the Denny area over 100 men enrolled in this period. Many of these had already volunteered their services to the Stirling and Clackmannan Joint ARP Authority, but felt that, with the worsening news coming from continental Europe, the need of the new volunteer army was far greater and more important. The ARP Authority requested that they should reconsider, as the prelude to any invasion would be bombing raids, which a depleted organisation would find it hard to cope with. The number of enlistments for the Local Defence Volunteers (henceforth referred to as the LDV) at Stenhousemuir Police Station was over 130 and the local newspaper correspondent wryly noted: "Yes, it's gone – that home front complacency".

Falkirk Police Station

The men turning up at the police stations came from every section of the community and from all ages up to, and beyond, the limit of 65 years. Richard Burns of Grove Street in Denny had served with the Royal Scots on the Indian frontier, the Boer War and in the First World War. A fervent member of the British Legion he answered the call for the LDV at the age of 72 years. Volunteer George Knight at Bo'ness was also 72 years old. He was a retired whale fisher and skipper and wanted to round his career off by having a shot at the Germans. Captain A W Steven, the first commander of 'D' Company that covered

Polmont, was only a few years younger. The men included accountants, clerks, clergymen, engineers, farmers, joiners, moulders, ploughmen, roadmen, shop salesmen and so on. The majority were relatively fit and over fifty years of age.

On Wednesday 15th May the British Legion in Denny held an impromptu meeting at which it was decided to throw the full weight of that branch behind the scheme locally. The Branch then arranged for another meeting on Sunday 26th May in the Drill Hall and this news was widely circulated. On that occasion the hall was crowded and John Paterson took the chair. Col. Connell Rowan of Kippen detailed the duties of the LDV, in so far as he knew them, and ex-Provost W Shanks spoke with pride about the need to defend their country. All agreed to set up a Denny corps of the LDV – but more details of the scheme were still needed.

Similar meetings were held throughout the Falkirk district. The following night, for example, Col. Alan Stein presided at an evening gathering in the Brightons Masonic Hall, when a substantial number of men enrolled. In Larbert the running was made by the portly parish minister, Rev J J S Thomson; and in Falkirk first by Major Alexander Anderson and then by John Farrell. The latter was the headmaster of the St Francis Roman Catholic School in Silver Row. Before long it was agreed from above that he would command the LDV platoon whose area embraced Falkirk, Glen Village, Shieldhill and Slamannan.

In the village of Slamannan word had been passed around that there would be a meeting in the Miners' Welfare Institute in Avonbridge Road. There was a good attendance, particularly by the coal miners. A considerable amount of debate and discussion followed. All present were keen for Slamannan to have its own LDV unit and it was decided there and then to elect its leaders – as yet there was no thought of officers in a voluntary body. The organiser and nominal head was George Ewen, the branch manager of the bank. His profession provided him not only with the requisite social status, but also with the unit's first firearm. The village bank had been robbed just a few years before and he had been provided with a shotgun and trained in its use to defend the safe, should occasion arise. He was also a single man with time to dedicate

Rev. J. J. Thomson of Larbert Parish Church.

Introduction 5

Boy Scouts at St Francis RC School in Meeks Road. 16th May 1943. Major Farrel is in his HG uniform. Back row: ——, Boyd, Bob Hawkins, ——, ——, Boyd, Jim Reilly, Watson, Benny Tortolano, Jimmy McKenna, ——, Dennis Hawkins. Centre row: ——, ——, Jim Moffat, Arthur Reep, John Duffy, John Finn, ——. Front row: Robertson, Dick Fyvie, Kenny Conlan, Alf Buchanan, Canon Welsh, John Farrell, Ronnie Clyde, ——, McLellan. Sitting: Jim Martin, Jim MacKenna, Peter Conlan, Bobby Robertson, McGuire.

to the administrative task of setting up the unit, and to cap it all he had a motor bike to lay at its disposal. The bike, it was agreed, would be used to rouse the volunteers in an emergency. Ewen was, however, an outsider, and for practical day to day purposes the man in charge was Tam Menzies, whose father ran a bakery in the village. Tam was then aged 28 years and had gone to the meeting with his younger brother, William, simply to find out what was happening. He had received a formal education, and in those days that made him a leader. When asked, years later, why the meeting had chosen him, Tam smiled and asked, "Why, don't you think I was good enough?" On a more reflective note he then added, "Because I had a car." Tam then appointed two of his close and capable friends, Rudy Kerr and Wilf Berwick, both miners, as assistants (later to be called corporals, Tam himself being a sergeant). The platoon headquarters at Falkirk was duly informed, John Farrell came out in his car and checked them out, and the Slamannan LDV was adopted.

One of the men at that inaugural meeting in Slamannan was Will Fyfe, the school janitor. He had fought in the Boer War. There were also a number of veterans of the First World War and such men formed the greatest proportion of the volunteers throughout the Falkirk district. They were keen to serve again in this desperate hour and the chance to do so released the pent up feeling of exasperation that they had experienced as they saw the German army striding across the map of Holland and Belgium into France. Indeed, the Government was actively encouraging this category of men to sign up and it was they that were the first to be approached when the registers were examined. As well as their enthusiasm they brought with them two invaluable assets – a knowledge of drill and musketry, and a strong bond of comradeship developed more than 20 years before in the trenches. They acted as a steadying influence on the younger men. When one veteran in Camelon signed up for the LDV his wife asked if had not already done enough for his country. He unhesitatingly replied that it was his duty to help on this occasion too.

The Slamannan Miners' Welfare Hall (left) was recently converted to housing.

Many of the major manufacturing businesses in the Falkirk district were run by local families with military experience as officers in HM Forces. Some felt compelled to establish, promote and aid independent LDV units to protect these vital industries – vital to the country as well as to themselves. Alan Stein was in many ways typical of these. He was born in Bonnybridge in 1888, joined the 4th (VB) Argyll and Sutherland Highlanders (henceforth referred to as A and SH) in 1906 and was gazetted second lieutenant in 1907 when the unit was amalgamated with another to form the 7th Battalion. In the First World War he served in France and was awarded the Military Cross. He was wounded three times and was mentioned in dispatches. On the reformation of the Territorial Army in 1920 he was appointed to command the 7th Battalion and became a colonel in the TA Reserve of officers. He succeeded his father as managing director of the family brick company in 1927 and was responsible for the creation of a new works at Manuel. As we have seen he was instrumental in the establishment of an LDV unit at Brightons and with an assistant from the

Introduction

Rudy Kerr of the Slamannan HG in his greatcoat. On the left he has just removed his L/Cpl stripe, and on the right replaced it with his two stripes of a corporal. Rudy, a coal miner, worked his way up through the ranks and eventually took charge of the platoon.

regular army he actively encouraged others at Bonnybridge. He also set up LDV units at both his brickworks – Castlecary and Manuel.

Later Stein became the commanding officer of the 2nd Stg HG Bn. Jimmy Rogers was the engineer foreman at Manuel, and was put in charge of the LDV there. "I found Col. Stein to be a different person altogether from what he was at work. Later on when the urgency for the Home Guard was not so urgent, when I was attending officers' meetings and listening to Col. Stein telling us all to be sure to attend on a special exercise next Sunday, he would also make a point of telling me later in the works to make it clear to the men that work came first.

For some time Col. Stein lent his car and chauffeur to the LDV to take ex-sergeant-majors around the platoons of D Coy, but all they did was to instruct the men on foot drill and later on arms drill, so different from what we were taught at the officers' meetings on the function of the HG. When Col. Stein stopped lending his car and chauffeur the sergeant-majors stopped coming too and some men withdrew from the Home Guard."

The clergy were very much to the fore of the movement to defend the homeland. They gave encouraging speeches and welcomed the LDV into their churches on parade days. Some took an active lead and became officers. The most senior of these was Rev John J S Thomson of Larbert Old Parish Church, who became the East Stirlingshire battalion's first commanding officer with the rank of Lt-Col. Lt. Gavin Boyd, the battalion's guide, was the minister of Larbert West Church, before leaving in January 1943 for HM Forces. In Falkirk Rev John A F Dean of the Erskine Church was a platoon commander in F Company, but was forced to retire due to his age – he was over 65. He was then able to continue his involvement with the volunteers by becoming the battalion's honorary chaplain. A few ministers were content to serve inconspicuously in the ranks, such as Rev. Neil McLean of Laurieston Parish Church. Scoutmasters too were prominent from the start. Major David Tough was the local butcher in Larbert's Main Street and a District Commissioner in the Scouts; he was important in establishing the battalion, serving as its second-in-command for a short time. His Scout hall at Larbert Cross was used as a temporary HQ, until the parish church hall became available. Dan Niven, a member of the Torwood Scouts, remembered many a night watch at the Barrwood in 1940, from which vantage point he was to spot enemy parachutists. Had they landed he was ready for them – armed with a stout staff!

Despite Anthony Eden's stipulation of age parameters for the volunteers, in the Falkirk area it was felt that anyone could serve the country at such a desperate and critical time and many men in their late sixties and seventies were accepted. It was generally around two years before they were weeded out. Similarly many under age boys tried to enlist in the ranks of the LDV. One of these was William Sharp from Smith Street in Bainsford. The nearest unit to his home met at the Falkirk Ironworks, but when its organisers learnt that he was only 16 years old, they told him to wait a year and then get back to them – the war would not be over. LDV units at Carron, Grahamston and Carronshore said much the same. William was desperate to do his bit and, after trying several other platoons he arrived at the Falkirk Burgh Stables in Station Road. Here he was asked if he was fit and answered to the affirmative. Then he was asked if he was of age, to which he replied in the like manner and was welcomed to the unit.

In the first week of June 1940 a young John Grierson was working in Falkirk High Street when he saw several dirty, dishevelled and exhausted men in the remnants of their uniforms walking up from Grahamston Station. Their eyeballs were prominent from lack of sleep and there was a look of terror on their faces. At the time the public had not heard of Dunkirk – but word soon spread. For those who saw the appearance of those utterly defeated soldiers, it, more than anything else, acted as a wake-up call. The following March, at the age of 17 years, John joined the Home Guard at Stenhousemuir.

When Rev J J S Thomson was appointed as the battalion commander for East Stirlingshire he was asked to raise 160 men, but had little trouble in enlisting 4,000 in just three weeks. Whilst the structure of the fledgling LDV was being evolved and imposed from above, the rush of enthusiasm continued the momentum from below. Whilst Lord Charles Hope, brother of Lord Linlithgow, the Viceroy of India, was agreeing to act as commanding officer of the West Lothian corps of the LDV, the Bo'ness Branch of the British Legion had taken over local recruitment and the numbers in the town rose to over 200 by 23rd May. Within two weeks the men at Bo'ness and throughout the Falkirk district were mounting guard duty throughout the hours of darkness – the dusk till dawn watch for which the Home Guard became so famous – watching and listening for any paratroops or any sign of an invasion using the cover of the night.

The main problem was always going to be the supply of equipment. The British Expeditionary Force had left most of the regular army's equipment behind during the evacuation of France and the Dunkirk debacle. Obviously priority now had to be given to re-equipping those forces rather than the new volunteer army. In the light of this the role of the LDV was slowly modified to that of an intelligence agency. The LDVs were to gather information by observation and then, without engaging the enemy, to report it to the regular army so that it could deal with it. They were, for invasion purposes, the eyes and ears of the Army. The public soon landed them with the appellation of the LDV Brigade – where LDV stood for Look, Duck and Vanish!

One Falkirk volunteer upon signing up was told that he would be supplied with a uniform in due course. He replied, "Never mind the uniform – gimme a gun!" Improvisation was very much the order of the day. At Slamannan, Tam Menzies approached the plumber, John Mathews, to get some lengths of lead pipe that the volunteers could use as clubs. In the workshop he was shown a plumber's tool, known as a 'dummy 18-inch bandier', which was used like a drain rod in soil pipes. It consisted of a short length of cane with a knob of lead on one end and it was agreed that it would make a more practicable weapon. So a few dozen were made up for the Slamannan LDV to face up to the enemy. These were augmented by the village blacksmith, Jimmy Meek, who welded some steel blades onto shanks and then stuck them into wooden handles to form pikes. Home-made pikes were also created at Bonnybridge, though there the knives and other bladed implements were lashed onto the poles with string. Elsewhere pickaxe handles, without any attachments, were carried on guard duty.

On 1st June 1940 the police made an appeal through the pages of the *Falkirk Herald*: "Shot guns or arms of any description, with all available ammunition, should be handed in, with signatures and addresses to Superintendent Turpie at the Police Station; and in particular all motorcars or motor lorries that can be made available should be reported. This force must to be effective be mobile. Will those who have small camp beds please hand these into the Police Office at once." The following week the hundred LDV members at Bonnybridge made a similar bid for travelling rugs, blankets and so on for their night quarters, as well as for old field glasses, sporting guns and firearms.

Only a few guns were brought forward. Some were old revolvers, cherished souvenirs of the First World War retained by officers. Old sporting guns and shotguns appeared in very limited numbers. Before the war Alec Forrester had supplemented his electrician's pay with money earned from removing vermin from his place of work with a shotgun. Early in the war he had been sent to work in the Docks in Grangemouth, where vermin control meant the use of dogs and ferrets – the proximity of a large number of fuel tanks would have made the use of guns somewhat hazardous. So Alec handed his gun over to the

Arnotdale House (later Dollar Park Museum),

police and hence the LDV. Most of the people who used shotguns – gamekeepers, hunters and poachers – kept them in the knowledge that they were useful for supplementing the meagre meat rations. At Falkirk the burgh museum in Dollar Park was visited and the weapons from the First World War display were taken out on loan, including a machine gun (the latter a Lewis Gun presented along with two ammunition cases by the War Office in the 1920s – accession number L755).

The three LDV units that sprang up in Denny were not directly connected to any of the town's works. They were in part based upon the geographical parts of the area, which also reflected a sectarian divide. Even in war it took time for the local divisions between Catholics and Protestants to be broken down.

At the age of 16 years Peter Graeme joined the Denny LDV shortly after its formation. The unit had managed to get together some smooth-bore rifles and practised on home-made targets set up in the Drill Hall. Peter enjoyed this, especially as he proved to have a natural ability at the game. On one occasion he shot five holes in a group no larger than a halfpenny piece from a distance of 30yds. He rushed home to show his father, who was unimpressed and pointed out that there was more to soldiering than target shooting. Peter's father then produced a medal that he had won some years previously with the Lord Roberts Miniature Rifle Club. That club was still active in Falkirk and Larbert and its members enrolled en masse into LDV units in those two places, giving them a strong competitive lead in subsequent years when shooting matches were arranged.

After their induction on the miniature range the Denny volunteers were taken to the Torwood Estate, where Kit Hannah gave them instruction with a 12-bore shotgun. Instead of firing the usual small pellets in a cartridge, they made up their own solid lead shot. There was no mistaking when these hit the target, for even at 40-50yds they tore

Jimmy Retson and Sgt. Sneddon both lived in Brewster Place, Denny, and attended the HG together. Here they can be seen sporting P17 rifles behind their houses. Note leather belts and gaiters and the A and S. H. cap badge. c1943.

huge holes in them. John Hannah was the gamekeeper for Denovan Estate and the Estate loaned the LDV a clay pigeon throwing machine. Even after their initial training most of the would-be marksmen found it hard to hit these moving targets, with success rates usually in the low range of one or two out of ten. John himself was able to achieve around 50% hits, but his son usually got 100%. He was in danger of losing this record when he only winged one of the clay targets, but smashed it to pieces when he hit it a second time before it reached the ground.

Denny LDV was quick off the mark, and guns were still scarce. On 11th June 1940 George Stirling of Glorat, the Deputy Lord Lieutenant of the county, renewed the appeal through the newspapers: "There is now in the county of Stirling a well organised branch of the Local Defence Volunteer Corps, ready to give immediate warning to the military authorities in the event of enemy invasion of this country. There is, however, an urgent and immediate need of rifles, shot-guns, cartridges and field glasses, to supplement those supplied from army stores, so that every man of the corps may be in a position to defend himself and to do what he can to oppose and delay the enemy until the arrival of regular troops on the scene. I appeal therefore most earnestly to the good citizens to place at the disposal of the nearest Local Defence Volunteer Commander, on loan, as many of the above articles as they can collect, as quickly as possible. He will give a receipt and see that they are properly looked after and that they are returned when they are no longer required. GEORGE STIRLING, HM Lt, Glorat."

Peter Graham of the Denny HG. He is seen wearing a greatcoat in a studio at the age of 17 years. For the occasion he is not wearing his gaiters.

For a strength of 355 men one of the Falkirk companies recorded at this time that its arms consisted of "5 rifles, 4 0.22 rifles, a few shot guns, 2 boxes 'Rebellion Swords', a number of broken bottles (for close fighting) and a great deal of enthusiasm." Clearly they could not rely on donations and the need for a greater Government issue was dire. Behind the scenes the Government was frantically trying to plug the gap by acquiring stockpiles of weapons left over from the First World War and still in the possession of neutral countries.

Some of the members of the LDV knew that the effective range of a glass bottle could be extended. Three of the coal miners in the Bo'ness LDV had taken part in the Spanish Civil War as part of the International Brigade. They had learnt a thing or two about guerrilla warfare waged with minimal resources and insisted on preparing Molotov Cocktails. They promptly set about making them there and then, and storing them in the old Court Room, which was then being used as their HQ, saying that there would not be time to assemble them in the event of an invasion. Such crude missiles were rather volatile and prone to exploding spontaneously and eventually the commanding officer's nerves got the better of him and he insisted upon their removal. They were taken to the old sexton's shed in one corner of the abandoned cemetery at Corbiehall. The ready availability of flammable fuels at Grangemouth Refinery and at the oil shale works at Pumpherston made these weapons an early favourite throughout the area. For several months they were, in fact, the most effective weapon that the LDV possessed.

The war veterans could remember the days when they had all manner of fighting equipment, including light artillery pieces, and most fostered hopes of receiving such items. In Zetland Public Park, Grangemouth, the local boys watched incredulously as the volunteers split into groups of three. Each group had a short length of cast iron rain water pipe salvaged from derelict buildings. One end of the pipes was then planted firmly in the ground and the upper end supported by one man in each group, so that the whole lay at an angle. Beside them a small pile of empty baked bean and soup tins appeared and the second man in the group picked one up and placed it into the pipe. The third man then shouted "BOOM" and the whole exercise was repeated. It took the children some time to realise that the adults were pretending to fire mortars. The LDV could not afford to wait for the weapons to arrive, as Sgt-Major J Fraser of Falkirk pointed out: "It was now a race against time – would they get the recruits trained in time to put up a good fight?" There were few illusions in those early days as to what they might achieve. At best they would be little more than nuisance value to the invading army, but they were determined to be a big nuisance!

Rifles did begin to trickle through to the LDV, but priority had to be given to those on the front line in such places as the south coast of England or the east coast of Scotland. As early as 28th May 1940 a small number of .303 rifles

Zetland Park seen from Grange School in August 1946. Two years later the war memorial was modified to take the names of those who died in the Second World War.

was allocated to West Lothian with 50 rounds of ammunition per rifle. Most units only received their first consignment a month later. This created a functional vacuum during which the leaders on the ground had to find things for the men to do. The old soldier element, with experience of barrack square drill, immediately set about square bashing. Even using imitation rifles and improvised weapons such as pikes or pickaxe handles, the men on parade would learn important lessons in discipline, team cohesion and character. Any hard smooth surface was suitable for this activity and school playgrounds, car parks and tennis courts were all put to use.

During the first few weeks of the formation of the LDV the volunteers at Bo'ness met every evening so that the numerous miners on shift work got some opportunity to attend. The meetings were well attended and the accommodation in the old burgh Court Room and an adjoining room proved to be rather cramped. Drill practice in the open air helped to ease the overcrowding. Rina Argent lived opposite the old Drill Hall in Corbiehall and saw the Bo'ness men with their wooden rifles sloped over their shoulders being inspected by "Johnson the butcher", before being put through their paces. Quite a few of these men worked at the Dock Pit and had spent what time they could spare practising inside the pit's power station, which had a concrete floor, prior to allowing themselves to perform drill before the gaze of the public.

Introduction 15

Ian Arthur, then only a teenager, remembered the embarrassment of drill training on the tennis courts behind the Slamannan LDV's HQ in the Welfare Hall. The villagers, including many young children, leaned or sat on the roadside wall and looked down on the volunteers (in more than one sense) as they took their first stumbling steps. In Grangemouth the public watched the LDV carrying spear-like weapons around the grounds of the High School. Nor were the grounds of the Territorial Hall in Bonnybridge much more private. There, the volunteers, dressed in civvies and carrying broomsticks with knives lashed to them, failed to impress the young boys. Unfortunately, it is the image of this activity, with this primitive equipment, that is often seen to represent the Home Guard and which is recreated on television programmes.

Despite the apparent absurdity of their situation, the one thing that the LDV had in abundance was enthusiasm. Without a clearly defined remit they were game to try anything to preserve law and order and to deter fifth columnists – much to the annoyance of the police. An incident that illustrates the 'have a go' attitude occurred at Falkirk bus station on 20th July 1940. Valentine Flanagan, a soldier with the 12th HLI protecting the BBC transmitter at

Members of the Falkirk Local Defence Volunteers at musketry practice. The newspaper caption calls them 'parashots'. There is a range of rifles in use, with a Lee Enfield in the centre and a P14 on the left, July 1940.

Falkirk Bus Station from Callendar Road, 1936. Doak's dance hall is on the right

Westerglen, was about to go home on leave. He was in uniform and carrying his rifle, as all soldiers did at the time due to the threat of invasion. However, he had been drinking in the town before going for his bus and ended up in an altercation with four young men. James Campbell, a bus inspector, was on 'guard duty' there, it being an important node in the transport infrastructure. He was sporting an 'LDV' armband, but had no weapon. Without hesitating he went to investigate and as he arrived Valentine turned the gun on him. As a bus inspector Campbell would normally have backed away from this situation, but with the authority of the LDV behind him he demanded that the rifle be handed over. Valentine considered this to be provocative and removed the safety catch. Fortunately, an army officer sitting in one of the buses saw the situation. He got off the bus and approached Valentine from behind and took the rifle away. It was found to be loaded. Valentine served 30 days imprisonment.

As well as improvising its own equipment and training, each unit of the LDV adopted its own methodology, which was amended as circumstances dictated or new situations arose. For its first fortnight the Bo'ness LDV was lacking in arms, except for a shotgun or two and a few revolvers, but the volunteers nevertheless turned out for duty whenever the sirens sounded an air raid alert. For battle stations the three sections reported to the Walton, Kinneil and the golf course on Erngath Hill. Yet the point in a full turnout

Introduction

'A' Company, 3rd Stirlingshire Battalion Home Guard. Winners of Battalion Drill Competition 1941.
Front row: Bobby Storrie, —, Alexander Hay, —, —, Jimmy McArthur.
Middle row: Alex McDougal, Robert Sinclair (councillor), Jock Dyer, J Scott, Alexander Sawers, Wilson, Wilson   Back row: —, McCafferty, —, Jock Forsyth, —.

seemed somewhat obscure and, after one memorable night when the call came no fewer than three times, that duty was discontinued. The Slamannan LDV had likewise realised the futility in having all its members turn out in response to the sirens. Any large scale invasion force would be detected long before it reached them, and smaller forces were more likely to be observed by the Royal Observer Corps or the ARP. Instead, a number of men were on standby duty throughout the night at the Welfare Hall. Not all of the public realised that the change in tactics had occurred and on a few occasions the slumbering men of the LDV were rudely awakened by people banging on the hall door to let them know that there was an air raid alert on.

Perhaps it was to obscure the rather hectic and haphazard way in which the LDV had sprung into existence, or simply because Winston Churchill preferred a different name, but on 23rd July 1940 it was announced that from henceforth the force would be called the 'Home Guard' (HG). In any case, the new name was more to the liking of its members, and it is how most people remember it.

Physical Exercise

While they were waiting for their arms and equipment the volunteers resolved to keep fit by undertaking physical exercises. The most popular form, with its military associations, was the route march. At first these were only over short distances, often with rest breaks built in and it was not unknown for tea to be organised. In October 1940, for example, the Shieldhill HG under Sgt Tom Stannage marched from Shieldhill to Falkirk, where they were entertained to tea by the Falkirk HG before returning on foot. Two of the Bo'ness platoons made their first route march the following month, when a pipe band led them up to the golf course where the third platoon (No. 13) was demonstrating its exercises. A far larger contingent met in the Hope Street car park in Falkirk that December, consisting of the two Falkirk companies, led this time by a military band. The novelty soon wore off and the bands disappeared, but short cross-country marches continued.

Meanwhile the Grangemouth men had, from their inception and without any pomp, been meeting at the Town Clock in South Bridge Street after work. They would then march down Dalgrain to Skinflats, picking up the boatyard employees on the way. This short walk, three miles in all, or five if they went on to Carronshore, kept them ready for action. They also conducted the occasional night march. On one of these they crossed the River Carron by Larbert Viaduct, camped at midnight around a fire, heating their drinks in billy cans, and then walked home.

Each night in public parks throughout the district, such as Anderson Park in Bonnybridge or Gairdoch Park in Carronshore, the old men of the LDV could be seen performing physical exercises to improve their fitness. Simple exercises could be conducted in the meeting halls even in wet weather. The young miners in Slamannan were particularly proud of their agility and stamina and soon instigated a routine that included circuit training. This involved such things as five minutes running on the spot, followed by press-ups, followed by sit-ups and so on. Six year old Leonard Kerr, three of whose brothers were in the platoon, eagerly joined in, only to find that he needed a long rest between activities. One of the exercises involved taking a broom handle and placing one end on the floor then, keeping it firmly anchored, the men ran around it – the lower the angle they held it at, the further they ran and the less dizzy they got. Another exercise used a chair. The aim was to stand first on the wooden seat of the chair, then on the back and down again without tipping it over. All of these were then done in full equipment, when it arrived.

The uptake of sports was actively encouraged. Football was the most popular and platoons formed their own teams. At first they played other teams within their company, but as they became more organised the winning team would represent the company within the battalion. At battalion sports days the teams were reduced to five-a-side for convenience. Matches were also arranged against local works' teams and those of the regular forces, a few examples are given here:

Oct 1940	Bo'ness HG v RAF Leuchars at Newtown Park
June 1941	Slamannan HG v Avonbridge HG at Slamannan Glebe (2:2)
July 1942	Bo'ness HG v Civil Defence at Newtown Park
Aug 1942	Carronshore HG v Services XI at Gairdoch Park (3:5)
Oct 1942	Carronshore HG v Carron Works at Gairdoch Park

These matches were open to the public and provided some entertainment. Sports days were organised at company level, with annual battalion competitions, and these became big events attracting large crowds, particularly as there was a great deal of public participation. In August 1941, for example, 'A' Coy (Denny) held its elimination contest for the 2nd Stg HG Bn event in Carronbank Park and was able to raise £30 for the YMCA canteen in the town. The following week the company's chosen representatives competed at the battalion sports day in Ochilview Park, Stenhousemuir, the money this time going to the Red Cross. These meetings had the usual array of events, such as flat racing, high jump, putting, five-a-side football, and so on, but there were also some that were adapted to the needs of the HG. These included obstacle races, grenade throwing (duds only), tug-of-war, pillow fighting, drill, clay pigeon shooting and a despatch riders' race. In the latter two teams of five or so riders competed with each rider cycling one lap and then passing a verbal message of about 20 words to the next rider. Marks were given for speed and accuracy of the final reported message. Competition was keen and it was noted that in the 100yds race James Scott of 'D' Coy was only just beaten in the final, despite being over 40 years of age. A championship shield, presented by the officers of the battalion, was provided for the company returning the highest aggregate of points for the individual and team items. 'D' Coy (Grangemouth) were the winners on that first occasion and were presented with the shield by Lady Orr-Ewing. The following week it was proudly displayed in the window of a shop in Station Brae, the premises of AH Stanners of the HG.

Such displays of athleticism from the older men inevitably took their toll. In July 1942 Lt Alex Hay of No. 1 Platoon (Denny) fell in a race and fractured a bone in his left shoulder. Owing to a disability in his right arm, due to a wound received during the First World War, he was completely incapacitated by the accident and had to receive treatment at Falkirk Royal Infirmary.

Progressively the tactical training exercises demanded greater physical fitness and companies were often divided up so that the fitter men formed mobile units. In June 1942 a reporter from the *Bo'ness Journal* witnessed one of the resulting exercises relating to urban defence: "Residents in Castleloan and other districts who have been intrigued and not a little mystified by unusual happenings in their midst following the visits of a platoon of the local Home Guard, such as the spectacle of soldiers apparently flying over high walls impelled by their own volition, have been witnessing the latest ideas in training. Climbing up the face of tall tenements by way of spoil-pipes or by the use of ropes and scaling high garden walls by means of improvised ladders formed by men holding rifles or wooden spars in such a position as to acts as steps, are among special features in the training of the ordinary soldier of today."

At Slamannan the 15ft tall wall that separated the schoolyard from a field was often used for this form of physical exercise. The men, in full kit, would run up to the wall, where two of their comrades held their rifles as a step and propelled them over. Waiting at the other side Willie Fyffe, the school janitor, would bawl "Left parry, right parry to the ground, get into him or he'll be into you!" And they had to thrust their bayonets into sacks before running down to Mosscastle Road.

The board reads "D Coy Home Guard / Grangemouth / Battn Shield Winners / 1941". This is the team that won the 3rd Stg HG Bn trophy. Pictured in the walled garden at the ICI Recreation Grounds.

Uniforms

Uniforms were slow in arriving. Some 'LDV' armbands and 30 field service caps were delivered to Larbert at the end of May 1940 – nowhere near enough for the 4,000 men requiring them. Further supplies of these articles dribbled in. One local man sarcastically suggested that regimental haircuts might usefully augment this 'uniform'; a comment that soon irritated the LDV leaders as it was repeated over and over again by other wags. The first trousers and blouses arrived in August and, although similar in style to the regular army's battledress, they were made of denim – reminding people of overalls. The sizes sent never seemed to fit anyone, detracting from the wearer's appearance. Outsize uniforms were allocated according to who they would fit, but the officers had to decide who they would give the regular size ones to. Some even resorted to the rather unsatisfactory solution of sharing them, so that as a man came off duty he handed over not just his weapon but also his clothes. The end of August also saw the appearance of the first great coats, extremely welcome with the winter approaching. Betty Baird was just one of the lucky children to benefit from this issue – her father's great coat was draped over her bed at night as an extra cover. In September the issue of denim suits was stopped and from thence the regulation serge khaki battledress was issued. Those who had considered themselves lucky to be amongst the first to get the uniforms now unhappily stood out from the crowd and in some cases it was over a year before they were replaced with the new fabric. Similarly some of the men had been provided with wrap-round gaiters. These were rather quickly replaced by leather ones with buckles. It was these that made members of the HG easily distinguishable from the soldiers of the regular army who wore canvas ones.

As well as battledress, great coats and leather gaiters, the men were informed that they would each eventually receive a free issue of leather boots, a forage cap, a steel helmet, a service respirator, a bandolier and ammunition pouch, a blanket and perhaps a cape. Being smart meant extra work for the guardsmen's families. After exercises the uniforms came back covered in mud, which their wives dutifully washed. Many of the men's daughters or younger sisters were roped into polishing boots and anklets.

The initial distribution of material was rather haphazard and without a quartermaster records were not always properly kept. At

The armband issued in 1940 to Wilfred Berwick of the Slamannan unit of the Local Defence Volunteers.

Ian Munn in his HG uniform standing at his back door in Jackson Avenue, Grangemouth. Note the "Home Guard" armband and fabric belt. Late 1940.

John Robinson, Grangemouth HG, with his wife Mary in their back garden at South Lumley Street, Grangemouth.

Grangemouth, for example, several large wooden boxes were delivered to the old Burgh Court Buildings in South Bridge Street for the HG. The volunteers were quickly informed of their arrival and duly assembled at the appointed hour so that the contents could be distributed. The crates were then opened and all found to contain boots. The men rushed over to try them on and they all disappeared – boots and men. Some men evidently took more than one pair. The chance of a free pair of boots spurred more men to volunteer. Willie Milne wore his HG boots for work, but this was normally frowned upon. In Willie's case it was all right because he was a member of the Manuel Brickworks Platoon, and its commanding officer, Jim Rogers, was a practical man who disliked parades.

Before long the allocation of uniforms became more disciplined. When Hector Maxwell joined the Slamannan HG early in 1941 he was sent to the HQ in the Falkirk Drill Hall to collect his uniform. Steel helmets were issued very tardily, supposedly because they were in short supply. This was particularly infuriating because the ARP wardens already had them and they were readily available to buy in the shops. In November 1940 HL Dickson of the Hippodrome in Bo'ness was presented with a helmet by the Edinburgh

Introduction

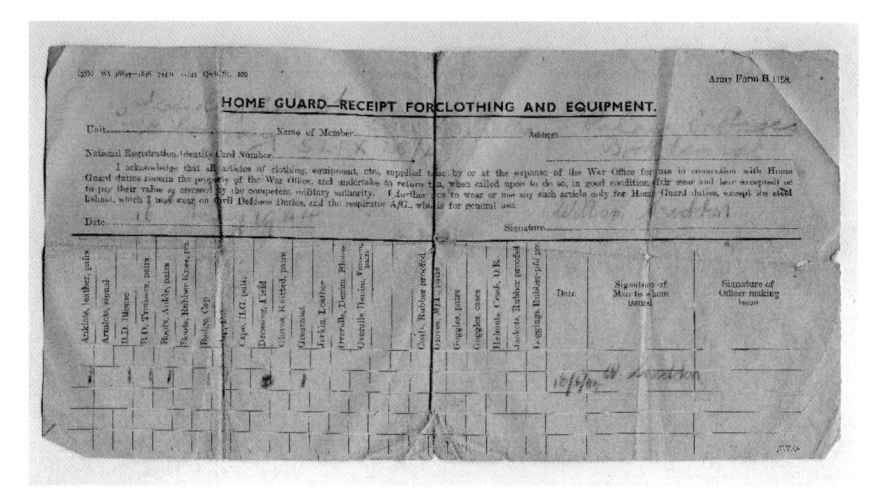

Receipt for equipment supplied to William Sneddon on 16th May 1944. He received 1 pair of anklets, 1 battledress blouse and pair of trousers, 1 pair of boots, 1 cap badge, 1 field service cap, 1 great coat and a field dressing.

Cinema Exhibitors for his services to them, which he found useful for his HG duties. Most of the time the men wore their field service caps and from 3rd August 1940 they were authorised to wear the cap badges of the local regiment, though they were rather hard to come by. Senior officers wore a Tam o' Shanter. These officers also had leather gloves and swagger sticks. It was some time after the receipt of the helmets that the men received netting to go over them in order to be able to add any necessary camouflage such as twigs and leaves. In the interim they used sticky tape to hold the plant material in place.

When Colin Sharp was directed into the Carron Platoon in 1941, he was sent to the church hall at Larbert to be kitted out with his uniform. He was issued with a full outfit, minus boots and a helmet, and had to wear his own boots on parade. One Sunday he was told to report for an exercise on Letham Moss. At the briefing, before they marched off, the officer in charge, a tall man, went over the forthcoming exercise and then asked for questions. Colin responded by pointing out that his brown civilian shoes were unsuitable for scrambling across the moss. The officer looked and agreed. So, instead of taking part in the war game, Colin was ordered to go to the houses of the guardsmen who had failed to turn up for duty and to find out why they were not there. He was handed a list of names and promptly set about his task. At a block of houses called 'Tipperary' in Church Street (later demolished to extend Larbert High School) he knocked at the door and it was answered by the absentee's wife. She took one look at the uniform combined with the brown shoes and shouted back into the house, "There's an officer here to see you. I told

Carron Home Guard photographed in a studio late in 1940. Note the denim uniform and canvas belts, the lack of leather gaiters and cap badges.

you that you should have gone!" Despite this very reasonable assumption, the officers wore the same type of ammunition boots as the rank and file.

By the end of that first year practically everyone had been provided with most of their uniform and the first parades could be held. Dressed for the part they now felt more like they belonged to a military unit and less humiliated in public. For those on the ball the first uniformed church parades fell on the day of the Armistice Day service in November 1940. Members of the Shieldhill and California HG had a parade at Blackbraes Parish Church before marching to the war memorial in Shieldhill to lay a wreath. The lament was played by piper Alex Bryce. Similarly the Carronshore HG marched to Bothkennar Church where the platoon commander, John Green, read the lesson. Green was a member of the Salvation Army and two weeks later he was part of the company that paraded to the Citadel in Bank Street, Falkirk. On that occasion the group formed up at Hope Street and marched behind the Falkirk and District Pipe Band by way of Newmarket Street and Princes Street to the hall. The battalion's minister, Rev J A F Dean of the Erskine Church, took part of the service. On the same day HG platoons from Airth, Bannockburn, Cowie, Denny, Grangemouth and Stenhousemuir assembled at the Central School playing field in Stenhousemuir. Nearly 800 uniformed HG were inspected by the sub-area commander, Col. W Maitland Dougall, and Sir Norman Orr Ewing, before marching to Larbert Old Parish Church, where Rev J J S Thomson addressed them.

Uniform inspections became part of the routine of the HG. On parade the CO would inspect the men's dress and equipment. On public marches through the town centres it was usually the provost or a senior officer in the Scottish Command. There was also the odd unexpected visit. Late in 1940 the Duke of Kent paid an early morning visit to Grangemouth Dockyard and called in to review a small HG party. He returned on 21st January 1941 to see for himself the progress at the nearby airfield.

The uniforms gave the men increased confidence. Shoulder titles bearing the name 'HOME GUARD' were authorised on 2nd August 1941, along with county designations and battalion numbers (regimental flashes, ie II STG, III STG or I WL in the Falkirk district). These slowly replaced the armbands and projected the image of a fighting unit. However, the local people never forgot the early days of the volunteer in civvies with his LDV armband. Until the end even the smartest HG was still viewed at large as not being a real soldier. Capt. W Clark of No. 1 Scottish HG Transport Column, the commanding officer of Walter Alexander's platoon, was so proud of his uniform that he would not let anyone in the family help him to clean it, or to polish his boots. There were two Italian POWs working on Strang's farm (Easter Carmuirs) near where he lived. Their names were Angelo and Inotino, and they often chatted with the children in the neighbourhood. They also became friendly with the Cifelli family who lived there. One day they saw Capt. Clark leaving his home in his neat military uniform, carrying a swagger stick. They automatically saluted him, only to be informed by the children on the streets, "Oh, that's only Mr Clark – he's only in the Home Guard!" They never saluted again.

Jimmy Retson of the Denny HG clearly proud of his uniform and P17 rifle.

Sleeve badges from the uniform of Wilfred Berwick, Slamannan Home Guard.

Part of the Scottish Dyes Section of the Home Guard, photographed just before leaving for church parade at Larbert. At least four of the men on the picture do not have uniforms. (Falkirk Herald 20th Nov 1940.)

The Duke of Kent inspecting an HG unit at Grangemouth late in 1940 on the same day that he visited the Dockyard. At this time there were no shoulder flashes. The men have Lee-Enfield Mk 3 rifles. In the background the Duke's motor car engine has been left running. (Bulletin 1940)

CHAPTER TWO

First Steps

At first the role of the LDV was poorly defined and most commanders on the ground improvised weapons and invented tasks for the men to perform. All saw their job to lie in military duties, which were of greater priority than the services of either the ARP organisation or the police. There was inevitably friction with these bodies. The LDV had a most important mission – to save the country from the German invader – and nothing should stand in its way, certainly not bureaucracy. A store room in Comely Park School was immediately 'requisitioned' without going through the appropriate procedure of form filling – a belief in the right of the cause and a new padlock were deemed sufficient. In Westquarter trees were cut down without the owner's permission where they interfered with machine gun sight lines. Men resigned from the ARP and joined the HG, against orders. Time was short and they simply got on with the job.

When the HG started to hold up traffic at temporary check points the police questioned their authority to do so, and were sometimes shown their rifles. In Falkirk Superintendent Turpie held frequent meetings with the HG commanders to discuss the rules of engagement and slowly they agreed roles and procedures. Such cooperation was vital, not least because the police had better channels of communication than the HG, many of whose platoons did not even have a telephone. For Bo'ness the police contact was Inspector Rankin.

Incidents did still occur. In September 1941 the Linlithgow Gazette carried the following story about Bo'ness:

Depute Chief Constable Turpie in 1946.

A Home Guardsman, fully armed, was taken into the Police Station and questioned on his credentials. He apparently had left his identity card in his civvy jacket pocket. He was not the only "absent minded beggar" on the job. The story goes that when taken into the Police Station the guardsman was not disarmed. So after being "put through his degree", he swung the point of his rifle in the faces of the well meaning police officers and dramatically exclaimed in a world of make-believe: "Noo, ye're a' shot deid!" And, shouldering his gun, our gallant home defender made his way back to the army headquarters.

In 1940 the attention of the LDV/HG was split between several activities, all of which contributed to their overall role of watching and reporting. One of the most onerous was the guarding of important buildings, such as works essential to the war effort, telephone exchanges, bridges and so on. The relative importance of this function increased with time and the theme will be explored in chapter four. Almost from the beginning the LDV made use of elevated locations as observation posts (OPs) from which to keep an eye on the area. At the same time night patrols were mounted in and around the centres of population. Both of these two activities petered out as the threat of invasion diminished, and by 1942 they had been abandoned as routine duties.

Observation Posts

For observational purposes it was realised that elevated locations were of great advantage. In Denny the LDV got permission to use the church tower at Dunipace UF Church. Two men were on duty at any one time, one of whom would act as a runner/messenger in the event of anything to report. It took six men to man the post through the night, with two hours on and four off. Two hours was more than enough on that exposed platform. Church towers were often used. The eighteenth century steeple on Falkirk Parish Church gave a good view of the town centre and was later used by firewatchers. Castles too were commonly occupied. In the northern area this included Airth Castle, Kinnaird House and Dunmore Tower. Even the Iron Age broch at Torwood was utilised, with its extensive views over Denny, Stirling and the Forth Valley. It suffered from lack of shelter for the observers as well as low visibility during low cloud or mist. It was soon realised that while it might be the first place to spot enemy activity, by the time that the runner had reached a telephone the activity would have been seen and reported by another OP. It was with a glad heart that the broch was abandoned. By contrast, the main OP for Bo'ness was at the golf club house on Erngath Hill and was quite popular. The Laurieston

First Steps   29

platoon made use of an outbuilding at Mumrills Farm. Many a beautiful sunrise was witnessed from these OPs by the volunteers on the 'dusk till dawn' watch.

Dunipace Church tower made a convenient observation platform for the north of Denny.

Torwood Broch had great views across the surrounding countryside, but poor communication to HQ.

The Steeple in Falkirk High Street looking east. Tall buildings such as this made good Observation Posts in the early years. Above, the view from Falkirk Steeple in 1950 looking towards Arnothill.

During the war two large cooling towers were added to Bonnybridge Power Station. A section of the HG worked there and so Major White was able to get access to the structures. The view of the Vale of Bonny from the top was magnificent. Major White's assessment was that while it was worth using as an OP, anyone up there would be silhouetted against the skyline and thus vulnerable to sniper fire. The very prominence of the structures also made them an obvious target for the enemy.

The observation posts had two main roles. Firstly they were to detect any invasion or infiltration, and secondly to monitor its progress. The use of boom defences in the Forth and the strengthening of the outer estuary defences ruled out a waterborne landing by small craft and the full establishment of a series of spotter posts by the Royal Observer Corps meant that it was better placed to watch for enemy parachutists. At the end of the summer of 1941 the HG abandoned its fixed OPs.

Patrols

The guard posts and observation posts were connected by patrols. In Denny the first patrols visited the small electric sub-station behind the Cinema de Luxe and the telephone exchange in Paris Avenue. Up the Braes the patrols were taken particularly seriously, as it was thought that German paratroops would land there on the open moors. At Slamannan the platoon was strong enough to allow a rota of eight men each night from 10pm to 6am. Two men remained by the telephone at the Welfare Hall (for the first few years they actually used the nearby telephone kiosk), whilst the other six patrolled the village and its outskirts carrying an air-cooled Lewis gun. The platoon had nominated a number of points outside the village, right up to the Lanarkshire border, to which they would patrol. Each night they walked to a different set point. Ham Row, a long single storey terrace of miners' cottages, was a regular stopping place for patrols heading to the south-west. This was traditionally seen as the village boundary, and a cup of tea was always forthcoming. Perhaps the most used route encompassed Hillhead Farm as it sat on a small hill overlooking the village, with good views up the Avon Valley.

A popular contemporary view of the Home Guard parading on the local golf course from an advertisement for Gillete razor.

The great advantage that the volunteers had over an invading force was that they knew the area better – or so it was thought. In point of fact it was found that such knowledge only applied to discrete areas and varied from individual to individual. The postman, for example, tended to know the urban area where he delivered mail, but not that of the adjacent beat. In either case the postmen knew the towns better than the poachers did, though they in turn had an intimate knowledge of local woodlands. The Balquhatstone Estate to the south-east of Slamannan had been closed to the public before the war and was not well known. The LDV officers decided to improve the overall level of geographical awareness of such areas by varying the locale of the night patrols. One night the Slamannan men were marched into Balquhatstone Estate. On a small knoll to the east of the house was the walled garden. In they obediently filed, recognising what a good place it would be to defend. As they walked across an open patch of ground the officer in charge of the patrol suddenly shouted "Company halt!" Evidently some lecture or manoeuvre was on its way. "Company – fall down!" came the next command. They had become accustomed to crawling along the ground on their bellies as part of their field craft exercises. "Company – get stuck in!" This was an unconventional command and one not too readily understood, until they realised as they peered in the moonlight that they were lying in a bed of ripe strawberries.

Patrols, night and day, were faithfully adhered to in Bo'ness during the summer months of 1940 at the height of the invasion scare. These patrols passed into desuetude as the threat diminished, until the following spring when some bright spark persuaded the powers that were that if anything was to happen, the likeliest time would be at dawn and so a dawn patrol was inaugurated. The Bo'ness NCOs took this task largely on their own shoulders. Despite the doubtful enjoyment of seeing dawn break from the golf course, this patrol also ran its short course. Instead, a system of quick 'calling-out' in an emergency was evolved and, on the few occasions that it was put into effect, this proved adequate.

To the vast majority of the civilian population, who spent their nights sound asleep, the nocturnal activities of the HG went unnoticed and largely unappreciated. For decades people recalled the impressive sight of the huge bomb craters beside Canada Row at Greenhill, but very few were ever aware of how close a HG patrol had been when the holes were created. A small patrol of six men had been doing their regular round by Lochgreen Road on the night of 7 April 1941, when suddenly their routine was interrupted. The sky lit up and they were blown off their feet, landing some distance away, where they were showered with mud. A stick of seven High Explosive bombs had gone off in rapid succession – four on the north side of the road by Canada Wood and three to the south by Seafield Farm. The incident provided quite a scare for the men, and more washing for their wives – but was quickly forgotten.

The Slamannan platoon maintained its night patrols longer than most in the continued belief that the wide open moorland provided an ideal landing area for enemy parachutists and gliders. On Friday evenings there were other distractions to tempt the volunteers off the patrols. One of the young corporals was not as streetwise as his mates and patrolled part of the village on his own, while they split up and patrolled the other parts – or so he thought. Unbeknown to him, as the war dragged on they had slowly, one by one, been drawn to the dances. It took some months before he caught on and joined them. Early in 1942 the night patrols ceased.

Vertical RAF aerial photograph taken in May 1950 showing the impact craters of three of the bombs near Canada Row.

Road Blocks and Check Points

It was widely reported, and believed, that German spies, Fifth Columnists and disguised paratroops had been largely responsible for the rapid downfall of Belgium, Holland and France. Such low level threats were pervasive and corrosive and any response demanded a large force spread throughout Britain, preferably one rooted in the community so that it was able to spot alien behaviour. This was clearly a task for the LDV and speeches emanating from Whitehall in June 1940 hinted at one of the methods. Night patrols and observation posts would catch the paratroops at the earliest opportunity, but through the manning of road blocks and the checking of identity cards the LDV would be "of the greatest value" in defeating the Fifth Column and enemy spy.

It is said that the first task undertaken by the West Lothian Bn had been to turn out on the night that Italy entered the war, 10th June 1940. The volunteers appeared in civvies and rolled empty barrels onto the Queensferry Road near Walton to act as a road block in the expectation of an assault by parachute on the Forth Bridge. Almost overnight makeshift road blocks were set up throughout the Falkirk district. Motorists and pedestrians alike were forced to submit their ID cards for inspection. Those absent-minded enough to have left their card at home were marched to the nearest police station, often at bayonet point. The LDV used whatever material was at hand to create the obstructions. A good example of an early road block was that established by the Maddiston HG on the main road south to Bathgate. The road went over the steep hill upon which Cairneymount Church stands and then down to the crossroads at Bowhouse. Just over the crest of the hill heading southwards the road was lined with earth banks surmounted by hawthorn hedges. About 50yds past the church there was a wooden farm gate on either side of the road. To close the road off the LDV simply opened both gates across it and chained them together.

The Falkirk Power Station HG were responsible for Lochgreen Road, which runs from High Bonnybridge to the southern suburbs of Falkirk. In the summer of 1940 everyone was very cooperative with them, even the farmers, and they had no trouble on Sunday exercises in rounding up a few tractors from local farms. These were placed across the road to form chicanes – the more tractors the more chicanes and the slower the traffic moved. Six tractors was considered a good number, though more or less were used according to supply. Once the vehicles using the road were moving slowly they were stopped by the volunteers and the ID cards of the occupants were checked.

The simplest form of purpose-built obstacle for use at temporary road blocks was the 'cuddie' – a wooden horse consisting of a pole stretched between cross-shaped frames and covered with coils of barbed wire. These could be left by the road side or in the adjacent field when not in use, and were easily lifted into position across the road. They came to replace the tractors on Lochgreen Road and could be found throughout the district at such places as the Bothkennar Road near Skinflats, or beside Thorneydyke Quarry outside Dunipace. At the latter the cuddie was located at an S-bend on the road and was accompanied by a 'pill box' or 'control point'. The control post consisted of a hole dug at the side of the road and lined with sandbags. These stood to the height of a man and had small openings or gun slits towards the top.

Not all road checks needed physical barriers and it was realised at an early stage that people would get accustomed to the locations where temporary blocks were mounted from time to time and spies would learn to avoid them. The road blocks were consequently augmented by ad hoc check points created by flagging the traffic down, or as one member of the Slamannan HG said, "We used ourselves as obstacles". One night they were told to stop every vehicle approaching from the south. The stopping place was near the back gate to Balquhatstone House, half way up the hill. Here the road was emerging from a cutting and so vehicles could not leave it. They also had to slow down to take the bend. Tom McCracken stood in the middle of the road with Danny Drysdale as a bus approached and shouted "Halt who goes there!" The driver, John Reid, an elderly man, was startled and took a while to recover his composure - he had been using the road all through the war and had never been stopped before.

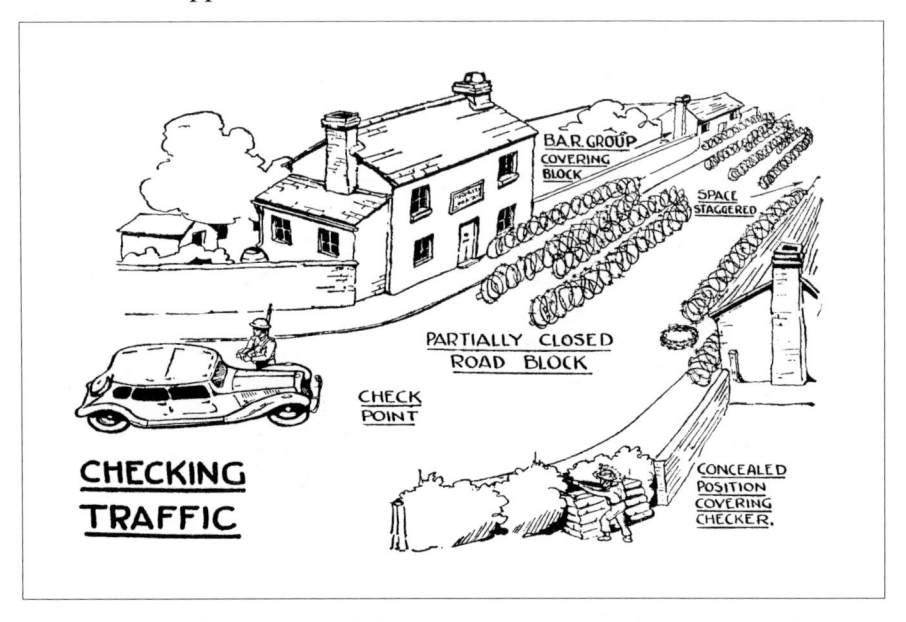

The set up for a typical road checkpoint (from Home Guard Instruction, No. 51, 1943).

On busy roads such checks created static queues, which acted to slow the traffic down anyway. Drivers soon became impatient at being stopped several times on the same journey by different HG platoons. Any attempt by them to ignore the demands of the individual HG units was risky, as at that time the paranoia infecting the whole nation meant that the HG would treat anyone being disrespectful as suspicious and were quite prepared to use their limited ammunition to shoot first and ask questions later. This phenomenon was highlighted on the night of 2nd June 1940 when LDVs elsewhere in Britain shot and killed four motorists in separate locations.

First Steps

Three members of the Carronshore HG in a back garden in the village.

Most suspicious of all were the vehicles using the roads after dark. This was perceived to be the time of greatest danger when the enemy would strike, and for the motorist it certainly was. The cover of darkness was the HG's natural hunting ground, when after a day's work they were on duty and in command. To flag a vehicle down in the black-out took a certain amount of courage and the guardsmen had to be prepared to jump out of the way if need be. One night in November 1940 a section of the Carronshore HG walked out from the village on a routine patrol carrying a single rifle between them. It was dark and when they got to the Bellsdyke Road the officer in charge decided on an impromptu road check. They duly waved a red torch at the first car to come along. It was a 1933 Morris 8 driven by Rev. William MacLaren of the nearby Bothkennar Parish Church. They recognised him, "Oh, it's only the minister – carry on!" Rev. MacLaren went on to visit some of his parishioners about family matters. While he was out another car approached the check point, but when flagged down it continued on without even changing speed. Rather irate, one of the guardsmen fired at it, but in the dark was wide of the mark. On his way back Rev. MacLaren was stopped again and heard all about it.

On another occasion Findlay Russell, a farmer from the Dennyloanhead area, was taking some of the lasses, who worked in his milk bar at Falkirk bus station, home after work. It was late and they had all been working hard. Findlay was not driving fast because the girls were sitting in the open back of the van with the empty milk cans and both were liable to fall off if he took the corners too quickly. At about 11pm he drove down the main street in Bonnybridge and everything appeared normal. He knew that there was a road block site at the Toll, but although he had to slow down because it constricted the passageway, he continued on as usual. Then he heard an almighty bang as a shot rang out so close that he thought that the van must have been hit. His foot hit the brake and the violence of the stop sent the milk cans flying into the

Bonnybridge Toll

girls and there was an awful commotion. Then there was some shouting as a HG approached. He had been waving his red torch at the road block site and being disregarded had fired a warning shot. Findlay was a special constable with good eye sight and even allowing for the black-out he could not believe that he had missed the signal. Using his authority as a policeman he was able to examine the torch and found that the battery was so low that the light, already partially masked for the black-out, was barely visible. Batteries were hard to come by. There is no record of the ensuing conversation!

The night time road blocks or checks seemed to catch a wide range of professional people in their net. They caused great inconvenience but were tolerated, due to the circumstances, by the drivers and even welcomed by the majority who were not car owners. Buses were included in the vehicles stopped. Due to the black-out they were usually behind schedule and the frequent inspections made them even later. Having stopped the bus, members of the HG would get on and check all the passengers' ID cards. The LDV platoon based at the Larbert Road Garage near Camelon was looking for things to do when it was formed. Wearing their armbands, and without a single weapon between them, they started stopping all the vehicles passing the garage after midnight, by which time all the buses were safely in. There was little on the road at that early hour, but they did have the pleasure of stopping Walter Alexander, the owner of the bus company, on several occasions. After four months this duty was suspended.

The night patrols gave the HG a new insight into the twilight world of traffic. The Haggs/Dennyloanhead HG found that one of the large cars that it caught was a hearse carrying a soldier's body north for burial. A lorry halted by the Redding HG at the Westquarter Gates turned out to have a full load of sugar for sale on the black market. This latter kind of incident caused a great deal of antagonism with the police, some of whose duties the HG seemed to be usurping without authority. Late one night the Slamannan HG stopped a car at the Avon Bridge as it approached the village from Falkirk. It was most unusual to see a car there so late at night and the guardsmen became very alert as it slowed to a halt. Several rifles pointed towards the driver's position as the NCO in charge of the patrol approached. A few short words were exchanged and then the patrol quickly melted away. It had been a policeman out on call and this had been the third time he had been stopped and delayed.

The police were not the only uniformed men on the move. At Grangemouth the HG stopped a car heading eastwards. It was only as the inspecting guardsman approached that he noticed that the driver was wearing the uniform of an officer in the regular army. Inside the car he had not been wearing his cap and so this fact had not been distinguishable from a distance. Just as the guard reached the car the driver pulled a revolver on him and asked what he was going to do about it. The guard's colleagues were too far away to even notice let alone assist. The driver had, it turned out, had a much interrupted journey and had finally reacted in this startling way. It was a salutary lesson for the guardsmen, and not one that they repeated.

James Frame wearing his great coat in a Falkirk studio. These coats were useful for the long night patrols in winter.

On another occasion a stranger in a car arrived at the west end of Allandale and was stopped by the Castlecary Brickworks HG. Suspicions were aroused when he gave no justifiable reason for being out so late at night and he was unable to produce any authority. He was apprehended, searched and escorted to the home of Charlie Taylor, the works' manager. Disturbing Charlie at dead of night required sound judgement. After further interrogation it eventually transpired that the stranger was a government inspector with responsibility for monitoring and inspecting the efficiency of the black-out at industrial sites in central Scotland, including the brickworks. He was making an impromptu visit, devoid of appointment or invitation. Much time elapsed before he was released from detention, only to find when he returned to his car that the HG had deflated all four tyres to prevent his escape.

It is not now possible to say how many of the makeshift road blocks were mounted in the Falkirk district. At least two more are known to have been placed in the area of the 3rd Stg HG Bn – at Todhill on the main road to Stirling (NS 8450 8408) and on the back road between Larbert Cross and Dunipace Bridge (at NS 8393 8192). In West Lothian this subject was handled differently. At first things progressed along normal lines and in June 1940 the Area Commander instructed Major Hope to arrange to have material such as

Appendix C

Road blocks.		Map reference
Kerse Lane	73/394022	[NS 895 803]
Belmont	392018	[NS 893 799]
Glenbrae	384013	[NS 895 794]
Grahamston Bridge	388023	[NS 889 804]
Hope St	385024	[NS 886 805]
Carron Bridge	382045	[NS 883 826]

Defence Scheme Dec 1942

farm carts available to form road blocks, but no clear picture was given as to where these should be. Even the company commanders were confused about what was being asked of them and whereas in Stirlingshire the local platoons took the initiative, here they sought clarification. Consequently the construction of road blocks in West Lothian was handed over to the County Council, which then had to liaise with the various interested bodies. When, in 1941, they eventually decided upon semi-permanent road blocks they took the form known as the 'double type', where brick end walls projected onto the roads leaving a gap just wide enough for a bus to squeeze through. Concrete cylinders were placed behind the walls and could be rolled into the gap and stood on end to close the road completely. In June 1942 Falkirk Town Council paid M Hunter and J Livingston & Company £800 each for cement used for road blocks – presumably those listed in the Defence Scheme in December of that year (see above). There was an additional expense in connection with these of £29.11.11 for covers and frames obtained from the Carron Company. Within the WL Bn area these were constructed at the following locations:

location name	coded grid ref	national grid ref	road
Walton	526 012	NT 0272 7932	A904 Linlithgow/ Bo'ness
Linlithgow Bridge	482 990	NS 9833 7715	A803 W of Linlithgow
Avontoun	482 982	NS 983 763	A706 S W of Linlithgow
Preston House	498 978	NS 999 759	B8047 S of Linlithgow
Hiltly	504 976	NT 005 757	—— SE of Linlithgow
Paper Mill	492 999	NS 993 780	A706 N of Linlithgow
Bonnytoun	508 996	NT 009 777	A803 NE of Linlithgow
Kingscavil	525 985	NT 026 766	B9080 E of Linlithgow
Slackend	469 941	NS 970 722	B792 Torphichen
Bathgate	471 908	NS 972 689	A89 Bathgate
Torbanehall	441 889	NS 942 670	B8084 Armadale/Whitburn
Fauldhouse	428 826	NS 929 607	B7010 Fauldhouse
Hareburnhead	539 818	NT 040 599	B7008 WestCalder/Lanark
Bankhead	431 812	NS 932 593	A71 Newmains/West Calder
Livingston	522 889	NT 023 670	A705 Whitburn/Mid Calder
Dechmont	531 923	NT 032 704	A89 Bathgate/ Broxburn
Pumpherston	568 912	NT 069 693	Pumpherston
Pumpherston Oil Works	575 915	NT 076 696	ditto

Whilst only the first two in this list are located within the modern boundaries of the Falkirk Council area, it is useful to be able to set them into context. The overall strategy of the HG in West Lothian is clearly reflected in the distribution of these road blocks. The vast majority of them are placed on roads that cross the county and are designed to restrict long distance travel. The layout of the road network meant that many of the roads led to the county town at Linlithgow and as a consequence it is ringed by the road blocks. Two of the locations, at Pumpherston, were there to protect the shale oil works.

The road block on the road between Linlithgow and Bo'ness near Walton was to the south of the farm of that name, where a farm track joined it. The Graham family, who occupied the farm, became accustomed to the presence of the HG. There were only a few on duty during the day, but their numbers increased at night and they soon came to recognise the Grahams and let them through without stopping. Robert Graham described the road block as "side wall with two concrete blocks placed in a staggered formation on the carriageway of the road. Tanks could easily have gone round it. One night a shot rang out and all hell broke loose. There was no vehicle there at the time and it appears that a rifle went off by accident."

Over subsequent years the list was augmented by individual companies. The Bo'ness Coy had concrete blocks laid out at the side of the Quarry Brae (NS 993 808 on the A993), which were put onto the road during exercises to slow the traffic down. Similarly, the engineer section of Stenhousemuir HG left a number of concrete cubes beside the Bellsdyke Road. Each cube had a steel ring fixed into the top and could be lifted into place on the road by a crane mounted on the back of a lorry. The vehicle had been adapted for this purpose by a local mechanic in his garage and was loaned to the HG for the duration of the war. It was kept behind the police station and required much form filling to get the petrol allowance.

Invasion Alerts

In that nerve-racking summer of 1940 it was not a matter of if the Germans were going to invade, but rather of when. Nervously expecting the enemy to drop from the sky at any moment it is not surprising that the LDV and HG patrols and observation posts should, in the eerie calm of the truly dark nights, mistake strange sounds, distant lights or moving objects as evidence of paratroops or spies. After an anxious moment or two a harmless explanation was usually discovered.

One of the earliest invasion alerts occurred at Grangemouth. A night patrol of the LDV left their HQ at the ICI Recreation Centre and made for the railway bridge on the Falkirk Road at Middlefield, which was seen as the burgh boundary and hence also the point at which a Falkirk platoon took over. They had done this for over a week without incident. As they approached the bridge they heard the church bells at Falkirk ringing. It had not long been announced that the bells were not to ring except in the event of an invasion, and even then it was only the churches in the immediate vicinity that were to sound them. The patrol rushed back to the HQ in a panic and alerted those on duty that night to call out the rest of the platoon. There followed many hours of frantic action and then inaction. Everything seemed remarkably normal and no one else had heard the bells. Eventually, after much investigation, it dawned on them that what they had heard was the bell in Falkirk Steeple chiming

First Steps

ICI HG in the grounds of Kerse House, June 1941. They have P17 rifles with bayonets sheathed. Their steel helmets cover their gas mask bags, which are slung from shoulder belts. J K Thomson, Bob Roberts, T Mitchell, J Paxton, A Silver, H W Deans, C Donald, W Hamilton, I Munn, A Cornwall, A G Rees, R P Chinn.

> **BURGH OF FALKIRK.**
>
> **"INVASION."**
>
> **A PUBLIC MEETING**
> OF THE CITIZENS OF FALKIRK
> will be held in the
> **REGAL PICTURE HOUSE, PRINCES STREET,**
> On SUNDAY, 13th SEPTEMBER,
> at 7.30 p.m.
>
> Mr D. L. SEATH, J.P., and
> Col. J. J. KINGSTONE, D.S.O., M.C.,
> WILL SPEAK OF THE
> NATION'S INVASION ARRANGEMENTS.
> Chairman—Provost HENRY BEGG.
> It is the duty of every member of the Community to attend this Meeting, so that he may be aware of his duties if the enemy should land in this country.
> APPROPRIATE FILMS WILL BE SHOWN.
>
> IN CONNECTION WITH THE ABOVE, A
> **Parade of Civil Defence Services, etc.,**
> will be held on the above date, at 3 p.m.
> The Parade will assemble at Hope Street at 2.30 p.m., and proceed via Newmarket Street, Vicar Street, Graham's Road, Wallace Street, Thornhill Road, Queen Street, Stewart Road, Kerse Lane, Callendar Riggs, and High Street, to the place of dismissal at Cockburn Street.
> ROBERT LYLE, Town Clerk.
> Falkirk, 2nd September, 1942.

midnight. It had been overlooked when the initial decision had been made to use bells to sound the alarm and was soon disconnected.

Another incident happened up on the high ground between Bonnybridge and Greenhill. Someone reported having seen an enemy parachutist walking along one of the back roads in the dark. The High Bonnybridge HG was called out and after many hours of extensive search they came across Willie Welsh, the farmer from Clayknowes, carrying a sick sheep over his shoulders – at first glance it looked like he had a parachute on his back!

Back in Grangemouth, still in 1940, a man going to work early in the morning by way of the Ice House Road spotted an empty white parachute billowing along the ground in the wind. Without stopping he rushed to the ICI Recreation Club and the duty HG immediately turned out. Tension was great as the men approached the area. At first nothing could be seen in the twilight, and then the parachute appeared, and disappeared. It was the white steam from the engines of the goods trains at the Fouldubs Shed, which due

The ICI Recreation Centre known as the Scottish Dyes Recreation Club, 1935.

to the atmospheric conditions travelled some distance along the ground. The people of Grangemouth had no doubts that the town with its airport and docks would be the place chosen by the enemy to get a foothold in the country. Early one morning a rumour went round the civilian population of the town that two uniformed German soldiers had been seen in the vicinity. The news spread like wildfire. Unaware of the rising tension John Bryce and Willie Marshall came off their HG night duty and instead of proceeding straight home they called in at a friend's house in the Old Town for a cup of tea. They were not in a hurry and chatted a while. They emerged into the street about three quarters of an hour later to the clicking sound of rifle bolts. Looking about they could see numerous weapons pointing at them. "Oh dear! What's all this!" exclaimed Willie as they hurriedly signified their surrender. They had been seen entering the house and reported as enemy combatants.

Land mines were also known as parachute mines because they gently descended to earth suspended from these silken canopies. Fleeting glimpses of these were seen in the dark skies on the moonlit night of 13th March 1941 when two fell at High Bonnybridge and another two in the vicinity of the Black Loch near Slamannan. The HG were asked to search the areas concerned to determine whether troops had landed at the same time as the bombs. It was easy enough to find the bomb sites, as three of the four blew up on impact leaving massive craters. The task of recovering the parachutes and thus accounting for the number reported to have been seen descending was made much harder by the local population, who took them into their own custody so that the silk could be converted into clothes. It took three days to find the last chute that had broken free, at Easter Whin Farm, Limerigg. It had travelled a considerable distance having been blown across the open moors into woodland in a sparsely populated area. Another time the Slamannan HG was informed that paratroops had been seen in the vicinity of Southfield House to the west of the village. It was a Saturday night and Hector Maxwell was sure that it was just another way for the officers to keep them employed and warm. In any case, they scrambled around in the dark, falling over fences and into ditches. Nothing was found.

Sometimes real parachutists did land in the Falkirk district. In the late evening of 25th August 1940 one descended in the area of Grangemouth Docks, where he was promptly arrested by members of the LMS HG. He explained that he was the pilot of a British Hurricane, number L1803 – but his name was Stein. He claimed that the plane had suffered a loss of oil pressure and that the engine had caught fire. As it happened, his story was easy to verify, as he told the guard that he was based at RAF Grangemouth, only a mile down the road. In the meantime he was charged with entering a restricted area without the appropriate pass.

A year on, a second pilot from the same stable landed at the end of his parachute on top of some trees near Island Farm, east of Skinflats. The local farm labourers retrieved him, unhurt, at the point of a pitchfork. They soon accepted his story and released him. Meanwhile, the parachute had been seen from Grangemouth Dockyard and the Grangemouth HG were turned out to instigate a search of the woods.

At the beginning of September 1940 the tides were considered to be favourable for a German invasion of Britain, which was expected before the winter weather closed in. GHQ Home Forces therefore decided to place the regular forces in the south of England on a state of heightened alert. On the night of 7 September it issued the codeword 'CROMWELL' to the Eastern and Southern Command to signify that conditions were right for an invasion. Before long the codeword was being passed throughout Britain in the belief that it meant that an invasion had actually taken place. At 22.05 hours CROMWELL was received at group 14 HQ in Bridge of Allan by Col. DG Sandeman and on his instructions the church bells were rung throughout Stirlingshire and Clackmannanshire. What an air of agitated excitement it created! The tension was palpable. Home Guardsmen quickly dressed in what uniforms they had and bade farewell to their loved ones. Runners were

Aerial view of Manuel Brickworks looking west, c1960.

sent round to inform stragglers who were unaware of the emergency, and by midnight all the anti-invasion posts were fully manned. Then came the long anxious wait.

G Bryson was in the Manuel Brickworks HG and recounted the night:

> The late Jimmy Blair and I were work mates together at Stein's. We were on night shift when it happened. Jimmy was a gas plant operator and I was a kiln foreman. The message came that there was a threatened invasion so we both closed down our respective plants and reported to the armoury of the works' Home Guard, of which we were both members, where we were issued with rifles and ammo. We were then detailed to a point in the field near the gas plant. We had orders to challenge three times and failing to get an answer, to fire. Time passed very slowly, but eventually we heard a noise which seemed to be coming closer. I challenged three times and did not receive an answer, but was very reluctant to fire. However, time passed and eventually I thought it was time for action but Jimmy suggested holding back a little longer — and it was a good job we did as it turned out to be a cow grazing on Haining Valley Farm. (Bryson, G 1981 *The Eastern Corner of Muiravonside Parish as Told by a Native*)

At the Gothic Foundry in Camelon the works' platoon was hurriedly mustering when a lorry from the regular army drove up to the gate. Boxes of ammunition were unceremoniously dumped on the ground and the lorry sped off into the darkness. Upon inspection it was found that there were approximately 10,000 rounds of small arms ammunition. No receipt had been issued, nor even asked for – and they were never returned! The men were issued with what rifles were available, 50 rounds of ammunition each and two hand grenades. They then rather soberly made their way to their post at the Three Bridges.

Sections of the Laurieston platoon manned the guard post and observation post at Mumrills Farm, whilst the main body of men stood to at the school to await instructions. Out at Greenhill by High Bonnybridge the Railway HG received news of the invasion. Having assembled they left in pairs, each pair equipped with a rifle and six rounds of ammunition, walking along the railway line to take up their posts in the Grangemouth Docks complex. The Brightons/Polmont HG went to the trenches that they had dug beside Weedingshall House to defend the airfield at Grangemouth from a landward attack. And so it went on, platoon after platoon, throughout the Falkirk district, thousands of men in a state of heightened alert.

It was 11am the next morning before stand down instructions were issued. By the end of the 'crisis' some of the volunteers from the Standburn/Avonbridge area were half dead. They had been informed that the Germans had landed at Queensferry and so they cycled all the way there without even a rifle! Presumably they would have been expected to pick them up from the battlefield. Cycling down to an unknown hellish encounter was one thing, but cycling back up hill in cold blood was another.

It should also be remembered that the numerous regular forces in the Falkirk district were also on alert that night. All three branches of the armed forces stood to. George Wardlaw was with 614 Squadron at RAF Grangemouth at the time. He had stood to on the night of 7th September 1940 and takes up the story early the next day with the dull clanging of church bells in the background:

> It was a Sunday and it rained all day. I had a greatcoat on and it felt like a ton. We went into a field, and in the middle of the field was a pit, which was full of canisters of mustard gas. There was a rigger, a fitter, all the RAF trades, and we loaded the containers onto a trolley and started to pull them out of this pit. I remember there was a canister, which had liquid oozing out of the seam, and a corporal put his finger on it. I remember thinking to myself "If that's mustard gas, you're daft". It wasn't till later that I read that somebody had had treatment at Falkirk Infirmary from that incident. We actually put those containers on aircraft and they were loaded up ready for use because we were under the impression that there was going to be an invasion. This was going to be the last resort – they were going to spray them with mustard gas.

Just as the plane was about to take off the crew was stood down – it had been a false alarm.

Some local men had mysteriously disappeared. They had literally gone underground. These were the men of the auxiliary units, an underground resistance movement, who would emerge from their secret subterranean operational bases after the Germans had overrun the area and carry out acts of sabotage. When the CROMWELL alert was signalled the auxiliary units in the rest of Britain prepared to go to ground, but in Scotland the men actually occupied their hideouts, where in most places they remained for at least five days.

The Scottish network of resistance cells was set up by Capt. Eustace Maxwell of the A andSH. Maxwell was given a brief course in sabotage techniques at Station 12, Knebworth, and then sent north to form the army of clandestine fighters. On 27th July 1940 he drove up and that same night established his headquarters in a sleepy little inconspicuous town called Falkirk. From here he masterminded the resistance movement, driving all over Scotland. Some of the best men were withdrawn from the ordinary HG units, but still maintained the outward appearance of being on special duty for that body. Within three weeks of his arrival at Falkirk more than twenty resistance patrols were in training, covering the most vulnerable stretches of the northern coast of Caithness and the entire coast of Sutherland. Most of the hideouts of the Scottish auxiliary units were near the coast, so that the greatest damage could be done to the Germans during the initial phase of the occupation before they had the time to dig in. Often they strengthened existing defences at strategic locations such as airfields.

No example of an operational base is known for certain in the Falkirk district, though there is one very good candidate. A small team of army engineers constructed what the few locals in the vicinity were told was an 'ammunition store' in the hillside beside Beancross village (at NS 923 796). The store was completed in a single day during the week. It was covered with earth and the turves were neatly replaced by the end of the school day when the boys living in the hamlet returned home. At the end of the war a bulldozer returned to the site to flatten it – and yet it was never seen in use. No one visited it as far as the villagers were concerned. The location would have been ideal. A little outside of the perimeter of the airfield by a busy main road, but hidden by the adjacent gardens. From here the resistance fighters could have blown up enemy aircraft on the ground using the captured airfield just yards away, or damaged facilities and vessels in the docks. It is known that there were also two inland operation bases in the west of Stirlingshire, to cover Glasgow, but these were not in the Falkirk district.

There is no doubt that the night of 7th September 1940 was the night that most HG thought that "the balloon had gone up". It was, however, just the

Looking down on the hamlet of Beancross from Mumrills with the flat ground of the airfield beyond, 1951.

most extreme example of a series of false alarms caused by the jittery circumstances that year. William Sharp of the Falkirk Power Station platoon recalled having to rush to the Burgh Stables on several occasions when the alert had been received. Here they would muster and await instructions and after, say, half an hour, an officer would call them to attention. Another hour could ensue before the order came to shoulder arms and they would march boldly off in the direction that they had been told to go. Such incidents tended to occur on the nights when there was a bomber's moon. At the time many of the public were still regaling the voluntary soldiers with the title "Look, Duck and Vanish", taken from the initials of the Local Defence Volunteers. The guardsmen had their own, more succinct, phrase, which was "hurry up and wait". It was all very exasperating and there was a single question on everyone's lips – "What's keeping the Germans?"

Apart from the so-called Cromwell incident, the best known false alarm in this area took place in the early morning of Friday 9th May 1941 at Bo'ness. At about 2.45am the Great Bell at the Parish Church started ringing in a subdued and intermittent manner, which persisted for around eight minutes. The residents in the Panbrae and Newtown districts were alarmed by the spasmodic nature of the strokes, which led them to believe that the invasion was not just imminent but actually under way. Most realised that it was only those church bells where the invasion was expected that were to ring. Needless to say, this threw many families into a state of fear bordering on panic. Some took to their air raid shelters. Margaret Neilson was a young girl living with her parents at Deanfield Road at the time. They were horrified to hear the bell and her mother made Margaret get dressed in case they decided to flee the house. Meanwhile her father dutifully lifted his steel helmet and long coat from their peg in the lobby and reported for action at the hall next to the Star Cinema – he was an ambulance driver with the ARP. As a stretcher bearer in the First World War he had hoped never again to see the carnage which he now knew was on his own doorstep. It was a clear night and Margaret sat at her bedroom window in the dark looking across Calder Park to the Firth of Forth. The water was calm and the moonlight reflected off it. Anyone coming from the coast and climbing the hill to the park would be silhouetted against the water and she quietly waited for them to arrive.

Peter McGuck was 14 years old and was surprised when, with the bell ringing in the background, his father came into his bedroom wearing his HG uniform. "I'm off now son," he said, and then added, "And I may not be coming back."

Rab Scullion was not much older than Peter. He lived with his parents in Avon Place, not far from the police station at Corbiehall. He too heard the bell ringing, but stayed in bed – after all what could he do? Indeed, civilians had been instructed through countless pamphlets and by the newspapers to stay put on such an occasion so as not to jam the roads and interfere with any response. From his bed he could hear the commotion outside. Most of the police, special police, war reserve constables and military police turned up at the police station to find out what was happening and how they could help. Just beyond that the HG were assembling. Two of the men from Camlouden Place had arrived at the HG HQ fully equipped in under ten minutes. They lived near enough to have heard the bell when it first sounded, but beyond the town centre to the east it was not heard. Nor was it audible beyond Douglas Park. Messengers were sent to collect the men from the east and south. John Mackie of Deanfield had heard the alarm and hurriedly dressed in the blackout. He was one of the first men at the Corbiehall assembly point, where there was much confusion. After several frustrating hours he was able to return home temporarily and it was only then that he noticed that he had put his trousers on back to front. On the other side of the road from the police station was the ARP Hall and here the turnout was absolutely remarkable. Within half an hour almost all the personnel were there waiting for news, waiting to do their duty.

Those nearest to the church could see that the tower was brilliantly lit as the light penetrated the windows causing a glare in the surrounding darkness. This was seen for miles around, not just in Bo'ness but up the Forth at Grangemouth and across at Culross. Ordinarily it would have made an attractive picture against the dark sky of an early May morning, but these

Bo'ness Old Parish Church looking south-west along Panbrae Road with the steep brae on the right.

were extraordinary times. The Bo'ness police spent many hours answering telephone calls from anxious observers all over the area complaining about the breach of the black-out.

The first house to the east of the church was occupied by George (known as 'Dod') Frank. His first instinct was to go to the church to find out what was happening, but being of German descent he believed that it would be unwise for him to explore alone. So he went to find his neighbour, John Collee, dentist and ARP warden, taking with him an ornamental sword from off the wall. John Bell, the church officer, lived just a few doors along:

> When I heard the pealing I refused to believe that it was our church bell, I listened, and convinced at last I rushed out of the house, saw the church was lit and imagined all sorts of things. I ran to the residence of Mr Collee to phone the police.

A few hundred yards down the road another member of the HG had been awakened by the first notes of the bell. He rose and dressed, but noticing that the bell was not tolling properly decided to investigate this circumstance rather than reporting direct to the HG HQ as he was supposed to do. He ran to the church, calling on the way at the home of the church officer. Mrs Bell informed him that her husband had already departed for the church. When the HG reached the church he could see no one about the place. The bell had stopped; although the steeple was lit up, all was quiet. The situation was worryingly strange and doubts and fancies began to assail his mind. Thinking that the church officer was in the church and perhaps in trouble, the HG, without any thought of personal danger, dashed up the stairs of the tower to the bell loft, which he found spookily empty. Considerably puzzled he descended the stairs to the church and at the opposite end of the building he saw, to his amazement, two naked female figures advancing hand in hand to the chancel steps. They stopped and knelt down on the topmost step in front of the communion table.

At that moment the police arrived. First in was Sgt. Campbell, who had been on patrol duty. As he and the HG approached the two women the older became terror-stricken and started screaming loudly. The men now had to restrain her and she struggled frenziedly. More police arrived and curtains in the hall were pulled down to provide wraps for her and her friend, who was standing by in a confused attitude. With the police were John Bell and John Collee. Their delay in arriving had been caused by Collee hurriedly bundling his wife and children into the air raid shelter at the back of his home. As his car was nearby it was used to take the elder woman away. It was now 3 am. The younger woman was walked back to her home, under escort, to Corbiehall.

Subsequent enquiry revealed that the two women were cousins, both over 30 years of age, living together in Corbiehall just down the hill from the church. On the previous evening (Thursday) they had attended the choir practice together for the first time for several months. At the close of the practice the members left the church by the door of the session house as usual, and unnoticed the women had stayed behind. They had waited for several hours in the growing darkness and in the early hours when all was quiet they had climbed the steep steps to the loft and pulled the rope. This was lashed to a post and by tugging at the taut rope they only got a weak clang to begin with. As it gathered momentum, and by a united effort, the bell eventually rang out louder, but still intermittently. What had caused the women to snap and to behave in this peculiar manner seems to have been the unbearable pressure of the constant threat of invasion and all the mayhem that would ensue – 'war strain' as it was called at the time. The older woman never really recovered and before the end of the week she was sent to the asylum at Larbert for specialist treatment. By the end of the war she had become institutionalised and volunteered to stay on as a sewing maid. The incident was the subject of gossip for many weeks – and not a few jokes about the behaviour of Bo'ness women! As far as the children were concerned, the worst aspect of the whole episode was the cancellation of the Saturday matinee at the cinema.

Five year old Nan Forrest did not get much sleep that night. When the church bell first rang the police called at the Stag Inn in Grangepans and woke the family – her father, the publican, was in the HG. The family had moved there from Dalkeith in 1938. James Forrest quickly donned his uniform and reported to his unit's battle station up the hill at the golf course. Many of the men there had no weapons and there really was an iconic pitch fork. Eventually word reached them that the scare was over and they each made their way home. James had never been at the golf course on a dark night and, the blackout being very effective, soon lost his way. It was some considerable time before he reached his worried family!

Elsewhere the alarms continued. The Castlecary Brickworks HG guarded the important railway junction just to the west of their works. Each night two men were on duty there at any one time. One night, just as dawn was creeping in, they spotted a group of men walking along the track in formation. Some say that a warning challenge was issued but the men were too far away to hear, others say that no warning was given. In either case rifle fire was heaped upon the mystery party. There was some irate shouting as the men took cover and were finally able to identify themselves as railway workers checking the line. Fortunately, it was either still too dark or the guardsmen were rotten shots (nerves no doubt), for no one was injured. Civilian casualties caused by the HG had not been anticipated, but the authorities were sure that many of the HG would die in the line of duty. Consequently, in February 1941, the local councils throughout the Falkirk district set aside lairs in their cemeteries for those killed in action – whether as a result of resisting an invasion or from aerial attack. While the company officers were aware of this allocation, the men were not told, as it was considered bad for morale.

As the war progressed and better news came from the fighting fronts the jitteriness of the home defenders decreased. Invasion scares became a thing of the past. The church and town bells remained silent even at New Year; they had last struck their peaceful summons to church in June 1940. They were heard briefly in November 1942 when, after due notification, they were rung to celebrate the victory at El Alamein. By April 1943 the situation was completely different and the bells were freed from their sombre role as indicators of impending doom.

The HG had developed its own system of call-out from the beginning, which in today's management parlance would be called the 'cascade method'. Those on duty at the various platoon HQs would receive the order over the phone. Some would head off to rouse more men, whilst some telephoned those platoon members with phones. Each volunteer receiving the stand-to

Aerial view of Castlecary Brickworks looking north-east, 1928.

command would pass the message on to two other named men before reporting in themselves, and so on until they were all aware of the situation.

The level of response was designed to reflect the level of perceived threat – both its intensity and certainty. If the threat was certain the men were called to ACTION STATIONS; if indeterminate the call was STAND TO. Each category was divided into two to take into account the intensity, with the word RAID added for the lower level. For a low level threat only the men most readily available were to be called out – these were known as List 1 men. The remainder, on List 2, were warned to be ready if required.

In April 1944 the Stirlingshire HG adopted the 'Snowball' system, whereby loudspeaker vans were used for calling out the men.

Police

Despite the odd conflict of interest with the police, there was a great deal of co-operation between the two services, as will be seen in the following chapters. One of the more unusual incidents in which the police asked for assistance from the HG occurred at Slamannan. A local man had returned from the army and then went Absent Without Leave. The police had been observing the movements of his girlfriend and knew he was hiding in the area near Balcastle – she had been taking him food. The HG search party then went to Balcastle Farm to scour the grounds. The deserter was found and dragged out of a hen house by the HG and handed over to the police (he survived the war.)

> 5. Calling out the Home Guard.
>
> (a) Unless otherwise specified, Home Guard Bns. will be mustered on receipt of the message "Action Stations". This message will be telephoned or sent by D.R. from H.Q. Stirling Sub Area, to Bn. H.Q. by day and to the C.O. by night. If by telephone, it (and all other important operational messages) will be checked back before action is taken, if there is any doubt as to the identity of the sender.
>
> (b) Company Commanders are responsible for ensuring that this message is acted upon with all possible speed. Personnel in List I will report at once; those in List II as soon as possible, up to a maximum delay of 48 hours.
>
> (c) Subsequently, personnel will be stood down only when authorised by Bn. H.Q.
>
> (d) The code message "RAID ACTION STATIONS" will signify that an enemy raiding force is known to be approaching SCOTLAND. Action will be taken as in (a) and (b) above.
>
> (e) The Home Guard may also be turned out any time on reliable information from H.G. sources, police, etc., that enemy parachutists or airborne troops, exceeding six in number or if less definitely identified as hostile have been seen to land in the vicinity.
>
> *(e) The Home Guard may also be turned out any time by the ringing of church bells by troops, Home Guard personnel, police, etc., to denote that enemy parachutists or airborne troops exceeding six in number or, if less, definitely identified as hostile, have been seen to land in the vicinity. [crossed out]*
>
> (f) In the case of H.G. being required to deal with armed raiders or paratps, this will be treated as a local muster.
>
>   [2nd Stg HG Bn Defence Scheme December 1942]

Compulsory Service

When it was formed the HG was entirely a voluntary organisation and commands relied upon consent. Most volunteers accepted that they were there to defend the country and as part of a quasi military organisation they took on this play role. There was, however, no such thing as military discipline and any volunteer could resign under what was nick-named the 'housemaid's clause' – all that was required was a fortnight's notice. The Government had been surprised by the initial response to its appeal for men, but towards the end of 1941 it was concerned that in some area the numbers were beginning to decline as the threat of invasion appeared to recede. By this time the HG was performing numerous valuable functions and the government intended to use this important human resource to free up manpower for the armed forces. The HG was to take over anti-aircraft batteries and coastal batteries, as well as the guarding of key Vulnerable Points. For this there had to be a dependable turnout and an ability to impose greater discipline. In November 1941 the government announced that conscription would be used for the HG. Under the National Service (No. 2) Act, any male civilian aged from 18 to 51 could, from January 1942, be ordered to join the HG and to attend for up to 48 hours training or guard duty a month, under penalty of a month in prison or a £10 fine. Once in, he could not leave until he was 65. Existing volunteers were given until 16 February 1942 to make up their minds whether to stay or to resign. In the latter case there was always the possibility, if they were under 51, that they would be 'directed' back in again.

The Government anticipated large scale resignations, but most of the old guard remained, determined to preserve the outward appearance and character of the voluntary spirit. Bo'ness was one of the worst affected places and a little under 10% took advantage of the housemaid's clause. Many of these resignations were made on the grounds of health or because their war work was more important than the regular commitment now seemingly required. What made the situation so bad in Bo'ness was that many of the HG were coal miners working long shifts and they could not guarantee their attendance on parades. Those that remained thought the Commanding Officer would consider their circumstances with some sympathy. The CO did, however, now have the power of courts-martial. At Falkirk the number resigning was closer to the national average at 5%.

At first all went well and the directed men made the most of their situation. Most joined in with the same enthusiasm

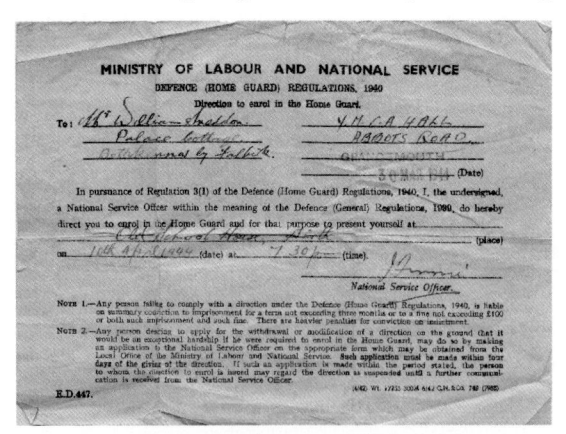

Form E.D. 447 directing William Sneddon of Palace Cottage, Bothkennar, to enrol in the HG based at the YMCA Hall, Abbots Rd, Grangemouth. He had to present himself at the Old School House in Airth, on the 10th April 1944 at 7.30pm.

First Steps

as the volunteers, though the bond of comradeship was always greatest amongst those who had joined in the early days. By 1944 the war situation was different and their grumblings grew louder. The COs were able to call upon the civil courts to compel absentees back to the parades.

The 2nd Stg HG Bn only had to use the courts for this purpose on four occasions:

July 1943   Robert Laidlaw, Camelon, 31 Platoon 32 absences in 6 months £10
July 1943   George Wallace, Maddiston, 20 Platoon 14 absences £8
Dec 1943   Jeffrey D Norris, Falkirk, 28 Platoon 18 absences £4
Jan 1944   Ditto

The West Lothian Bn used it more often, though one cannot help sympathising with the men:

Feb 1943	John Russell Bo'ness	£5	
Mar 1943	Alex McGregor	£5	Working long hours
April 1943	Cornelius Guthrie Kinneil	£5	Absent from coal mine
May 1943	John C Stirling	£4	
Aug 1943	Bernard Hampson Stoneyburn	£2	Miner
Aug 1943	Thomas Hampson ditto	£2	Miner
Oct 1943	Robert Livingstone Bo'ness	10s	Officer absent
Dec 1943	Bernard Rooney	£2	
Dec 1943	Robert Gilfinnan	£1.10	
Dec 1943	Peter Boyle Bathgate	£1.10	
Mar 1944	Bernard Rooney	£3	Getting married.
May 1944	John C Stirling	£6	Worked long shifts in a pit 12 miles away.
July 1944	James Duncan, Linlithgow	£1	Turned up late for guard duty of restricted area.
July 1944	George McLay, Armadale	£5	Volunteer almost from inception – now gastric trouble and back dermatitis from working in mine.
July 1944	10 more each fined	£5	Working in the mines

Aug 1944	Charles M Neil	Grangepans	£2	Doctor's note invalid – Guardsman should have been checking IDs at protected area.
Aug 1944	Daniel McDonald	Uphall	£1.10	
Aug 1944	Anthony McVeigh	Bathgate	10s	

For men doing demanding hard physical work on long shifts it was vexing to be heavily fined for failing to turn up to unnecessary parades by officers who were also absent. There is little doubt that tensions were getting strained. Then, in September 1944 the HG was placed back on a voluntary basis. Many breathed a sigh of relief and the old volunteers rallied around yet again.

CHAPTER THREE

Weapons

The early improvisation of weapons by the LDV has already been described. These varied from the home-made knobkerrie, pike and Molotov cocktail to the borrowed shotgun, sporting gun and museum exhibit. They were first augmented and then slowly replaced by conventional infantry weapons, which were made available through official channels. In time new weapons specifically designed for the HG were added to the arsenal. Although necessarily 'cheap and nasty', they gave the body an immediate light artillery capacity. These had strange names like Northover Projector and Blacker Bombard and were in the process of being replaced by more reliable, proved and tested equipment handed down from the regular forces, when the HG was disbanded. Throughout this period the principal weapon was the rifle and it was only when every guardsman had ready access to one of these or a sub-machine gun that the units considered themselves as fighting fit.

The progress of the 2nd Stg HG Bn in respect of the issue of weapons was typical. In the first weeks of service the scale of arms was very limited. In September 1940 there was an issue of rifles, on a scale of one per four men; and ten Lewis Guns (Air) made their appearance. Next to arrive was a consignment of Browning Automatic Rifles providing for two per company. Much has been heard about the notorious 'pikes' issued in October 1941, but they, like the rubber truncheons, were kept in reserve at Battalion and Company HQ. Three more Lewis Guns were welcomed in March 1941, and the following September Tommy Guns were listed, but were subsequently withdrawn. It was not until 1942 that grenades and anti-tank mines became available. The beginning of 1943 saw a marked development with the arrival of Spigot Mortars, EY rifles, and Smith Guns, and then came the 'Sten' to ensure that before the end of the year every man had a personal weapon. During the last year, 1944, the Battalion was well equipped with 6 Smith Guns; 26 Spigot Mortars; 13 Lewis Guns, 6 heavy Brownings, 20 BARs, 850 rifles and 430 Stens for a total strength of 1450. 2-pounder guns were promised but never reached the Battalion.

Shotguns

The principles of shooting could be (and in the early days of the LDV they were) learnt by practice on a shotgun. The basic elements, though different in detail from gun to gun, were there – maintenance, loading, aiming, firing, recoil, range and so on.

The Denny LDV, as mentioned earlier, were trained by the gamekeeper from the Denovan Estate using shotguns. They then graduated to the miniature rifle and eventually to the standard rifle. Even when the latter started to arrive in reasonable numbers the shotgun was retained as a useful close-up weapon. It also had the distinct advantage of being much easier to find ammunition for. To hone their skills in its use the Bo'ness HG found a practical use for the shotgun. In May 1941 they received permission from the Town Council to use it on its woodland at Kinneil Estate to eradicate the rooks there. The birds were considered a threat to national security because they fed on the crops in the neighbouring fields. Weekly shooting parties were organised, usually on a Sunday, and procedures were agreed to safeguard the public walking in the area. A storm of protest ensued from those interested in the preservation of this all too common birdlife, but the shoot went ahead in the belief that it was contributing to the preservation of people's way of life. It had one further benefit not yet mentioned. The dead birds were gathered up and delivered to the Model Lodging House on the corner of Main Street and Dock Street. Here the cook removed their breasts and made crow pies, which were gratefully received by the occupants of the lodging. News of this philanthropy soon leaked out and the chance of extra unrationed meat brought out private shooting parties, but they were turned away from Kinneil Woods because the HG had been given sole shooting rights. However, despite the precautions taken, a young boy from the town managed to infiltrate the shoot and was injured. Crow shooting on the Council's land was banned in June 1942. The hunt merely moved westward to the Craw Yett and to Nether Kinneil, where the farmer was a member of the HG and liked crow pie.

Clay pigeon shooting remained a popular sport amongst some of the HG. At one of the sports days held in Callendar Park for all the local platoons it featured alongside five-a-side football and the like. Marcus Rodgers of the Falkirk Ironworks platoon had never fired a shotgun before, but was happy to join in the spirit of the occasion and had a go, especially as there was a prize of so-many cigarettes. Much to his astonishment, and without giving it much thought, he hit three out of three. He had been surprised by the speed of the release and had automatically responded. He found that he was the only private

Weapons

Falkirk Ironworks Platoon, 'B' Coy 2nd Stg HG Bn, in Callendar Park, c1942. The photographer is standing with his back towards Callendar House. The absence of weapons and ammunition pouches suggests that this was a social occasion. The men with Tam O' Shanters are company and platoon officers.

Man with no cap, back row 4th from left — Tom Brown, trainer of Falkirk Lions Ice Hockey team and Falkirk Football Club, worked in foundry. Man in row in front of Tom Brown, just to his left, again no cap — Jim Isdale. Man standing isolated at back — Dick Sharpe, foreman polisher. Front row, first complete youth from left — Harry Rodgers. To right of Harry Rodgers — Harry Wilson, manager Falkirk Iron Works. Man directly behind Harry Rodgers — Jock Lane, lived at Hayfield. Front row, at crack in photo — Major Bob McNair, plasterer. To right of Bob McNair — Rattray, managing director. Front row, 6th from right — Alex Logan, foreman moulder.

soldier to make it through to the second round. The rest were officers who, like Lt-Col. Stein, shot for sport. Marcus decided to concentrate on his game this time and inevitably left his shot too late.

The local gamekeepers and poachers were not only accustomed to the use of firearms, but also to stalking their prey. They had developed stealth and tracking abilities. They were able to form an unholy alliance to become the nucleus of special units aimed at ambushing small parties of any invasion force.

Molotov cocktails

Apart from broomsticks with various bladed implements attached, the earliest weapon of the HG was the Molotov cocktail. These could be readily improvised using old bottles, which were filled with an inflammable liquid. A rag soaked in paraffin was then pushed into the neck and left protruding to act as a fuse. This was lit with a match and the bottle thrown at the enemy as soon as possible. Upon impact the bottle broke and its contents burst into flames – or so the theory went. There was a good chance that the flame would travel down the rag and ignite the fuel prematurely. Their range, of course, was only as far as they could be thrown so it was always useful to seek out an elevated location for an ambush.

Some of the coal miners in the Bo'ness HG were already familiar with this rather crude weapon from their recent experiences serving in the International Brigade during the Spanish Civil War. As good socialists they had volunteered to fight to preserve the elected left wing government in Spain against Franco's fascists. They soon started producing Molotov cocktails in large numbers, though they did not know them by that name, which had only been coined in Finland a few months earlier. During that country's valiant resistance to the Russian invasion the Fins would shout "That's one for Molotov!" the Russian Foreign Minister, as they hurled each one.

Tom Gardiner of the Slamannan HG in his back garden in New Street.

The West Lothian HG adopted the Molotov cocktail with a will and enlisted the help of Scottish Oils Ltd in their manufacture. The Stirlingshire battalions became equally enthused after an experienced regular officer from Stirling Castle gave then a demonstration. It filled the men with renewed confidence and brought home to the HG officers the advisability of demonstration before the issue of any new weapons.

In February 1940 the Slamannan HG decided to hold what they called a 'Bottle Party'. They marched 2.5 miles (4km) to Darnrigg Moss carrying the bottles of flammable liquid. Each man then got a chance to try them out, which meant setting the oily rag in the mouth alight before throwing it. When it came to Tom Gardiner's turn, he duly set the flames going and then hesitated. "For God's sake throw the thing or we'll all go up! yelled Rudy Kerr. He did. Oddly enough Tom had the same momentary lapse when it came to hand grenades.

Rifles

The initial shortage of weapons for the LDV and the rather vague uncertainty concerning its role in the event of an invasion – sometimes restricted to mere observation and reporting – led to various attempts by other organisations to take on the military role. In June 1940, for example, the Camelon ARP built a shooting range behind their headquarters at the Gymnasium in Union Street. The concept, in so far as the people of Camelon were concerned, was that these men of the Civil Defence organisation would switch from air raid duties to fighting ones in the event of an invasion. Personnel in the ARP services had been asked not to leave in order to join the LDV and this was their response. Elsewhere they did switch allegiances.

At the same time in Larbert David Graham, a gymnastics instructor at the RSNI, decided to give instruction in the use of the rifle and in physical training to anyone over 17 years of age and willing to resist the Nazi invader, regardless of occupation or sex. He had previously served in the army for 16 years with the rank of Corporal-Instructor. The lessons were held at the Village School at 8pm on Mondays and Tuesdays, or 6pm on Wednesdays, Fridays and Saturdays.

The first consignment of arms and ammunition for the East Stirlingshire Battalion of the LDV arrived on a Sunday morning, just two weeks after the original appeal for volunteers. It consisted of 30 rifles and a very small quantity of ammunition, together with 30 field service (FS) caps and LDV armlets. These had to be spread over almost 4,000 men. The rifles were issued to those volunteers going on guard duty in the evening, and were duly handed over to the relieving sentries, together with the caps and armlets.

The Falkirk Ironworks platoon doing duty at Bainsford Bridge only had a single Lee-Enfield rifle amongst its 30-40 members for the first month. At the end of each two-hour guard shift it was passed on, along with the single clip of five bullets. The latter was put into the pocket of the guard, but few members of the public noticed that and it was amazing just how much confidence could be gained from holding an empty rifle. As the platoon got more rifles they were kept locked in the armoury next to the guardroom in the ironworks. The key for this was kept by the officer on duty.

The combination of gun and uniform inevitably bred a deal of pomposity and the HG had a tendency to stretch its remit. There were objections from the public over the number of times that they were asked to show their ID cards. Drivers were particularly irate over the increased journey time caused by HG road blocks. The standard response to these and many other challenges was "Don't you know there's a war on?" Increased vigilance was essential, but it often went too far. Surely it was not necessary to stop people you knew to demand their ID cards?

A well-known example of this behaviour occurred at the Dock Pit in Bo'ness. The miners used to walk to work through the Docks and across the closed lock gates. However, when the Admiralty took over control of Bo'ness Dock this route was closed off. All pedestrian traffic to the pit had to pass over a long footbridge over the numerous railway sidings to the east. At the south end of this bridge was a large wooden sentry box and here was posted the guard, which at various stages was manned by the HG. Each employee within the restricted area was given a blue enamelled badge with the initials 'B D & H' on it to signify that they had the permission of the Bo'ness Dock and Harbour authority to be there. The sentry could also demand the national ID card of anyone attempting to gain access, as these had to be carried at all times. To begin with the men on duty did not possess a rifle, but sported a revolver with a black hand grip. This was prominently displayed in a holster attached to the

Brass badge with blue enamel. The initials BD&H stood for Bo'ness Dock & Harbour Trust and the badge was used to show that the bearer was on legitimate business within the restricted area of the Docks.

Weapons

Aerial photograph of Bo'ness Docks showing the location of the Dock Pit and the access to it.

belt. The guard was rotated, but with a limited number of volunteers to draw from it was not long before they became familiar with the miners working at the pit. Indeed, some of them worked there themselves. Tommy Murphy, 'Spud' to his friends, was late for work one shift and sped up the steps to cross the bridge. However, the sentry was not to be bypassed and he challenged Spud to come back or be shot, at the same time removing his gun from the holster. Spud was in a dilemma. He believed that the gun was not loaded and that the man, who clearly recognised him, was not likely to shoot him anyway – but could he take the chance? He swore vehemently and retraced his steps. He came face to face with the sentry, who was expecting more vitriolic language. The sentry was not expecting the violent punch that hit him in the face and sent him reeling. He was still staggering when Spud was telling him never to take his gun out again unless he intended to use it. By the time that he had recovered Spud was clocking on at the pithead.

With a large number of guard posts to man the Bo'ness HG were not initially able to issue a rifle to each. A small number of .303 rifles had been allocated to the West Lothian Battalion on 28th May 1940 with 50 rounds of ammunition per rifle. They were soon dispersed and further distributions were made in June and July, in some case with 20 rounds per rifle. Most of these later rifles were .300 gauge and had been shipped from America. By the end of November 1940 the number of rifles held by the West Lothian Battalion was 1,544 .300

and 89 .303. The East Stirlingshire Battalion seems to have held similar numbers, though the only figure available at the end of December 1940 is for the 3rd Stg HG Bn, which had been formed by splitting the original battalion in two. It possessed 757 .300 rifles and 83 .303 rifles. The bulk of these had been issued in September providing roughly one rifle to every four guardsmen.

The standard British infantryman's rifle of the time was the modified short Lee-Enfield, which fired the standard British bullet of .303 calibre. These were reliable and accurate, making them trusted by the regular army. Being only 44.43ins long and weighing 9lb 1oz, they were better balanced and less cumbersome than previous models. Unfortunately, most had been left behind in France and for the next few years all those that were produced went to replace them and to supply the rapidly expanding regular forces. Fortunately, alternatives were available within a relatively short period of time, albeit they were older models.

Soon after the short Lee-Enfield had been introduced in 1903 it was criticised in some circles and so a longer version, the Pattern 14, was designed just in case there was any justification in such views. The new rifle was designed with an eye to rapid production in wartime. It happened, of course, that the 1903 rifle was of a very high standard, but the shortage of rifles caused by the First World War led to the production of several thousand P14s on contract in the USA. After that war they had been put into storage and the British Army continued with the Lee-Enfield. When the LDV was formed the P14s were taken out of storage and distributed around the country. Hugh Baird of the Brightons platoon remembered it was a good rifle that was quite accurate. Its only problem was that if fired rapidly it got warm and the recoil increased giving it a kick like a mule.

When the USA had entered the First World War it was found that it had a problem with its own rifles. This was solved by redesigning the P14 to take the standard US .300 cartridge, and then getting the manufacturers of the P14 (the Remington Arms Company and the Winchester Repeating Arms Company) to produce them. This version was called the 'Pattern 17' by the British, and the 'M1917' or 'Enfield' by the Americans. It was 46.25ins long and weighed 9lb 10oz. In all 2,193,429 P17 rifles were produced before the contracts terminated in 1918. After the war these too were placed in storage. To protect them during this period they were coated in heavy grease and packed in wooden crates. After Dunkirk Winston Churchill negotiated to have them sent over and they first arrived in late June and July 1940. They were delivered to the individual units still caked in grease and the first job that their recipients had was to spend hours removing it with the aid of rags and hot water. Whilst this task was dirty and wearisome, the men were jubilant to have real guns.

Weapons

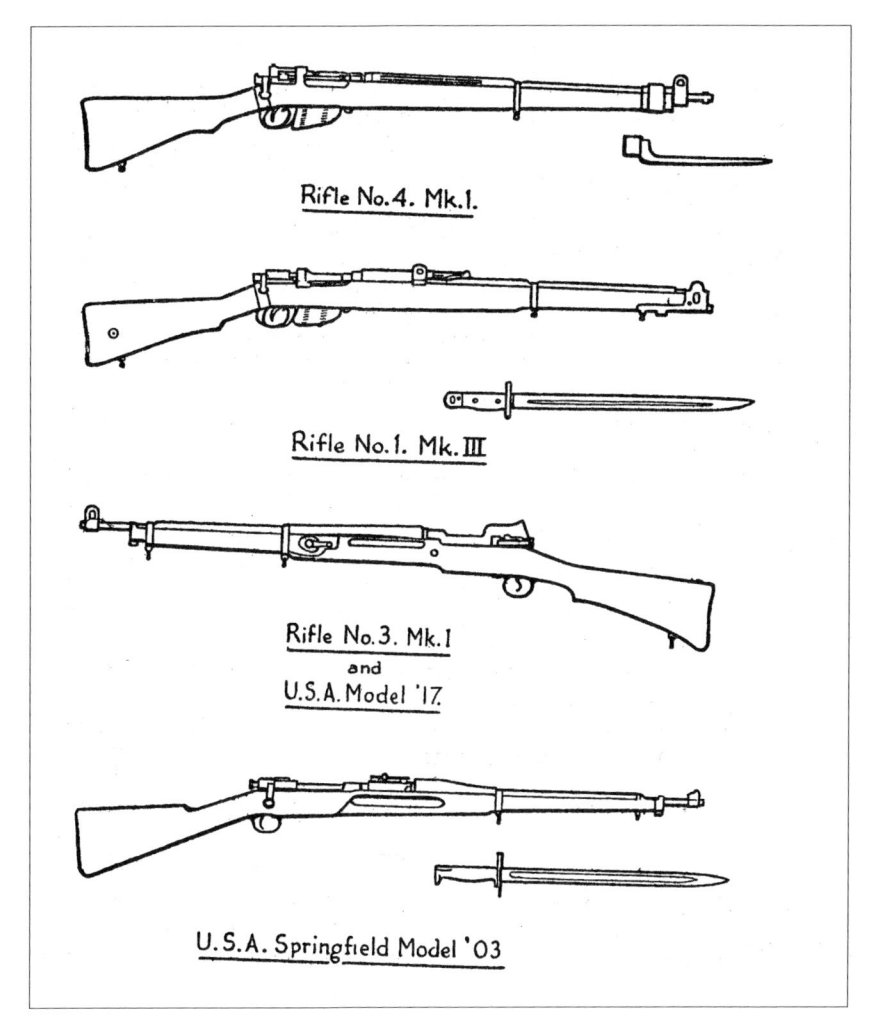

Drawings of the short magazine Lee-Enfield (SMLE) Mks I & III, the P17 and the Springfield rifles (from Small Arms Manual, Lt-Col. J A Barlow & Major REW Johnson, Nov 1942).

Another foreign rifle at this time was the Canadian Ross rifle. It was the longest of the rifles and weighed almost a pound more than the Lee-Enfield. When the Falkirk Power Station platoon received its Ross rifles they had neither bayonet nor sling. The men made their own slings from leather belts. The rifles were prone to jamming if the tiniest grain of grit got into the mechanism. The longer barrel gave the Ross rifle a high degree of accuracy in the right hands. John Grierson of the Stenhousemuir platoon recalled that it was very good at 100yds, and with practice (requiring a change of sighting criteria) it

BROWNING LIGHT AUTO RIFLE

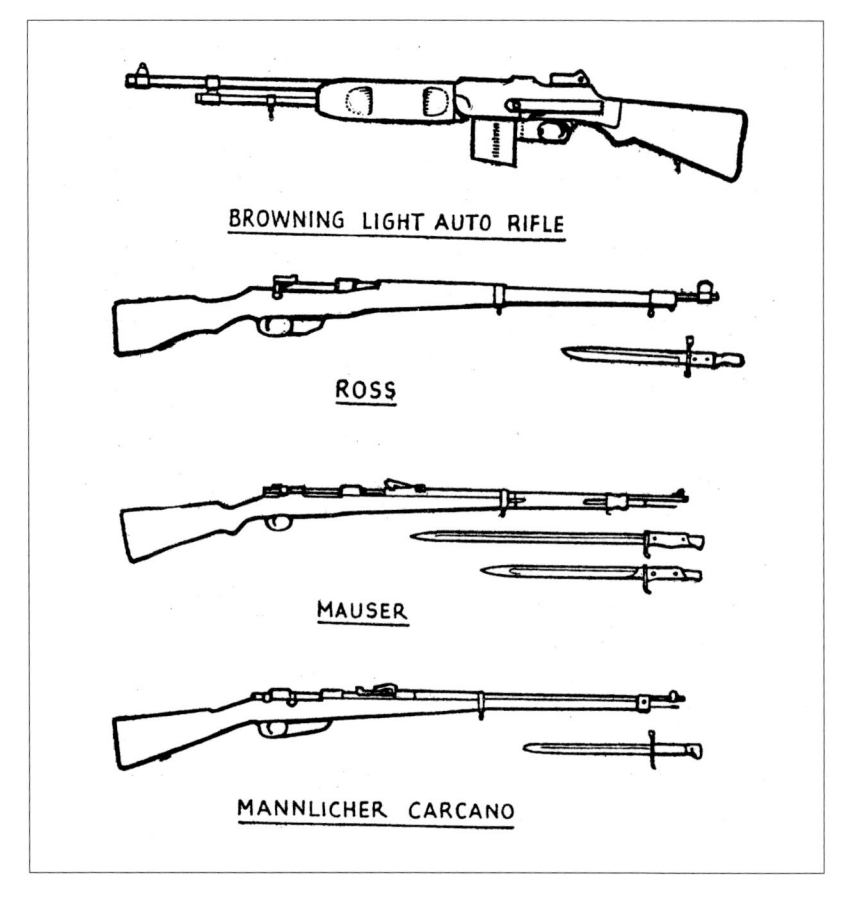

ROSS

MAUSER

MANNLICHER CARCANO

Drawings of foreign rifles with the Ross rifle second from the top (from Small Arms Manual, Lt-Col. JA Barlow & Major REW Johnson, Nov 1942).

was pretty accurate at 200 and 300yards. The sight consisted of a small vertical pin with a spherical swelling at the end of the barrel and a hollow ring at the breech. The rifles also looked impressive on parade, but not in confined spaces, as the Laurieston HG discovered. This platoon met in the woodwork shed at Laurieston School and decided one night, due to the appalling weather, to do a full drill practice indoors. The long bayonets were fitted in preparation and then the call came to shoulder arms. Up went the rifles as quick as you like, all in unison. And down came the plaster and paint from the ceiling. The rifles were rapidly lowered, but they were now somewhat unbalanced by their impact "and poor Webster got a fright when one just missed slicing off his ear."

Ross rifles were issued to a number of local platoons, including those based at Manuel Brickworks, Falkirk Power Station, Stenhousemuir, Falkirk Ironworks, Laurieston and Grangemouth. The P14 is known to have been used by the platoons at Denny, Larbert, Bonnybridge and Brightons. It too could be used with great accuracy and 16 year old Peter Graeme of the Denny platoon found that it suited him. It had a long V-shaped back sight above the bolt and an aperture sight at the end of the barrel, which he used to good effect. When he later joined the army and was given the short Lee-Enfield to use his accuracy plummeted. Most of the platoons were issued with some Lee-Enfield rifles, though the Slamannan platoon is the only one that I know that was completely equipped with them. This may have been due to the unusual youth and mobility of this unit, combined with its unique role at a nodal point (of which more later).

There was considerable variation in the places that the rifles were kept for safekeeping. The armoury at the ICI Works in Grangemouth was near the main gate where there was a guard and it was protected by a steel door. Similarly, the armoury at the Falkirk Ironworks lay next to the unit's guardhouse and had a separate entry to which only the officers had the key. These works' storage facilities, and those of Smith and Wellstood in Bonnybridge, were at the top end of the range and it was rare for the guardsmen of these platoons to take the rifles home. However, Jim Young, whose father was in the Falkirk Ironworks platoon, can recall his father keeping a Ross rifle in his bedroom cupboard.

When it was first formed the East Stirlingshire Battalion only had the use of a small side room and two police cells in Stenhousemuir Police Station as an office, armoury and HQ. The police assisted in the issuing of the weapons to those on duty. The police station at Grangemouth was also used as an arsenal and strictly administered. At Slamannan the platoon met in the Miners' Welfare Hall and some rifles were kept locked in racks there, whilst the ammunition and explosives were stored in a lockfast magazine in the wood behind the hall. Ian Arthur was studying medicine at university at the time and was only able to attend the Sunday meetings of the HG. As a List 2 man he never got to take a rifle home. Most of the platoon did take them home so that they were ready in the event of an invasion, including Barney Schoneville and Hector Maxwell, both of whom kept them in presses in the halls so that they were handy for picking up on the way out. In neither case was the press locked, though ammunition was always kept separate. Barney, for instance, had ammunition pouches that were put away with his uniform. William Wilson of the Larbert platoon kept his P14 rifle in the hat stand in the hall, like a walking stick.

The Ross rifles of the Manuel Brickworks platoon were only issued when required for drill or guard duty. At other times they were kept locked in racks inside the foreman engineer's office. The foreman engineer was the platoon commander. Perhaps the worst stores were the wooden huts used by a number of platoons, such as those at Laurieston, Redding and Carron. The Redding men responsibly took their rifles home. Robert McNab kept his in a locked cupboard so that his two younger sisters would not get at it. The bullets were in his great coat, which hung at the top of the stairs. Many mothers objected to their young sons bringing such equipment home, but circumstances demanded. Peter Riddell's mother was one of those unhappy by their presence, but once she was out of the house his father, a sergeant in the Carronshore HG, would teach his young son how to dismantle and then reassemble rifles or Sten guns. Occasionally other members of the HG would call round at Keswick Cottage for a meeting in the front parlour and Peter would impress them by the speed with which he could strip the guns down.

William Clark with a P17 rifle, c1940. He is still wearing an armband.

To prevent the wrong calibre ammunition being used many of the American .300 rifles had red bands painted on them. This was particularly important for those platoons that had a mixture of the two calibres, such as the Falkirk Ironworks platoon that had Ross and P17 rifles, or the Grangemouth platoons that had P17 and Lee-Enfield. In an effort to avoid such a mix up in ammunition, and to maximise the use of that available, on 3rd September 1941 the 1st Stg Bn based in Stirling exchanged twelve .300 rifles for the same number of .303 rifles from the 2nd Stg Bn based in Falkirk.

Ammunition was scarce. At first the Ross rifles of the Falkirk Power Station platoon were kept in the HQ and only issued to the men on guard duty. The first firing practice they got was at the Policy Bing at the top of the Glen Brae. Here makeshift targets were set up so that the spent bullets hit the side of the waste tip. There were only enough bullets to let each member in the platoon

Weapons 69

have one shot. The officers naturally wanted to have more than one go themselves and intended to omit the younger volunteers. The threat of mass desertion forced them to change their minds – a sign of discipline before compulsion.

In the early days the allocation of small arms ammunition (SAA) was only ten rounds per rifle on average, to be used exclusively for operational purposes – that meant there was no opportunity to practice shooting. Over the first three years few men of the 2nd Stg HG Bn fired more than five rounds on a range, which, needless to say, was a considerable handicap for their training. The 3rd Stg HG Bn was in a similar position, with the available ammunition for practice purposes not even permitting one round per man. They were all as keen as mustard to have a shot and, having been granted permission to use the Greenhill Range, they 'borrowed' ammunition from the regular soldiers billeted in the area and bought it off the 'open market'. The end result was that they too got an average of five rounds off.

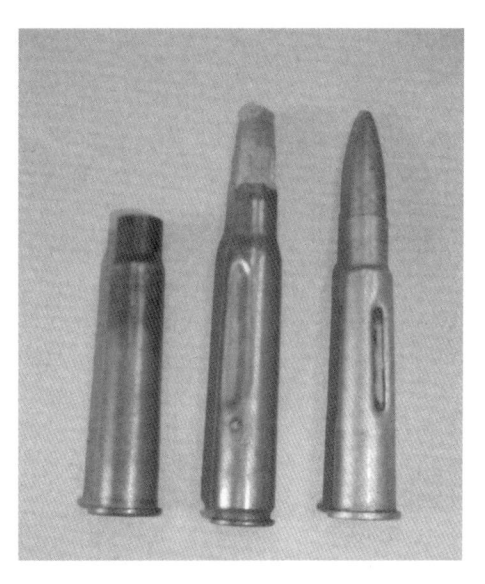

Three bullet cartridges used by the Falkirk HG to demonstrate their action and the differences between rimless and rimmed examples or .303 calibre and .300.

In May 1942 two of the more youthful members of the 2nd Stg HG Bn got into trouble for using their initiative to procure extra rounds of .22 ammunition to put in some extra hours of shooting on their own miniature rifle range. The 308 rounds that they were able to lay their hands on were not obtained through the usual channels – in fact they were stolen. The two young men, William Duncan aged 17, and John Harley aged 18, had been the guests of the Polish Army at Callendar House. They were shown into the stores at the stable block and it was only a few days later that it was noticed that the ammunition was gone. They were fined £5 each.

The West Lothian HG Bn seems to have been more fortunate in respect of SAA, for in July 1940 it was invited to share facilities at the Dreghorn Barracks to the south-west of Edinburgh. In practical terms this meant that a handful of men from Bo'ness went by rotation on Sundays to the shooting range there and had an opportunity to practise with live rounds. This programme continued until the end of August, when transport difficulties closed the range to them over winter. It resumed the following year and the Bo'ness platoons became proficient enough to compete against other units on the range. By all accounts they acquitted themselves well.

Each platoon in the Falkirk district seems to have produced a few crack shots who became quite enthused with the new sport of target shooting. Somehow they too managed to find sufficient SAA to participate in competitions. Inter-platoon rivalry was positively encouraged. National newspapers vied with each other to sponsor events, which they rightly claimed would improve the standards of HG shooting. As the papers provided the ammunition the guardsmen were happy to enter. In October 1941 the Bonnybridge Power Station section of the HG found itself in the final of the Landscape Target Competition organised and sponsored by Country Life. The objects and salient features of the target were not discernible to the naked eye and a leader was appointed who, with the aid of binoculars, was able to give directions and aiming points to the other members of the team. Although they did not win, the section was highly commended. William Wilson of the Larbert platoon remembered this type of shooting: "We were all part of an inter battalion rifle shooting competition where an officer or NCO with binoculars would point out a target, say 'a house at 400yds, target is at 10 to 12, five rounds fire.' Practice for this took place in the Lord Roberts Rifle Club in East Croft Street, where there was a 25 yard range for a .22 rifle."

That same month, October 1941, Capt. Curran of Bonnybridge set up an HG miniature shooting league. Each team comprised eight shooting members and four reserves and the rules conformed to the Scottish Miniature Rifle Club standards. Score cards were printed and before long the teams were accepted into the Stirlingshire Small Bore Rifle Association. The following year replicas

Shooting trophy presented to 'D' Coy 2nd Stg HG Bn for internal competition by Mr Muirhead. (Now in Falkirk Museum.)

of the Scottish National Cup for miniature shooting were presented to the winning team from 'A' Company and the British Legion gave the 2nd Stg HG Bn. a cup for annual competition. The teams that became prominent in the next two years were Bonnybridge, Milnquarter Works, Castlecary Works and the Falkirk Post Office. Indeed, the 2nd Bn. came to dominate local competitions. Outwith that battalion, 'B' Company of the 3rd Stg HG Bn. did well.

Miniature rifle shooting with .22 calibre was well established in the Falkirk district before the war. The Falkirk Rifle Club had its own indoor miniature range in Oswald Street formed from an old factory. Such ranges were relatively small, being only 20-30yds long, and were found in the most unlikely places. One existed, for example, in the basement of Bainsford Church in Smith Street and a complex system of pulleys was rigged up to allow the targets to be inspected at close quarters. The most famous of these pre-war clubs was the Lord Roberts Rifle Club in East Croft Street, Larbert, where many fine marksmen were trained.

At the establishment of the LDV it was found that the .22 rifles and ammunition were more readily available through private channels than standard rifles were through any means. They also had the advantage of requiring smaller ranges and so training was conducted on them throughout the war. The Territorial Drill Halls at Bonnybridge, Denny, Falkirk and Grangemouth all had plenty of space for internal ranges and were each made available to several platoons of the HG. Elsewhere miniature ranges were improvised. At the west

Annual shoot for the Kinnaird Trophy and county individual championship at Falkirk Iron Company's recreation ground. Each marksman has a telescope by his side to check the target. (May 1939.)

end of the county they emulated Bainsford and set up a range in the basement of Haggs Church. A basement of sorts was discovered below the Miners' Welfare Hall in Slamannan, which was already the base for the HG platoon there. It was not tall enough to stand up in, but that did not matter. The dwarf walls supporting the floor ran lengthwise along the hall and provided three discrete alleys. One member of the unit later noted that it was only the officers and 'so and sos' that got to use it. The three Bo'ness platoons shared a miniature range at Bridgeness. This belonged to P & W McLellan the shipbreakers and was located at the south end of their yard, lying parallel to the main road to the east of the Bridgeness Pottery. It was rather an unusual structure, being only one storey high but long and narrow and made of plate steel. It had been created by the shipbreakers using deck cabins from redundant vessels, joined end to end. Home Guardsman McCaig taught the local army cadets how to shoot here on Sunday afternoons.

The team of eight shooting members from the Smith & Wellstood HG platoon pictured outside the back of the work's office with the trophy it won in the miniature rifle shooting league. C1942. Cpl James Torrence in centre of the front row. Reginald Fife-Smith, on the right, was a director of Smith & Wellstood.

Weapons

The commander of the R & A Main work's platoon, Lt G Wortley, was a managing director there and a member of the Lord Roberts Rifle Club and encouraged his men to take up miniature rifle shooting. To this end a long open alley way between a moulding shed and the pattern shop was converted into a range. A target was placed at one end and the men spent their free time there. Jim Greig became a good shot. Competitions were arranged between platoons. One of these was against the Sunnyside platoon and was held at Alexander's Garage in Stirling Road, where there was another miniature range. Each man got five shots. Jim fancied his chances, but knew that he faced sharp competition from a local man who had honed his shooting skills as a rat catcher. Jim fired his five shots and then went off to enjoy the evening with his mates, not bothering to wait for the results. The next day, much to everyone's surprise, Mr Wortley appeared on the shop floor at the works. He was searching for Jim and when he found him divulged that Jim had won the shooting competition. He was evidently a little annoyed that Jim had not stayed to take the credit for his excellent shooting – and of course had not passed that credit on to the platoon.

The principal armoury of the 2nd Stg HG Bn was at the Drill Hall in Falkirk and naturally the .22 firing range there got most use. Platoons from all over the battalion's area used its facilities. Hugh Baird of the Brightons platoon was there one day with two other men from that unit. One of them really fancied

Falkirk Drill Hall in Cow Wynd is now a gymnastics centre.

himself as a splendid marksman and took the central galley so that his mates on either side could see how well he was doing. They took their positions and each let off five shots at the same time. The fancy shooter knew that he had done well, but was rather annoyed when he discovered 15 holes in his target. Then the man who looked after the range challenged them to a competition. By that stage they knew better than to accept. He often did this and the younger recruits, being less level-headed, usually took him on. There would be a small wager, each recruit putting in a small sum of money to make a prize pot of say half-a-crown or so – winner takes all. The man in charge always won and kept himself in beer money for the rest of the war.

Women had always been eager to join the HG and in August 1942 a group of them were able to share in the shooting part of the training by forming the Falkirk Women's Rifle Club. At the inaugural meeting held in the Erskine Church Hall the committee was elected. It consisted of Mrs Blackadder (wife of the engineer John Blackadder), Mrs Callander (wife of the architect James G Callander), Mrs Loxton, Miss M McIntosh and Miss Johnston. Rev. J A F Dean of the HG agreed to act as an instructor. Representatives from the men's rifle club were then asked to join the committee and their range in Oswald Street was made available.

It was not until the spring of 1943 that ammunition became available in sufficient quantity to permit the HG to attend regular courses at open firing ranges. Thereafter there was no holding them back. At the end of the year the HG throughout the Falkirk district found itself in a position whereby every member had either a rifle or a Sten gun of his own and with sufficient ammunition to train thoroughly and use it if necessity arose.

1943 was the year of the open range. The Bo'ness Company had been using facilities at Dreghorn in 1940 and 1941, which lost a lot of time and fuel in travelling. In 1942 it had shared a range at Hutly near Linlithgow. Now that it had sufficient equipment of its own, the Bo'ness HG constructed its own rifle range in the early summer of 1943. It successfully sought permission from the Forth Conservancy Board to use its land on the coast to the west of Bo'ness at Dykeneuk. At Bainsford the HG hollowed out an area in the side of Cinder Hill at Bankside, placing old wooden railway sleepers and sandbags against the resulting scarp. The targets were set up just in front of the sleepers and the hill absorbed all the spent bullets. The HG at Slamannan did the same thing with an old pit bing at Salterhill Farm, to the south of the village. After church service on a Sunday the men would collect a bag of ammunition and walk up to the range. Over at Denny the home-made shooting range lay on the south side of the River Carron, to the west of Dales Bridge, making use of a disused railway embankment as the butts. It was always useful to have such large artificial banks behind the targets for bullets that went astray. At Caldercruix they simply set the targets against the side of the hill until one day when a horse grazing in the background suddenly jumped into the air with a loud whinny. It had been shot in the butt! The range at Callendar Park appears to have been little better and it was not unknown for the dull thud of a spent shell to be heard in the back gardens of James Street in Laurieston.

Like the Bainsford and Slamannan platoons, that at Castlecary Brickworks fired into a bing, though its was adjacent to the works at its west end. Local children from Allandale relished the pleasure of collecting the copper cartridge cases that were to be found in the heather and extracting the lead bullet heads from the wooden railway sleepers in the target area. Their parents were not enamoured at finding these treasures on the floor with their bare feet as they crept around the darkened rooms. Some of the boys would lay their prizes on the steel railway lines in the shunting yard and watch as the wagon's wheels compressed them into new shapes.

Known miniature rifle ranges:

1st West Loth. Bn	McLellan's Yard, Bridgeness
2nd Stg Bn	Castlecary Brickworks – canteen & bowling club
	Falkirk Drill Hall
	Slamannan Miners' Welfare Hall
	Avonbridge HQ
	Park Ave, Laurieston
	Manuel Brickworks canteen
	Bonnybridge Drill Hall
	Bainsford Church basement
	Alexander's bus garage
	Gothic Foundry
3rd Stg Bn	Denny Drill Hall
	Haggs Church basement
	Grangemouth Drill Hall

Known open ranges:

1st West Loth. Bn	Dykeneuk, Kinneil (800yds)
2nd Stg Bn	Greenhill, Lochgreen (1000yds)
	Salterhill, Slamannan
	South Bantaskine
	Callendar Park

	Cinder Hill, Bainsford
	Shieldhill (30yds)
	Avonbridge
	Bonnybridge adjoining school playground
3rd Stg Bn	Dales Bridge, Denny
	Shelly Bank, Grangemouth (600yds)
	Polmont Hill, Grangemouth

In the last six months of its existence the 2nd Stg HG Bn. had twelve 30 yard ranges in regular use, in addition to the open range at Lochgreen. The latter lay to the south of High Bonnybridge and was known as the Greenhill Range. At first the men were driven there in small numbers by their officers, but before long army transport was arranged. This usually meant lorries from the Motor Transport pool provided by regular units in the area, or buses from the HG's mobile column at the bus garage in Brown Street, Camelon. The Slamannan men hired buses from Reid in the village. Such shooting was nearly always done on a Sunday so that there would be a large turnout, and because to use the range meant closing the minor road between Cadgersloan and Lochgreen. Before firing could commence a man had to go to each end of

Laurieston HG Platoon in Callendar Park. 1940. The men include Ian Grant, Geordie Erskine, Douglas Haston, Charlie Dunn. Alec McNab third from right in the back row; George Main 6th from right in the back row; Jack Abernethy 3rd from right in front row.

the road to place red flags into position. The targets were set at the top of a small stone cliff, at the foot of a sloping hill with an earth bank or butt. It was run by staff from the regular army who gave instruction and set up the targets. William Barron was employed as range warden.

The targets could be raised and lowered from behind a concrete shelter fronted by a stone dyke. This meant that results could be relayed either by marking the targets with large symbols, or by field telephone. The majority of the shooting was done at a distance of 200 yards, but by moving to a number of stances it was possible to vary this to up to 1000 yards. Some of the platoons ran sweepstakes for the highest score – only coppers, but it made it more interesting. One thing that they did not want to do was to be on the course too long, for approaching dusk the midges were voracious.

The most unusual thing about the Greenhill Range, which gave it a unique character that endeared it to the users, was Mrs McNellie and her tea trolley. She lived in the adjacent farmsteading at Cadgersloan with her daughter, who helped her to prepare sandwiches, buns and so on for the men during their break. The tea trolley was really a bogey and the prepared tea had to be reheated on a Primus stove when she got to the shooting stances. Somehow she had been able to arrange to get extra rations for this purpose and she would cycle to the bakers in High Bonnybridge, opposite to St Helen's Church, to pick them up each weekend. She was doing her bit for the war effort and has her place in history.

After years of frustration Colin Sharp of the Carron platoon was finally allowed to practise with his rifle at Greenhill. He got his shots away and then went to take his turn standing at one end of the closed section of road to stop the public using it. To his surprise he was soon called back by Capt. Johnny Watters. Apparently Colin's shooting had been quite accurate and he was given another opportunity to handle the rifle. The following Sunday he was told that he had been selected to become a sniper. Along with a select few he was taken in an army truck, driven by a member of the ATS, to Glenbervie Golf Course. They dismounted and walked up the hill to the west until the instructor stopped them and asked if they had seen anything unusual in the area below them. None of them had and so to break the silence Colin pointed out a small group of cattle on the golf course. The area had been set aside for this purpose, but it was still a little odd. To everyone's surprise the instructor congratulated him, he was right – but it was only as the instructor explained that the cattle were crowded into one corner of the field because someone had disturbed them, that Colin realised why. As snipers it was such apparently insignificant things that they should be spotting.

The 'Targets' at Lochgreen in 2005, looking east. The area has been planted with trees. The front of the building, to the left, takes the form of a stone wall. Behind is a shelter for the operators to work in relative safety.

In the six months leading up to December 1944 the 2nd Stg HG Bn. was able to fire off over 50,000 rounds of SAA to good effect as far as training was concerned and over 400 men from the battalion completed the full battle course. At this late date, with the risk of invasion greatly diminished, an emphasis was placed on training sniper screens. That the training had not been wasted was shown by the fact that 150 of those completing the battle course passed out as "marksmen". Four of them actually found places in the 'King's Hundred' for the HG. This had been a nationwide competition organised by the National Rifle Association at Bisley. Places were decided on the highest individual scores in the rifle course, shot on the open range. As only 17 places were secured by Scottish marksmen this was quite an achievement. The successful competitors, who each received certificates, were Sgt. George Robertson, Sgt. McLay, Pte. A M Kelly – all of Falkirk, and L/Cpl Kyle Penman of Shieldhill. The first three scored 135, and the last 132, out of a possible 140 points. George Robertson of the Battalion HQ in Falkirk was also a leading member of the Falkirk Lord Roberts Rifle Club. In September 1944 he was awarded the Scottish Championship for small bore rifle shooting. He was at the top of his form and within days he capped that prize by winning the Individual Championship of Britain.

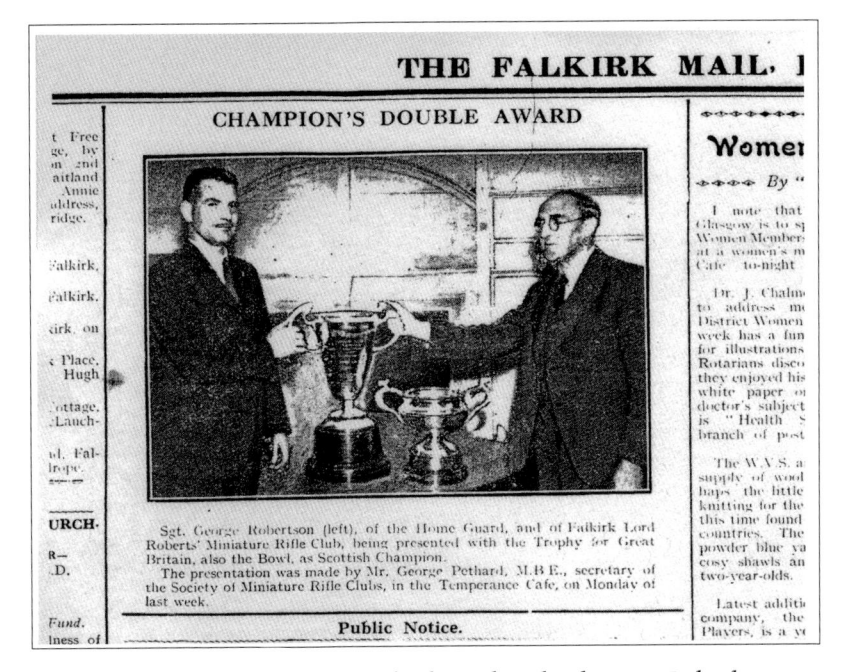

Sgt George Robertson (left) being presented with a trophy and cup by George Pethard, secretary of the Miniature Rifle Clubs, in the Temperance Café, October 1944. (Falkirk Mail)

Shooting competitions provided not only a way of improving the marksmanship of the HG, but also a way to keep them interested in the organisation beyond the initial enthusiastic outburst at its formation. Miniature rifle competitions began as early as 1941 and continued for some years after the war. When the HG was being stood down in December 1944 many of its members wished to continue to meet socially and the most obvious focal points for such meetings were the rifle ranges. Some clubs simply continued to meet as before and others were set up under the new civilian conditions. The Grangemouth HG Rifle Club, for example, was only inaugurated on 19th April 1945. Although it met in the Drill Hall, which they had been accustomed to using, a brand new miniature range was laid out and opened with much pomp but little ceremony by Provost Murray who fired the first shot. Lt. J Christie, ex HG, was the president.

At first the rifle competitions were held within small areas due to the problems of transport and organisation. This meant that they were limited to the section or platoon level. Early in 1941 Lt. J M Miller of 'C' Company 2nd Stg HG Bn presented a silver cup to the company for inter-section competition. Each section from Shieldhill, Blackbraes and Avonbridge had a team of ten men and the total score of the ten counted to the team result. The Shieldhill section, led by Dan Penman, won in the first two years. After that Slamannan entered and won.

With a large number of regular army units in the west of the district it is not surprising to find the odd shooting match between them and the HG in 1942. Once the area league was set up the platoon teams started to move further afield and it was only a matter of time before inter-company and inter-battalion competitions were established. Officers donated prizes and trophies and the number and variety of shooting events continued to proliferate. At one shooting match William Sharp of the Power Station platoon found himself in the final against his own brother, who was in a different company. At 200 yards they matched each other shot for shot, bull for bull. The range was increased to 300 yards and William, firing a P17, duly adjusted his sights to take this into account, but observed that his brother failed to do so. The next shot was a bull for William, but a magpie for his brother. "Lift your sights", he advised. There followed a brief moment of confusion, not to mention anger, before his brother realised that he had not said "Little Shite!" Once the message had been clarified and the sights duly adjusted the competition continued. The next four shots were evenly matched, but the lost shot gave William the prize.

In February 1943 Sir Norman Orr-Ewing, Zone Commander HG Glasgow Area, gifted a trophy for miniature shooting in the Stirlingshire area. This was augmented by others and an inter-battalion prize was competed for by the three Stirlingshire battalions and that from Clackmannan. Each battalion hosted one meeting a year. The Stirlingshire battalions all used Greenhill as the venue, with Mrs McNellie doing the catering. The 1st Clackmannan Bn. arranged its event at the Hillend Range in Alloa. In 1944 the 2nd Stg HG Bn won three out of the four events, and came a close runner up in the fourth. These all-day events attracted other competitions. Firing could be done from various distances using a variety of weapons, including service rifles as issued, at fixed or moving targets. The men too could move from one stance to another and rapid firing was introduced. Novices were separated off and given their own competition, whilst officers could be handicapped in several ways. The battle course presented the ultimate combination of skills, weapons and exercise.

The Craigieburn/ Auchengean area south-west of Falkirk was often used for competitions as well as field training. All sorts of weapons were used on these exercises, including rifles. Jim Kirkland, who lived on the adjacent farm at Newlands, would explore the area with his brother after the men had departed.

Weapons

The two boys found a shell cartridge that appeared to be complete and took it back to the farm. They jammed it point first into a joint in the masonry of one of the outbuildings. Jim's brother then put a 6ins nail against it and hit it with a hammer! This set off the percussion cap and drove the bullet into the wall, thankfully not all the way through to where the livestock were. The small explosion had surprised the boys, but it was only later that night, as they sat down to a meal, that Jim's brother noticed that a finger was bleeding. Closer inspection showed the presence of a metal splinter in the finger. His father took him to Falkirk Hospital, where they cut a slit in the finger and removed the small piece of shrapnel. This was kept as a souvenir – and as a lesson.

One element of rifle training that did not appear at these competitions was the use of the bayonet. The men were all taught how to fit them on the command and then how to use them to the accompaniment of the regulation loud screams. At Slamannan they packed some old sacks with straw and suspended them from trees on a small knoll on the opposite side of the Culloch Burn from their headquarters. This was easier than rigging up a tripod arrangement on the adjacent tennis court. Barney Schoneville became the bayonet instructor. Unfortunately for him many of the men, instead of letting out a blood curdling yell and cursing the sack dummies before stabbing them, got the giggles, as

A Grangemouth HG platoon passing Wallace Street as it marches along Lumley Street, Grangemouth. The men are carrying P17 rifles with bayonets attached. The platoon commander at the head is accompanied by four corporals. The march has attracted a small crowd of onlookers, who are being supervised by an air raid warden wearing his steel helmet.

did the attentive young audience. Eventually this subsided and they were able to get on with the serious business of disembowelling the evil sacks. Likewise an evacuee from Glasgow recalled the HG in Avonbridge attracting an interested audience of children by running up with eldritch cries as they stuck their bayonets into sacks. When they became more organised, bayonet practice became part of the weekend camps at Craigieburn Farm. Here they speared stuffed sacks hung from a proper wooden frame. Guard duties were usually performed with the bayonet already attached, as it showed both friend and foe that the soldier was ready for action.

BARs

At the same time that the Falkirk HG were being issued with their first sizeable consignments of Ross, P17s and P14s in 1940, they received smaller numbers of a heavier American automatic rifle. This was the famous Browning Automatic Rifle (BAR), which was fed from a clip containing 20 rounds of .300ins calibre bullets. Like the P17s these were manufactured right at the end of the First World War and placed into storage and were therefore available for the HG. The 3rd Stg HG Bn had 20 BARs by the end of 1940 and kept them until stand down. They had rather a violent action in use and the men were therefore trained on the 200yds ranges in a lying position. In the final practice the target was exposed for 40 seconds at a time and after ten single shots the last ten rounds were fired in a burst.

Alex Anderson had good reason to remember the arrival of one of the BARs. He had just left school at 14 years of age and was working at Smith and Wellstood's foundry in Bonnybridge. The HG quartermaster, McCordle, worked in the foundry office and asked Alex if he would pass a rifle on to another member of the platoon, Sgt. David Nimmo. Nimmo worked on the farm up Bonnyside Road, not far from Alex's parents' house. Alex was delighted to be entrusted with such a task and readily agreed. However, he had assumed the weapon to be an ordinary rifle weighing under 10lb. By the time that he had carried the 22lb BAR up the road his arms ached.

EY Rifle

The beginning of 1943 saw the arrival of the EY rifle (the initials stood for Edward Yule, its inventor, but local HG took it to be Extra Yield). This was actually a 'cap discharge' fitted into the end of an ordinary rifle, but fired using a special cartridge. A grenade was fitted into the cup and could be projected anything from 80 to 200yds. A variety of grenades were available, but the most commonly used was the No. 68. This weighed 1lb 15oz and detonated upon impact. It was a hollow-charge weapon, which meant that it was able to penetrate thin armour plate and this made it a most welcome addition to the HG's arsenal.

Initial training with the EY rifle was undertaken in the grounds of Kinnaird House, Larbert. Even today the ground is still littered with fragments of fins, gas check plates and bodies of No. 68 grenades and they are common finds for metal detectorists. Further practice was conducted on weekends at Craigieburn Farm. The user knelt within a half-moon mound of earth, having attached the cup discharger, he placed the butt of the rifle on the ground and angled the rifle according to the trajectory that was required. On one occasion one of the men from the R & A Main platoon in Camelon "placed his cup on the end of the rifle, but did not put the metal plate that retained the gasses into position (the gas cork slot was open instead of closed). He pulled the pin out of the stick grenade and put it onto position and pulled the rifle's trigger. Instead of launching the grenade at high velocity it merely pushed it out of the cup and onto the ground at their feet. Training grenades had a seven second fuse. Fortunately, the regimental sergeant of the Argylls, who was conducting the session, with great presence of mind, merely picked it up and threw it into the distance."

By stand down in 1944 the 2nd Stg HG Bn had 850 rifles; the 3rd Stg HG Bn had 666 .30 rifles, 110 .30 EY rifles and 54 .303 rifles. Senior officers were issued with pistols, usually Colt 45s.

Flame Barrels

From an early date the HG experimented with the use of burning oil and petrol on a grander scale than in the Molotov cocktail. This led to the invention of devices for spraying narrow lanes with the burning liquid supplied by hidden oil drums on either side. One version used in 1941/42, the Harvey Flame Thrower, actually used stirrup pumps. Although it had the advantage of being mobile, it was found to be impracticable and was soon withdrawn from service. The urgent necessity of the moment soon led to a workable solution that was adopted by the Scottish HG in early 1942. The new device was graphically called the 'hedgehopper', or flame barrel. This was basically a fuel-filled oil drum concealed by the roadside with a built-in explosive charge designed to

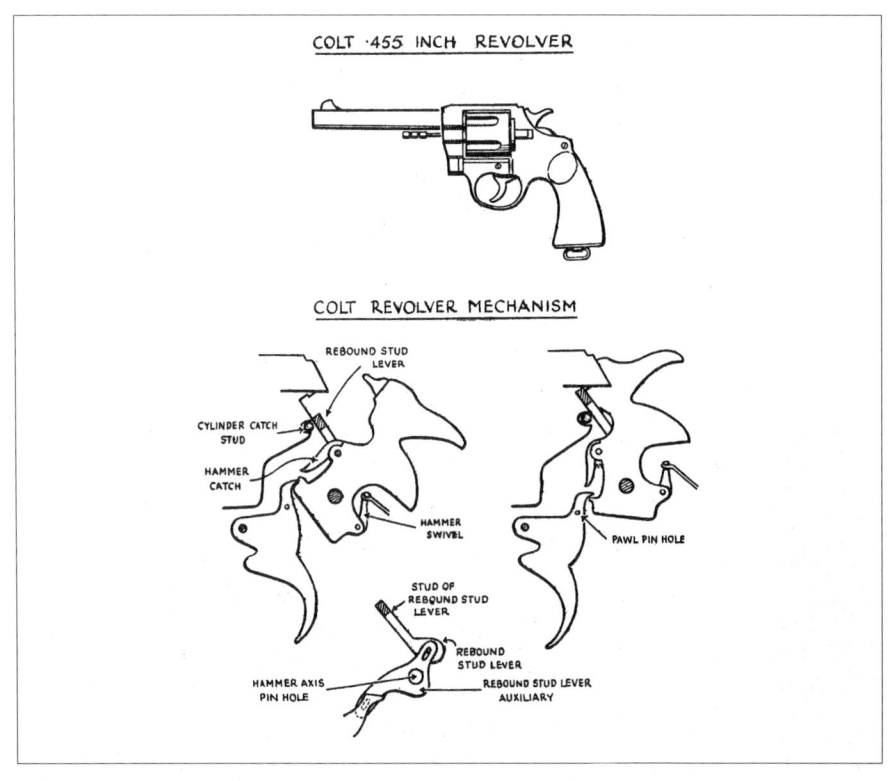

*The Colt revolver issued to most senior HG officers
(from Small Arms Manual, Lt-Col. J A Barlow & Major REW Johnson, Nov 1942).*

hurl it over a hedge or wall into the path of the oncoming enemy vehicle.

Each of the HG battalions in the Falkirk district formed engineer sections in 1941 to learn about this form of warfare and they then set to with a will to install flame traps on all the main roads. Within the area protected by the 3rd Stg HG Bn alone some 96 barrels were set in place. Working for the 2nd Stg HG Bn John Grierson helped to install three on Lochgreen Road – on the back road from High Bonnybridge to Falkirk. A hole was dug in the bank at the side of the road just the right size for the barrel. A small explosive charge with a fulminate of mercury detonator was then placed in the base of the trench and two wires were led from it away from the road. The 40-gallon oil drum full of petrol and oil was then slotted into position. It was important that it should fit snugly into the excavated trench, which inclined towards the road at the top, as this would help to guide its journey when used. Then a thin layer of earth was placed over it and capped with the original turf, so that it was not visible to the casual passer-by. The two wires were led about 25 yards away

Weapons

and the ends set into a cork and bound with black tape. In use the tape and cork would have been removed and the wire terminals set into a detonating box with a plunge handle. The operators would have lain on their stomachs concealed behind a hedge or a wall until the enemy vehicle came along. When the vehicle was opposite the trap the plunger would have been depressed and the explosive would have flung the barrel out onto the road, where it would burst into flames and hopefully engulf the vehicle.

The first of the three was installed on the south side of the road (at NS 8678 7882) almost opposite to Greenbank Road that leads down to the monument of the 1746 Battle of Falkirk. There is a sharp S-bend at this point and any vehicle using the road has to slow down momentarily. A low stone boundary

Photo showing the line of Lochgreen Rd. to the south-west of Falkirk. FB indicates the location of a flame barrel.

wall provided cover and the detonating wires were led through it. Lying in wait the home guardsmen had a clear view from here along the straight stretch of road to the west. The second barrel was placed on this straight section of road, 250 yards west of the first. It lay on the north side, practically opposite to the track leading to Seafield Farm (at NS 8618 7863). The final one was near the first of the houses on the outskirts of Falkirk (approx. NS 8723 7890). Again a bend would have slowed the invading traffic.

The minor road from High Bonnybridge to Falkirk occupied the high ground and was thought to be a probable invasion route into the town. Above Bo'ness there was a similar road overlooking the town, running from Bonhard to the Flints. Locally it is known as the Thief's Road. The Bo'ness HG placed their flame traps a little to the east of an old quarry where this road enters a cutting (NT 005 793).

Embankments of this kind were favoured because it confined the area of the conflagration and placed the barrel already some distance above the road. Bridges under railways and canals provided ideal locations. An example of the latter occurred at the recently named 'Radical Pend' at Bonnybridge. Here

The Pend under the Forth & Clyde Canal at Bonnybridge. This view shows the south side where the flame barrels were placed into the bank on the right.

Weapons

Bonnyside Road passes under the Forth and Clyde Canal to emerge on the north side in Bridge Street. The entrance to the Pend from the south was protected by three 40-gallon barrels planted in 1943 in the earth bank on the east side (NS 8247 8014). They were about 5-6ft up, almost level with the top of the arch. This was quite similar to the point at which the Union Canal crosses over the main Edinburgh road to the east of Linlithgow, where more barrels were placed, this time beside a hedge (NT 012 770).

The local platoons would have been responsible for operating the traps in the event of an invasion and were therefore given a lot of say in their locations. 'A' Company (Bonnybridge) of 2nd Stg HG Bn was responsible for five sites as well as the one at the Pend. Some of these must have been at road junctions.

Known locations of flame barrels:

Lochgreen Road, Falkirk	NS 8618 7863	
Lochgreen Road, Falkirk	NS 8678 7882	bend in road
Lochgreen Road, Falkirk	NS 8723 7890	bend in road
Thief's Road, Bo'ness	NT 005 793	road cutting
Radical Pend, Bonnybridge	NS 8247 8014	road under F & C Canal
Linlithgow Pend, Linlithgow	NT 012 770	road under Union Canal
Callendar Road, Falkirk	NS 8929 7980	road junction
Denovan Road, Dunipace	NS 8242 8307	bend in road & cutting
Bellsdyke Road/ Alloa Road	NS 8757 8411	road junction
Alloa Road/ Bellsdyke Road	NS 8756 8408	road junction
Three Bridges, Camelon	NS 8560 8083	railway embankment across road
Three Bridges, Camelon	NS 8558 8083	bridge over road
Three Bridges, Camelon	NS 8540 8105	cutting at road junction

CHAPTER FOUR

On Guard

On the eve of the declaration of war, on 2nd September 1939, the Stirlingshire County Police force placed men at the southern end of the Kincardine Bridge to monitor traffic and to keep a wary eye open for saboteurs. The bridge, along with several other locations in the Falkirk district, such as Grangemouth Docks and Nobel's detonator works at Westquarter, was designated as a Vulnerable Point (VP) in the event of a war. The threat level was seen as low and for the period of the 'phoney war' this was certainly the case. After Dunkirk this had to be reassessed, as did the entire sphere of home defence.

Upon its formation the LDV immediately took upon itself the responsibility to guard many of the works where they were based. From these nodes the organisation's control slowly permeated across the surrounding landscape to encompass the transport infrastructure, often in association with the police. Contact was also established with the ARP services and guards were allocated to protect Report Centres and other vital posts. These were soon dropped as reviews of the military situation dictated that the HG had to concentrate upon anti-invasion defences. Existing road blocks and guard posts were reorganised into stop lines, which in turn evolved into a network of strong nodal points. As the war entered its final stages the HG also assumed responsibility for guard duty at the Vulnerable Points previously undertaken by the regular army, such as Grangemouth Airfield and the Kinneil petrol can factory.

Guard duty was always undertaken by two men at a time, one of whom was initially usually an ex-serviceman. In this way they were able to pass on their experience and keenness. Often the couple were already acquainted. Joe Duncan, for example, had been a soldier in the Boer War. He eagerly joined the LDV and was soon given their only rifle with which to guard the Report Centre at Arnotdale House in Dollar Park. This became a weekly night stay and so Joe talked his young son-in-law, James Mailer, into accompanying him. He would call round at Jim's house on the way to his night duty to have a cup of tea with his daughter. Over the nights that they spent together Joe taught Jim the rudiments of rifle drill and the two got to know each other better.

Tucked away behind Arnotdale House is the old Report Centre – its flat concrete roof and brick walls contrasting with the cream coloured sandstone of the house built in 1832. The house used to accommodate the burgh museum and is set in Dollar Park.

Two examples of the dedication of the ex-soldier and his willingness to 'do his bit' are given during the first week of June in Bo'ness. "One man did a guard in the late evening and the same week was put on the 4am to 6am guard. The 'orderly sergeant' visiting this man's post at 5.30am was met with "you slipped it across me this time." On being asked what was wrong, the guard replied that he had only finished work at one o'clock that morning and was due to start again at six. This man, it should be noted, had had some eighteen hours' warning of his duty, but did he complain? – not a bit of it. The second man did an early forenoon guard, and as it is very often difficult to fit men into the forenoon hours he had to be called upon the following day to turn out at the same time. The 'orderly sergeant' visited the post and casually remarked that he was glad the guard had received his message all right. "Yes," he replied, "I got it just as I came home from work." The ex-soldier had come out without a grouse to do a four hour guard after a night down the pit!" *(Bo'ness Journal 7th June 1940)*

Transport

Learning from the German invasion of France it was realised that the protection of the transport infrastructure was vital to the repulsion of any invasion. Road and rail links had to be maintained in order to get the regular army reinforcements to the landing place. At the time the role of saboteurs and paratroops in the German successes had been overestimated and the fear was that these could strike anywhere. With a huge length of coastline open to potential invasion its hinterland was massive and beyond the means of the rather scattered and disorganised regulars to watch and guard. This was where the HG could plug the gap in resources.

The Avon Viaduct carrying the Edinburgh-Glasgow Railway at Linlithgow Bridge

The importance of rail links was probably heightened by the false belief that the air raid on the Forth shipping on 16th October 1939 had the Forth Rail Bridge as its intended target. Both the LNER and the LMS established independent sections of the LDV in the area, the former based at the Polmont Goods Yard and at Falkirk Station, the latter at Grangemouth Docks and the Greenhill Yard at High Bonnybridge. The railway companies provided facilities for those on their period of rest during night duties, such as tea-making equipment and bunks, heating and lighting. Each night the LNER had a rota of sentries guarding the two ends of the Falkirk Tunnel beyond the High Station. The lofty railway viaducts were obvious targets for saboteurs and they too were watched by static guards. At the Avon Viaduct near Linlithgow Bridge this task was shared between the Manuel Brickworks HG and the West Lothian HG. The farmer at Manuelhaugh cultivated fields on either side of the railway and had to take his tractor along the road under the viaduct. At first he was stopped on each occasion to have his ID card checked, but eventually the HG got to recognise him and waved him through, whilst keeping a wary eye open for strangers. The Larbert HG guarded the Larbert Viaduct over the River Carron from on top as well as below. The static guard at the end of the structure was soon replaced by periodic patrols walking along it and visiting other VPs on the route. Half way across the structure they would meet the patrol from the Alexander's Bus Garage platoon.

The LMS HG at Greenhill protected the main Edinburgh-Glasgow railway, though responsibility for the important railway junction at Allandale was assumed by the platoon at the Castlecary Brickworks that lay adjacent to it. In the event of a full scale invasion alert involving seaborne troops, the Greenhill men were to make their way along the line to Grangemouth to supplement their colleagues there in its defence, which was considered a greater priority than dealing with paratroops in their own area.

In the summer of 1939 a small unit of Territorials attached to the A and SH had been billeted in the dock complex at Grangemouth. When war broke out

Some of the LNER HG in Princes Park, Falkirk. These men were based at Falkirk Station and helped to guard the tunnel. They are wearing armbands printed 'HOME GUARD'. Late 1940.

Men of the LNER Home Guard being inspected on a Saturday by Superintendent J McKenzie, Glasgow The location is probably Polmont Goods Yard. (Falkirk Herald 11th Dec 1940)

they were supplemented by special constables and the Docks became a Restricted Area, with permits required to gain access. The police, backed up by the soldiers, manned the access gates into the area and verified the right of those wanting to enter to do so. With the worsening war situation in the early summer of 1940 the port was declared a Protected Area and security was reviewed. In the First World War local Volunteers had guarded the docks, manning the gates and patrolling the large area within. It was only natural that with the formation of the LDV the Grangemouth volunteers should once again assume responsibility. In August 1940 the War Office considered that the protection of the Docks was indeed better suited to the HG than to the police. Seventeen policemen would still be used at the entrance gates, together with five LMS police on internal traffic duties, but the LMS HG would patrol the dock complex. Oddly enough the main objection to this proposal came from the LMS officials on the ground. Mr Trotter, the Dock Superintendent, and Major Price, Security Control Officer based at Leith, both considered that the Admiralty should retain responsibility for its own plant – the Mining Stores Depot and the oil distribution tanks. Major Price wrote to Scottish Command saying that the LMS would not be held responsible for the security of these facilities and so the regular military guard was retained at these points until the summer of 1941.

The HG also took a share in guarding the docks at Bo'ness. The whole complex was surrounded by a high new perimeter fence with gates manned by naval personnel. The HG's job was to patrol the east fence, keep guard on the footbridge over the railway lines leading to the Dock Pit that was inside the complex, and watch the shore. The latter was a preferred job. Usually two men were on duty at any time and old Alex Bell was often one of these. At first he did not have a rifle, just an old service revolver. They patrolled from the coast to the railway bridge, where they hailed the guard at the southern end. To provide some rest they made themselves a small lean-to shelter beside the shore where they sat looking out to sea, listening for the sound of approaching craft. During the day Alex's grandson would walk along the beach from Grangepans to take him some soup and sandwiches. He often took a wheelbarrow, not because there was so much food but because once there he and his grandfather would gather coal that had washed up on the beach. This much sought after fuel was then wheeled home.

As well as the Docks, Grangemouth had an important airfield. The defence of the airfield was placed in the hands of the Black Watch and the HLI, later replaced by a unit of the South Lancashire Regiment consisting of six officers and 113 other ranks. They in turn were replaced in January 1942 by No. 2799 (Defence) Squadron of the newly formed RAF Regiment, whose officers actively promoted the involvement of the Grangemouth HG in the RAF station's defence plan. Having established a training school at Avonside with a firing range at Polmont Hill, they made these facilities readily available to the HG.

The greater portion of the efforts of the HG in the early days was focussed on the local road system. Temporary check points were soon created and before long evolved into road blocks and more permanent barriers, often forming defence lines. These are dealt with in a separate section. Here it is sufficient to mention the guard post that was established at the Falkirk Ironworks at the southern end of Bainsford Bridge. It was formed for two reasons. First and foremost because it covered the main road northwards out of Falkirk at a crossing point of the Forth and Clyde Canal. This line of navigation formed an obvious barrier in its own right. Secondly because the Falkirk Iron Company had established its own platoon, complete with armoury, and the guard post was able to protect the works at the same time. The actual post itself was split in two. One man stood guard in the firm's existing security office at its gates, whilst his partner occupied a makeshift pillbox on the other side of the road. The security office was a wooden extension built onto the north end of the work's office block and before the war had been occupied by the night watchman, with whom the HG now shared it. The main difference was that he was paid. Here, during the day, the foundry workers clocked on and off. It had a slow combustion stove and was

Photograph showing Grahamston at the bottom, with Bainsford at the top on the opposite side of the Forth & Clyde Canal. The main street running across the picture is Grahams Rd, which led to Bainsford Bridge. 1938.

relatively comfortable. The pillbox was created by placing sandbags across the front of a narrow passage between the electricity sub-station and a tall boundary wall. A sloping roof was placed over the passage to provide shelter from the worst of the weather. The platoon was large enough to man the posts with each man on duty one night out of five. As usual the two men were on active duty for periods of two hours and then went to the platoon's HQ for their rest period, where they were still on call. Here they could sleep, chat or play cards according to their mood. Two hours on guard and four off was normal practice for HG units. The hours covered varied according to the time of year, but were essentially from dusk till dawn. Up until midnight the guard would mount random checks of people's ID cards, but thereafter they would stop anyone. This delayed many a journey and not all the public appreciated the value of the work. On the evening of 28th June 1940, for example, Alexander Cruickshank, a furnaceman living in Carron Road, approached the LDV post at Bainsford Bridge after a night out and, recognising one of the guards as he passed, started swearing and making a disturbance. He had been drinking and was subsequently fined £1 for a breach of the peace.

The judge told him that "the LDV are carrying out essential duties and nothing must be allowed to interfere with them in the course of their duties."

Fifth columnists came in all forms and disguises and so anyone who was out late at night was stopped. This included people in uniform. George Gray remembered travelling home on embarkation leave from the RAF to see his family. Trains did not run to timetable due to the difficulties of wartime requirements and it was very late by the time that his train pulled into the station at Falkirk. Even off duty he had to wear his uniform and carry his rifle in case of an emergency. He walked up Grahams Road in the dark and as he approached Bainsford Bridge he heard the challenge "Friend or Foe?" shouted from the shadows to his left. He had left the district before the post had been set up and was surprised to see the sandbagged structure. The HG saw the uniform and insisted on inspecting George's form 1250. In the darkness he had to scan it with his torch before handing it back. The HG was unarmed and on his own, as far as could be seen, and George often wondered what would have happened if he had wielded his rifle.

The guard post also had an influence on the social and criminal activities of the area. When, for example, one young woman was on her way to a dance in Falkirk, all dressed up, she was recognised by a friend of the family who was on guard duty. He knew that she was still just under 16 years of age and that her father, who was on night shift, would not have approved of her being out on her own. He told her to forget the evening out and to return home. She was evidently feeling a little guilty anyway and unquestioningly did as she was told – because that was the way you behaved in those days.

Few people were up and about between midnight and 6am and so anyone crossing the bridge in this period was treated with suspicion. In mid September 1940 the Falkirk HG throughout the area was asked by the police to be vigilant for the presence of a gang of men from the south side of Glasgow. The men were not suspected terrorists, but bank robbers, and intelligence had been gleaned that they were in the area. On the night of 15th September guardsman Alexander Christie of Grange Drive was on duty. Shortly after 3am he saw a man running towards the bridge as if to cross it. This was just the kind of thing that a saboteur would do and Christie sprang into action immediately. The man was halted in his tracks by the point of the bayonet on Christie's rifle. William Bishop, who was also on duty, came to assist his colleague and together they demanded to see the stranger's ID card. It appeared to be valid, but the man came from the Glasgow suburb for which they were watching. He was arrested and taken to the guard room at the Iron Works for further questioning. Shortly afterwards they were disturbed by a small group of agitated men. The new arrivals included police constable James Fergus, the officer on the local beat, and William Coleman, an ARP warden who had been on night duty at his post near the corner of Grahams Road and Dalderse Avenue. With them was a second prisoner whom they had just apprehended. The two prisoners were subsequently conveyed to Falkirk Police Station by car with a joint escort of police and HG. It transpired that PC Fergus had been on his beat along Grahams Road when he had heard a violent explosion that appeared to come from the premises of the Falkirk & District Co-operative Society at 200 Grahams Road. After enlisting the help of Coleman he went to investigate and upon approaching the rear of the premises they disturbed a man who immediately fled the scene. The two men gave chase and after a short distance they caught up with him and brought him down. They were concerned that he might make another break for freedom and so took him to the guard house for extra security. An examination of the Co-op premises revealed that access had been gained by forcing a window at the rear. Carpets and pack sheets had been laid against the safe to deaden the sound of the explosion used to blast it open, the upward force of which had discoloured the ceiling. The handle of the safe was off and some of the strong steel rivets had snapped, while the lock had been badly damaged. The door had, however, jammed and denied access.

Despite these odd flurries of activity, guard duty at the post was mostly routine and mundane. Peter Monro was 18 years old when, in 1941, he took his place there. All he remembers is standing for an hour or so on the bridge itself, then going to the sentry box beside the electricity sub-station, before returning to stand guard again. He had no specific instructions to stop anyone or to defend the bridge. He did, however, have a .303 Lee Enfield rifle and a clip with five rounds of ammunition, which he kept in his pocket. The men on duty at Bainsford Bridge were often greeted by patrols from the Bainsford HG as they left or returned from their base beside the AFS in the old Burnbank Foundry. There was always a friendly rivalry between the two neighbouring platoons, especially as the Falkirk Iron Works platoon also had guards on the gates at Castlelaurie Foundry and Abbots Foundry on Bankside, which was considered to be part of Bainsford.

The Pay Brig at Dalgrain over the River Carron also had a semi-permanent guard post. The Grangemouth HG arranged with the Town Council to take over a newly completed but unoccupied upper flat nearby at 9 Devon Street for those members of the watch on their rest periods. This too proved to be a relatively quiet post, only enlivened by an odd incident such as the one involving the ICI chemist George Drever. Much important wartime research was undertaken at Grangemouth by the industrial chemists of ICI and they were given a relatively free hand to explore new avenues. One evening George Drever was experimenting with the production of carbonate free caustic soda. He had a large glass aspirator full of distilled water under a 3 inch layer of ether. He then cut a piece of soda and dropped it in. It touched the water and came into contact with the ether. The reaction did not seem to be going fast enough and so he cut another half inch square chunk off and added it. There was a bang and the ether caught fire, producing an unholy mess in the fume cupboard. The sodium had sparked on contact with the water and continued to do so. Naphtha was introduced to neutralise the effect. The question now was how to dispose of the naphtha-coated sodium in its wide-mouthed jar. Pollution regulations were not as strong in those days and another chemist took the offending substance a short distance down the road and, standing in the middle of the Pay Brig, he threw it into the river. As it hit the water it burst into flame again and the chemist was promptly arrested for trying to blow the bridge up – though if this had been his aim the arrest had come rather late in the day!

The two HG on duty at the bridge would walk backwards and forwards across it for their two-hour stint. After dark any travellers were challenged. One local tradesman always hailed the guard first, "It's the baker from Skinflats," to make sure there was no mistake. At the end of the night, usually around 8am, all the men would report to the council house. Here they would clear their rifles, which had been loaded during the guard with a clip of five rounds, plus one up the spout. Far too often the one up the spout was forgotten and before they vacated the building the ceiling was peppered with little holes (a good thing that it was the upper flat). At 8am they went home, had breakfast, and then went straight out to work.

In France the German infantry had commandeered civilian vehicles to get them around far quicker than if they had been stuck on foot, helping themselves to petrol from whatever pumps they came across. The HG therefore made arrangements in the event of an invasion to, in the first instance, guard all pumps. Each platoon took responsibility for the petrol stations in its own area and the owners were made fully aware of their responsibilities. It was important to keep these resources open as long as possible for the home forces, but if the situation became dire, the HG were given instructions on how to destroy them. The HG also took on the task of aiding the police to check any parked vehicles to make sure that they had been immobilised. This could be done, for example, by removing the rotor arm. A number of prosecutions followed. The local councils were one of the largest groups of users of motorised

17. Immobilisation Policy.
The general policy will be of immobilisation rather than destruction (the latter will only be taken as a last resort), with the intention of denying the enemy stocks of food, etc., which would be of immediate use to him and to deny him transport and the means of communication.

18. Immobilisation of petrol and fuel.
Separate instructions dated 10th January 1941 have been issued to Company Commanders and to those in charge of personnel responsible for the immobilisation of petrol and fuel oil in the Battalion Area. J M Millar Section ("B" Coy) is now responsible for the immobilisation of all petrol and fuel oil pumps in the Falkirk and Camelon Area.

20. Immobilisation of motor vehicles.
See Appx. I.
(a) The civil police are primarily responsible for seeing that this is carried out in the case of civilian transport. All non-military vehicles NOT showing an Emergency Label will be immobilised.
(b) Local military comdrs will be prepared to take action on their own responsibility in the case of any civilian transport which has not been immobilised and which is in danger of falling into enemy hands.
(c) All drivers of military vehicles (incl. civilian vehicles earmarked for military use) will be prepared to immobilise their vehicles in the last resort and must be instructed how to do it. (For details see Appx. I).

Appendix I. Immobilisation of vehicles.

1. Policy.
(a) The responsibility for ordering immobilisation of transport rests with the regional Commissioner until the area concerned becomes the scene of operations, when the Military Commander is entitled to order the immobilisation of any transport in imminent danger of falling into the hands of the enemy.
(b) In the case of civilian transport the civil police are primarily responsible for seeing that this is carried out, but any police constable or soldier in uniform may carry out the immobilisation of the user had not done so.
(c) In the event of immobilisation of civil vehicles being ordered in the Bn. Area this will apply to all such vehicles with the exception of those to which E.L. labels have been issued and which are necessary to maintain certain essential services. If, however, such vehicles are in imminent danger of capture they will also be immobilised.

2. Method of immobilisation.

Complete destruction.

(i) If fire is permitted petrol will be poured over the vehicles and set alight.
(ii) If fire is not permitted and time allows:

(a) Smash radiator at bottom tank.
(b) Smash sump if possible; if impossible, pour dry sand into the oil filter cap and
(c) Run engine on full throttle till it seizes.
(d) Smash carburettor ignition and other delicate components.
(e) Perforate bottom of petrol tank.
(f) Mutilate tyres.

(iii) If time does not allow for above:
(a) Smash carburettor, ignition and other delicate components.
(b) Smash radiator at bottom tank.
(c) Perforate bottom of petrol tank.
(d) Smash sump if possible.

Immobilisation with a view to further use or re-capture.

(i) Remove distributor lead and all H.T. leads.
(ii) Remove or destroy carburettor or injector.
(iii) Puncture bottom of petrol tank.

All parts removed will be taken away or securely hidden, and it will be at the discretion of the Officer Commanding at the time to decide what complete destruction or immobilisation only is to be carried out.

vehicles and the HG units based at the transport depots or 'burgh stables' in Cow Wynd, Falkirk and Main Street, Stenhousemuir, were able to mount watch on these at night. The Post Office HG likewise guarded the fleet of vehicles used by the Royal Mail, and at various works with their own HG platoons, these controlled the movements of the works' vans and lorries.

During the first week of June 1940 the local HG also helped with the removal of any signs that might be used by an invading force to guide them about the country. Road signposts were uprooted. Mileposts were obscured and the nameplates at railway stations and above shop windows were painted over. Much later in the war this meant that the HG had to undertake points duty. Hugh Baird of the Brightons platoon, for example, was one of those who directed traffic at the crossroads at the foot of the Quarry Brae when large convoys of army vehicles and tanks passed from north to south under the cover of darkness. Traffic control had formerly been conducted by a special branch of the army, but in 1943 these responsibilities were taken over by the HG in order to release more men to the fighting front. Transport and Traffic Control Officers were appointed in each battalion. At Bo'ness the post was taken by 2nd Lt W G Findlay of No. 3 Company and men from his company trained for the duty. They had their first full-scale exercise on the first Sunday of December 1943, when a rash of red arrows suddenly appeared throughout the town.

Water Supply

One of the obvious targets for a low intensity but devastating attack that could incapacitate a large section of the population was the drinking water supply. As with the Docks at Grangemouth, these too had been guarded in the First World War by volunteers. Yet again it was the water works' employees who knew the locations thoroughly who were given this task. They were issued with rifles and co-opted into the HG. In November 1940 J Russell of the Sauchie sector HG resigned because he was expected to undertake HG duties elsewhere. It was agreed that he should stay on and that his guard duty would be restricted to the reservoir at Sauchie from the embankment down to the entrance gate.

Carron Reservoir, c1955.

Communications

Communications were vital and the Falkirk Post Office formed its own LDV unit to guard the telephone exchange as well as its fleet of vans. Wireless communications were scarce and land lines were necessary to transmit information on the enemy and to direct the armed response and ARP services. Outside of Falkirk the local area platoons protected the exchanges. The Falkirk post office and telephone exchange was located in Weir Street, at the junction with Vicar Street. It seemed strange to the employees to be in the premises after working hours, but they knew its strategic value. The exchange was still manually operated and the women who manned it were made aware of a large axe fixed to the wall where they worked. The axe, they were told, was to be used to destroy the equipment if the Germans entered the town. The nightly guard duty undertaken by the members of the HG was unrelentingly tedious. The guards spent most of the time waiting for something to happen; drinking tea, playing cards and sleeping. Although the Falkirk Post Office platoon was good at marksmanship, they were rather low on energy and efficiency. One of its younger members remembered being so bored that he listened in to telephone conversations late at night, particularly those from Italian POWs to their girlfriends. He said that he had learned a lot from their patter, but refused to be drawn on whether or not he had put any of these points into practice.

Extra telephones were put into Report Centres in each of the burghs so that the Civil Defence could gather current information and properly coordinate its responses. Direct lines were laid to the fire brigade, police, ARP posts and first aid posts. Rest centres, information centres, the HG and so on also needed to be contacted and slowly the network expanded. It now seems hard to believe that at the beginning of the war very few schools had telephones and those installed for the war were intended to be removed at the cessation of hostilities. At first the HG maintained a nightly guard on the Report Centres, but it was soon realised that this was unnecessary and they were only guarded during air raid alerts when they were fully manned. In such instances the guard acted as the HG liaison with the Civil Defence authorities. The Report Centres in the Falkirk District were:

> Arnotdale House, Dollar Park, Falkirk
> The Town House, Glasgow Road, Denny
> Seaview House, Corbiehall, Bo'ness
> Burgh Stables, Wood Street, Grangemouth

Through headmasters eager young boys were recruited from the high schools to act as messengers if the telephone lines were interrupted by enemy action. Each provided his own bicycle. They were selected according to the teacher's knowledge of his pupils and were keen to play in the war games. They took part in some of the early exercises, but like their counterparts in the ARP they were soon dispensed with. One lesson learnt at Clydebank was that the messengers were very exposed to danger and it was found to be extremely bad for morale to have a high percentage of deaths in this age group.

When it came to wireless transmission the newly opened BBC transmitter station at Westerglen was clearly important. This lay to the south-west of Falkirk on the Slamannan road. During the first year of the war it was protected by small sections from the 12th HLI and the Pioneer Corps, but as these regular soldiers were pulled away for duty elsewhere the task was delegated to the HG. The nearest unit was at Shieldhill and the duty fell on it. The BBC had a green van at Westerglen and it was given over for their use. A sentry box at the entrance housed the men guarding the gate.

The building in the foreground was the reserve transmitter station at Westerglen. It was to be used in the event of the main building being destroyed by enemy action. Both buildings were protected by the Shieldhill HG. In the background the transmitter masts can be seen. The coniferous trees have grown up since the war.

Jim Kirkland was familiar with the area, having been to school at Auchengean on the other side of the road. He lived at Newlands Farm and in his mid-teens used to play in the area of the transmitter. One day late in 1940 he and his friends were playing in the woods next to the transmitter when they saw that the soldiers had placed wires around the outside of the boundary fence of the station. The wires were connected to tin cans with stones in so that anyone trying to approach would catch a wire and set the cans rattling. This was tantamount to challenging them to beat the system. As the small group of adolescents walked around the perimeter inspecting it, they noticed an old waste pipe set in a culvert coming out of the station into an adjoining drainage ditch. The challenge was accepted and in a spirit of adventure they crawled along the pipe into the grounds of the station. As they emerged, one by one, they were confronted with a HG pointing a bayonet at them. He interrogated them to find out how they had gained entry and then escorted them off the premises. The pipe was soon sealed off.

Government Property

Not far from Westerglen was the ordnance depot in Lochgreen Road, which had been built just before the war in anticipation. The depot was surrounded by a high chain link fence and in the centre of the compound was a large building with a store bungalow attached. Wooden huts were dispersed around these. Initially the army had administered and guarded the depot, but as the men were moved onto front line duties they were replaced by civilians, leaving just two or three members of the ordnance corps and an officer. The latter travelled in from Edinburgh each day and was picked up from Falkirk High Station in a utility car. John Clapperton was the storekeeper in charge of the storemen and Bill Tilsley was responsible for the civilian clerks. Tilsley had been in the army for 20 years before retiring and was then brought back for this job. Although he was given a housing allowance he found it almost impossible to get accommodation locally and so partitioned a section off in one of the wooden huts, though this was not officially sanctioned. The stores included gun sights, binoculars, compasses, light ack-ack guns, searchlights, trucks, army cars, parabolic dishes, range finders, gun barrels, barrel liners and so on. The larger equipment was kept outside under covers.

Two civilian watchmen were paid to look after the main building at night. They did not have uniforms and in fact never left the entrance room except to inspect the interior of the stores. They were rather comfortably off, with a coal burning fire and facilities for making tea and toast. Only these two were allowed into the stores at night and they had timetables to follow around them. At set points there were time clocks attached to the walls and the watchman took his key from his chain to insert it into each clock in turn, thus marking his progress on a chart within its casing. The LDV or HG guarded the buildings from the outside. Each night six men and an NCO (usually an older man) would form up at the Burgh Stables in Cow Wynd and then march to the ordnance depot in all weathers. At the depot the section divided into twos with two hours watch per pair. The younger members were given first turn from 10pm till midnight, so that they could get some decent sleep afterwards. In the early days of the LDV they only had one gun amongst them, with five rounds of ammunition. This was given to whoever was on watch at

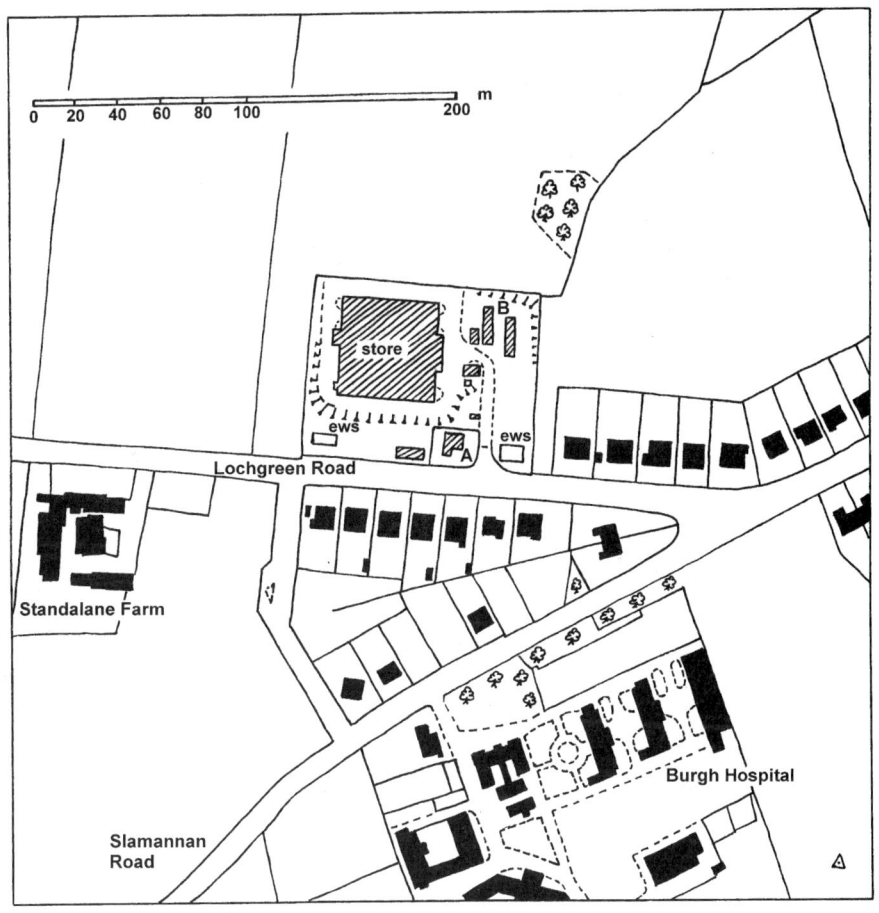

The Ordnance Depot in Lochgreen Road. A – guard bungalow, B – administration & sleeping quarters.

the gate. This man was told to stay out of the dim light that lit up the main gateway, so as not to present himself as a target to the enemy – in the blackout even this faint glimmer seemed to blaze like a beacon. Meanwhile, the other man on duty together with the NCO patrolled the perimeter, which could take up to half an hour. There was no sentry box for the man at the gate and he stood there in all weathers, whilst his companion, having finished his tour, would stand in the doorway, which provided but little shelter. Each man was out once a week. It seems strange now to think that these men undertook this uncomfortable work voluntarily for years – and that despite the fact that the two men who were being paid were snug inside. During the rest period the HG shared the bungalow fire.

The 'old hats' soon settled down to the routine, but the raw recruits were a source of constant amusement to them and the cause of the odd panic. Like the time when 'young Peter' was given the rifle by the NCO, who that night was William Sharp. Sharp told Peter that if there was any trouble he was at hand. "Okay Bill," came the reply. "It's Corporal to you!" was the rejoinder – the boy was bound to be trouble. Sharp had been in his billet for about quarter of an hour when there was a loud bang! This was followed in rapid succession by four more reports. He ran out to the main gate and found the rifle lying on the road and Peter frantically waving his arms in the air as if to say "It wasn't me!" It transpired that Peter had heard some rustling noises coming from the fence not far away. He had shouted out "Halt or I fire." No answer and the rustling continued. "Halt or I will fire!" No change. Peter was now very scared. "Halt I am about to fire!" and he did, five times. Five times he missed the cow that was rubbing itself against the fence.

A light rain or high humidity would produce a mist over the floor of the Forth Valley. At the end of a night watch it was very picturesque seen from above at the ordnance depot. The mist veiled the valley below like a massive lake and in the silence of first light it was rather eerie. There were no lights to interrupt its waters – it was pure white. One morning it was so bright that the NCO, full of the joys of spring, got all his men together for an hour's gymnastics. He roused them from their sleeping bags, but once they had formed up he changed his mind and they did drill instead. The men were also feeling perky and did not object. He barked out the orders and the men attentively performed the various manoeuvres. Suddenly the NCO noticed that they had attracted a small crowd of onlookers. About 50 residents from the locality were watching through the fence in a bemused way, curious to find out what was happening. Did it fill them with confidence to see the HG so well disciplined? I have no idea! At the end of each shift the section formed up again and marched back to the Burgh Stables, where they left their rifles before going on to their various employments.

The local people certainly had good reason to know of this platoon's guard duty, for there were one or two zealous "incidents" along the line of march. One night, at the height of the invasion scares, a section was marching up the hill led by Sgt. Strang. Strang was a gamekeeper who lived up by Hallglen and was blunt in his manners, but to the point. As usual this band of brothers were singing and whistling cheerfully. As they approached Princes Park a room light glared at them from a house on the north side of the road. The LDV rang the door bell, they banged on the door, they shouted and roused the neighbours – but they were unable to gain entry or get the light extinguished. The owner was evidently out and the men had to be elsewhere. They had no equipment with which to force entry, which they never doubted that they had a right to do. They did not even have a rifle and were dependent upon Strang's shotgun for a weapon. Strang simply lifted the gun to his shoulder, pointed it at the window and blasted the light out. A curt note was left pinned to the door,

Falkirk Power Station with Comely Park School in the foreground to the right.

signed in the name of the LDV. The section reformed and continued its march and the whistling.

Colin Robertson lived with his parents in a new bungalow not far from the ordnance depot. Indeed, it was so new that there were snagging problems for the first two years of the war. One of these was a faulty light switch in the living room. Vibrations from the heavy lorries going to and from the depot would cause the light to go on. One evening the family went out whilst it was still daylight without putting the black-out blinds up. When they returned after dark they found a small chunk of glass missing from the bottom left hand corner of the living room window. On the floor in the centre of the living room was a small scatter of shattered glass from the light bulb, and a gun pellet. They concluded that the electric light had come on and that the HG had "done the necessary". The small hole in the window glass was filled with putty and was none the worse for its incident, lasting for many years. It would seem that the HG had refined its tactics from experience.

Another government establishment that made increasing use of the HG as the war dragged on was the petrol can factory set up in 1943 on the Grangemouth Road at Kinneil, west of Bo'ness. Its official designation was 'Satellite Can Factory S.1' (S.2 being at Caernarfon in north Wales) and it was capable of making 10,000 cans per day shift. Fuel was pumped to the factory along two pipelines from Grangemouth – one from the tanks of Scottish Oils and the other from the Air Ministry depot. The newly manufactured cans were filled at the works, loaded onto lorries, and then taken by road to Bo'ness Docks for shipment overseas. The factory was an obvious target for a raid, whether landed by parachute or by small craft on the coast less than a hundred yards off. At first the Bo'ness HG supplemented regular troops at the gates and patrolling the perimeter. Before long they were on their own. The heavy smokers amongst them found it somewhat tiresome, as they were not allowed to smoke during their periods off – for obvious reasons. Jenny Arthur of East Kerse Mains Farm used to go to the works to deliver milk, which was given out to the paint sprayers to counteract some of the chemicals. She had to show a permit at the gate to Sgt Smith of the HG in order to get access, even though she had become quite a familiar visitor.

Very early in the war the Royal Navy made a decision to disperse its ordnance stores for the provisioning of ships at Rosyth and in the Falkirk district a depot was established at the old railway sidings at Causewayend, Muiravonside. There were no elaborate underground bunkers or earth-bound structures, rather the shells were simply kept in railway carriages in the sidings. At first the area near the old Almond Foundry next to the Union Canal was utilised as it had a large number of lines and was partially sheltered by the cutting. This area soon became too limited and wagons started to extend back to the other side of Bowhouse. The Navy provided a small guard, but in 1940-1943 these were supplemented by men from the Manuel Brickworks HG. The rota meant that each man was on duty about twice a month, with four on duty each night. To begin with they had no hut and were supposed to spend the whole night patrolling the perimeter, but they were later given accommodation in one of the railway vans. The public footpath that went from the gates of Muiravonside Estate to Muiravonside School had to be

Satellite Can Factory Number 1 – the petrol can factory at Kinneil Kerse on the Bo'ness Road with the Forth Estuary in the background.

The large Nissen-type huts of the factory seen from the side.

closed because it crossed the railway line. For the pupils living to the south this meant a slightly increased length of journey to school. In 1944 a special naval unit was set up to take over the guard duties.

The RAF also made use of the HG for the defence of the airfield at Grangemouth (see separate section below) and of the decoy establishment for Grangemouth Refinery. The latter was officially designated as a QF decoy, that is to say a decoy that used fires at night, and was located at Upper Kinneil.

An aerial photograph of the petrol can factory taken in the late 1940s.
The Forth is on the right and Bo'ness Road on the left.

Large concrete basins were constructed in an open field and flammable fuel stored beside them. In the event of a night raid on the refinery the fuel at the decoy was poured into the basins and set on fire. Some of the basins were circular, mimicking the storage tanks at Grangemouth. Hopefully this would deceive the second wave of enemy bombers and they would drop their bombs in the open fields around the decoy. The Bo'ness HG had a guard hut, just a simple wooden shed, at the entrance to the field. This was next to the underground control room that operated the decoy. The concrete structures and storage tanks in the field were covered with camouflage netting and made the area difficult to patrol. However, the greatest problem that the armed guard had to face was the local children, who were able to penetrate the barbed wire perimeter at will in order to enter this unusual playground.

Perhaps the most unusual government property that the HG in the Falkirk district was asked to protect was the Royal Train. When the royal family visited Scotland they usually travelled over the railway network here and each viaduct and bridge had to be checked before the train passed over or under it and was then guarded until it had passed through. This was a task which the police had always performed before (and indeed after) the war, but with the increased threat level the HG was called in to help. The frequency of these semi-secret trips increased as the royal family did its best to provide encouragement to the beleaguered population.

Not only did the King pass through the area, but on numerous occasions he stopped over night. With the wartime vagaries of rail travel, when journeys were delayed by air raid alerts and priority was given to ammunition trains, it was necessary for the Royal Train to travel north the day before the appointment and to stop for the night in central Scotland, before finishing the journey the following day. Here the train would pull into a siding and the royal family would sleep in it. The spot chosen was at Carmuirs on the Denny Branch line. During the day this branch was still used for goods traffic to the paper mills at Denny, and indeed it took newly arrived Italian and German POWs to Denny Station for forwarding to the Castlerankine Camp. At night it was as quiet as the grave and not being a true siding it attracted little suspicion. The Royal Train rested less than 200yds from the mainline and could easily proceed north through Stirling, west to Glasgow, east to Edinburgh, or south again by Carstairs. The train was guarded by a special detail that accompanied it all over, but the perimeter was patrolled by a combination of regular soldiers and the HG. Men from Larbert walked over the viaduct, towering above the River Carron. The Camelon men manned their posts at the Three Bridges along to Bogton, and the Bonnybridge Power Station section kept a wary watch on the roads to the west. These all-night operations were seen as a welcome change by these men, as they felt part of the national scheme and believed that they were doing something of great importance for the country's war effort.

Another task associated with the RAF was the guarding of crashed aircraft, of which there were far too many (see *Grangemouth: from Airlines to Air Cadets – the story of the 'drome*, Bailey G 2006). The local HG were usually amongst the first on the scene of any crash, as part of their remit was to intercept airborne troops. Their presence denied the children of their prize mementoes, though where the impact had been considerable the debris would be strewn over wide areas and some souvenir could usually be gleaned. How long the HG were in attendance depended upon circumstances and the platoon commander. In theory the wreckage should have been handed over to the police upon their arrival, but in rural districts the police were happy to let the HG carry on. However, once reported, it did not take long for the RAF salvage crew to arrive from Grangemouth and then they took over the scene. It was this hardened crew that had the grim task of investigating the accident and retrieving the bodies.

RAF Grangemouth

Although arrangements had been made to provide anti-aircraft cover, the ground defence of airfields in Britain was not taken seriously until after Dunkirk. Indeed, it was 21st January 1941 before the Black Watch arrived in Grangemouth to man the newly erected pillboxes around its perimeter. Avonside Farm, to the south-east of the airfield, was converted into accommodation for the 200 men and 7 officers. This complex had lecture rooms for training, and a firing range at the foot of Polmont Hill. The successful German invasion of Crete in May 1941 stressed the importance of defence in depth and as well as the six perimeter pillboxes there were gun posts and trenches. Should these be penetrated there was a 'keep' near the hangars, consisting of three interconnected pillboxes and three Picket-Hamilton forts (retractable pillboxes) were positioned next to the runways.

Despite this the number of troops at Grangemouth Airfield was reduced when, on 31st May 1941, the Black Watch was relieved by a detachment of the South Lancashire Regiment consisting of 6 officers and 113 other ranks. The diminution of numbers and the need for defence in depth led to meetings with the HG and a new defence plan was drawn up for the airfield. It was arranged that 'D' Company (Grangemouth) 3rd Stg HG Bn would protect the western or town side. Here, in its familiar urban landscape, the HG would have been able to mount a fierce resistance to any attacking force. Not long after the LDV had been formed the Grangemouth men had dug slit trenches at the top of Newhouse Road to halt any advance up Abbots Road. These trenches were manned during exercises, attracting crowds of children, giving away their position to whatever 'enemy' they faced. Threats from the men made little difference to the boys and it was only when the novelty wore off that the HG was left in peace to practise their pretend war. More trenches were dug besides the Grange Burn. A hut at the junction of King Street and Bo'ness Road acted as a guard post for some of the HG on night duty. This post

Aerial view showing Grangemouth Airfield at the time of its official opening in June 1939. During the war the approaches to the airfield through the town (bottom and left of the picture) were protected by the HG.

allowed the nearby concrete road block to be quickly manned and also provided dispersement for the troops so that they could quickly reach their battle stations.

The ridge to the south of the airfield was to be defended by platoons from the 2nd Stg HG Bn:

Platoon	battle station	reference	grid ref
No. 5 (High Bonnybridge)	Radio Hill	444 013	NS 945 794
No. 4 (High Bonnybridge)	Reservoir Hill	442 013	NS 943 794
No. 20 (Maddiston)	Old Polmont	435 013	NS 936 794
No. 22 (Polmont)	Old Polmont	435 013	NS 936 794
No. 18 (Redding)	Dollhouse	428 014	NS 929 795
No. 19 (Brightons)	Beancross	424 015	NS 925 796
No. 17 (Laurieston)	Mumrills	417 016	NS 918 795

The number of platoons involved reflects the perceived importance of the airfield. Those platoons from Bonnybridge had to be provided with transport

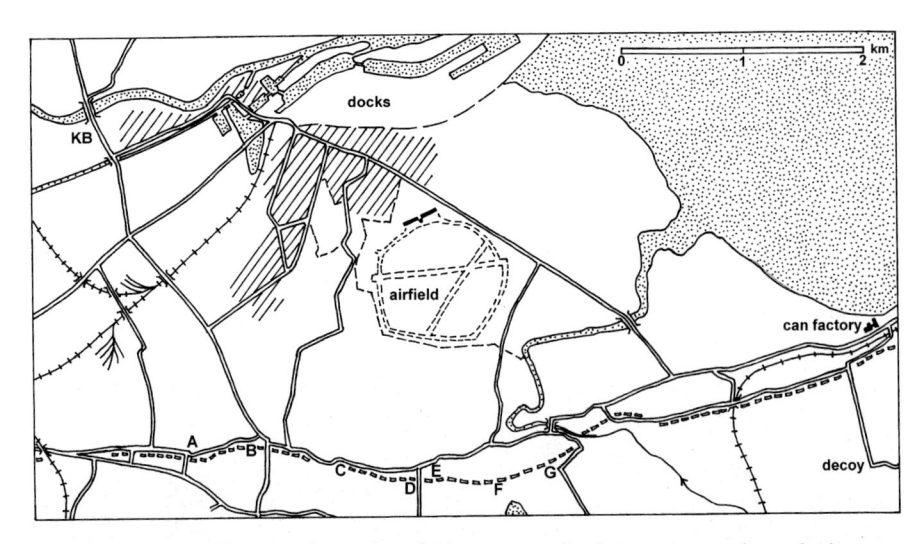

Plan of the Grangemouth area. To the east the airfield was protected by the River Avon, to the west by the town and to the south by the HG posts along the ridge occupied by the Roman Wall (shown as a dashed line). A – Mumrill's Farm; B – Beancross; C – Dollhouse; D and E – Old Polmont; F – Reservoir Hill; G – Radio Hill

from Company HQ. In the event of an invasion alert these platoons from 'A' and 'D' Companies were to be formed into a new company, designated 'G', under Major A Sharp with Lt Robert Harvey as second-in-command. They would act under direct orders from the officer commanding RAF Grangemouth and after the first day they would draw their food supplies from the airfield.

In most cases the platoons were to occupy prepared positions in the form of trenches. Robert McNab remembered doing his hand grenade practice in the trenches dug by the HG just along from the RAF hospital at Polmont Park. Another section of defences appears in an aerial photograph of the Roman temporary camp at Polmont Hill East, which shows a series of zigzag trenches across it from west to east that must surely be the handiwork of the HG. These lie east of Millhall Reservoir, somewhat south of the position that we might have expected (at NS 946 790) and suggests that even here the HG was preparing to defend in depth. Presumably a second line lies along the Antonine Wall itself, near the crest of the hill next to the underground reservoir referred to as 'Reservoir Hill'. At Beancross there was a slit trench on the north side of the road just west of the village, with a hollowed out sand pit part of the way up Mumrills Brae on the opposite side. At Mumrills it was the farm buildings that were fortified.

It is an amazing coincidence that all seven defensive points listed above are within a stone's throw of the Antonine Wall, for in 1942-44 the line faced

Four of the gun loops in the south wall of Polmont Churchyard can be seen in this photograph. Some of the houses of Polmont appear over the top of the wall.

south rather than north like its Roman predecessor. In 1942 it was essential to deny the high ground overlooking the airfield to the enemy, but it was also useful to be able to extricate the defending forces from the ridges in the face of overwhelming odds. That seems to have been the reason why the Weedingshall peninsula was abandoned – lying in the centre between two narrow valleys it might easily have been overrun. By placing the defensive line on the lower ground to the north the HG were giving themselves a clear killing zone.

In May 1942 the Commanding Officer of RAF Grangemouth made a formal request to the local council for permission to make 20 loopholes in the south boundary wall of Polmont Churchyard. These were duly made, facing the direction in which it was anticipated that the enemy paratroops would advance, that is to the south. At the same time a battle headquarters was formed in a Victorian villa at Old Polmont, called Northfield. This building had a superb view of the airfield and its surroundings and so could be used to coordinate the defenders on the airfield itself. Underground telephone lines were installed from the villa to the 'keep'.

During that summer an underground battle headquarters was built nearby, to a standard Air Ministry design. It consisted of five rooms, including a command post with an elevated observation cupola and became operational in August 1942. By this date the regular army had already left the airfield. Indeed,

Two gun loops made in the re-entrant angle of the churchyard wall. This corner arose due to an extension of the graveyard – but it made a useful position to provide enfilading fire along the front of the wall to the east. Until about ten years ago there were concrete blocks at the foot of the walls for the men to stand on when shooting.

in January 1942 the South Lancashires were replaced by a unit of the specially formed RAF ground force known as No. 2799 (Defence) Squadron. These 149 men formed the mobile force for the airfield. At the airfield the static force consisted of the station personnel – engineers, mechanics, clerks, and so on – who were put through intensive training by 2799 Squadron at their headquarters at Avonside. 2799 Squadron was itself withdrawn in July 1942, leaving the HG to maintain the defence of the perimeter and the new battle HQ. Over the following year concrete bases for the HG sub-artillery and anti-aircraft guns were installed in the back garden of Northfield. Regular exercises were held to test the over-arching defence plan.

The trained manpower available for the defence of Grangemouth was substantially augmented in 1943 and 1944 by the build up of Polish forces in the Falkirk area. As the men of the Polish army were expected to be deployed overseas at any moment, it was sensible to form them into a mobile force. Consequently it was arranged that on the issue of the order "Man V.Ps." the 1st Polish Army Corps would send 33 men under Lt Biedanowiec to Grangemouth Drill Hall. The men were to be armed with three Bren guns, 21 Sten guns, grenades and pistols. This mobile reserve then came under the command of Major J S Thompson of 'D' Company 3rd Stg HG Bn.

Works

Many of the HG platoons in the Falkirk district started life as independent works' platoons with the concept of defending vital, and not so vital, industries. Most were already formed before the HG was given a distinct role in home defence and actually suited the idea of static defence then in vogue. Guards sprang up at the gates to the works and the initial patrols were of their boundaries and internal yards. The variety of industries involved ranged from chemical works to brickworks though, given the history of the area and their importance during the First World War, it is not surprising to see the iron foundries in the vanguard of this movement.

We have already looked at the Falkirk Iron Works HG and its watch over Bainsford Bridge. This foundry incorporated men from Castlelaurie Foundry and slit trenches were dug by the HG on the top of Cinder Hill with barbed wire protection, presumably for the defence of that site. Foundrymen from Callendar Abbots Foundries also signed on with the platoon. Curiously enough, so too did those at Carron Works. It is rather odd that the Carron

Stirlingshire Home Guard. 'C' Section - Falkirk Iron Works Platoon. Photographed in JC Brown's studio. Back row: ——, ——, R Turpie Front row: ——, Robert Murray (RN in First World War), Harry Young

Iron Company, which was doing more war work than any other foundry, never had its own HG unit. The clock tower of the main office block was used by the Carron village HG in 1940/41 as an observation post, but the men were not directly associated with the foundry. Arrangements were made to defend the

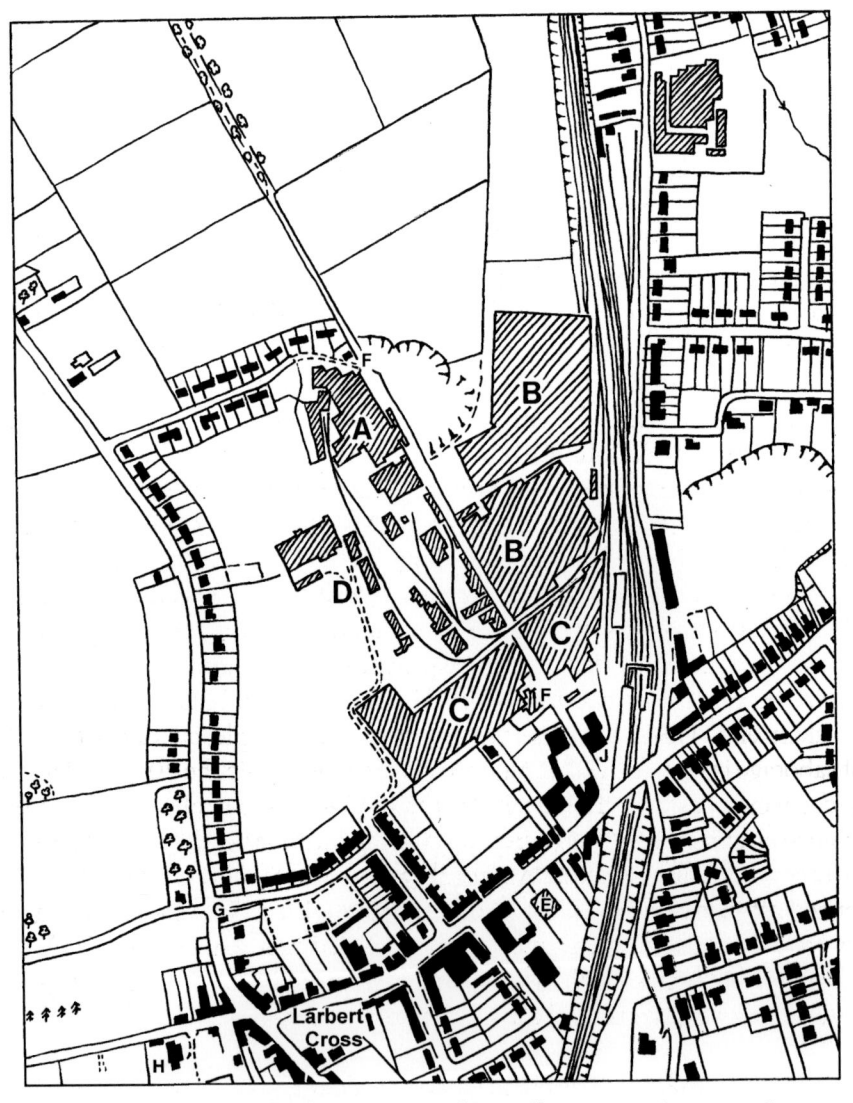

Foundry Loan was a private lane housing A – Scottish Enamelling Co; B – Larbert Ironworks; C – Torwood Foundry and D – Jones' timber yard. Guard posts were established at either end – F. Some of the guard enjoyed a drink at the Station Hotel – J. The HG HQ was at the parish church hall – H. Regular troops were billeted at the Village School – E. There was also a gun post at the end of Pretoria Road – G.

works with miles of barbed wire and a few trenches. The Carron Company, however, never saw the need for its own unit as its following statement makes clear:

> In the event of an emergency being anticipated or arising in the works, it will be the duty of constables and guards to raise the alarm and cause communication to be immediately sent to the local police office, where, according to the nature of the report received, arrangements will be made to send to the works a Home Guard detachment or regular troops.

This situation contrasts sharply with that of Jones & Campbell in Larbert. The company owned both the Torwood Foundry and the Scottish Enamelling Company's works (SEC) in Foundry Loan, and had close family connections with the adjacent sawmill of James Jones & Co. Also in this short length of road was the Larbert Foundry of Dobbie Forbes & Co. Together these made a complex about the same size as the Carron Iron Works, and like that works the SEC had just won a government contract to machine artillery shell forgings. When the call went out Jones & Campbell had no hesitation in forming a unit with John Logan of SEC and Willie Reid of the Torwood Foundry as officers. Due to delays in receiving weapons and equipment, the platoon could do little over the summer of 1940 other than keep a wary watch on the locality. By the time that these arrived the threat had been reduced by the onset of the winter weather and in any case it was Christmas before the SEC Shell Factory was turning out large numbers of projectiles. Beyond the Station Hotel the Foundry Loan was a private road belonging to the foundries. After 400 yards it turned into a small farm track with large trees lining its northern end. This was a favourite walk with local people, but due to the risk of sabotage it was decided at night to close to the public the 400 yard length in the hands of the foundries. In March 1942 it was entirely closed, but re-opened after protest at the end of May during the hours of daylight. The SEC factory was totally enclosed by tiers of barbed wire fences and "the Loan was fenced off just beyond Larbert Foundry gate with a Guardhouse and gate controlled by full-time personnel who were retired men. The sergeant, I believe, was named Menzies, walked with a slight limp, and then in the evenings we part-timers would do guard duty two hours on and four hours off" (William Wilson)

The gate for closing the north end of the Foundry Loan was just south of where Campbell Drive is now and Sgt. Bobby Rollo of the HG was also on duty there in the evenings. The gates at the south end lay just to the north of the Station Hotel, with a wooden hut for the HG near the gates to the car park

Station Hotel at the head of Foundry Loan, Larbert. Behind the hotel on the left is the Torwood Foundry of Jones & Campbell with a wooden hut in the car park.

of Torwood Foundry. Inside the hut were night rations and bunks for those not on watch. In the winter months the guard was maintained from 8pm until 6am, requiring up to ten guardsmen on duty each night for each gate, giving a watch of two hours. The area between the gates was made a restricted area and only those in uniform or with a pass were allowed to enter. Those HG who were due to go to work straight after the night's guard duty would usually take the first three shifts. On watch each had a rifle and five rounds of ammunition and at the end of the shift he passed it on to the next man. A bandolier containing about 30 bullets was kept locked in a box inside the hut under the control of a corporal. If there had been an alert the corporal would have issued this to the men.

> There was one daft bugger from Stenhousemuir who, when on duty, always had his gun in his hand. Well, one night he handed his bullets over and was mucking around with the rifle when it went off and the bullet just missed the other guardsmen in the hut and went through the roof. Discharging a firearm in such a confined space created a huge noise and as well as deafening us, it woke everyone in the area up. We were rather hard on him after that! (John Grierson)

One of the Bonnybridge platoons was based on the staff of a foundry there, that of Smith & Wellstood at the Columbian Stove Works. Major James White from the office was the commanding officer of 'A' Company 2nd Stg HG

No. 3 platoon, "A" Company, 2nd Stirlingshire Battalion HG. Based at the Columbian Stove Works of Smith & Wellstood. The photograph was evidently taken on a field exercise with other platoons, which may be seen in the background. Most of the men are wearing their haversacks containing gas masks on the chest and others have rattles, suggesting that the exercise included the use of gas.

Bn, while his second-in-command, Joe Curran, worked in the sales team. So too did Sgt Robert Bellingham of No. 3 platoon and Tom Aitken (later transferred as a lieutenant to Falkirk). The platoon commander, Alex McLaren, was an assistant clerk of works with Smith & Wellstood. John McArdle, the platoon's quartermaster was a manager. Ordinary members of the platoon included George Gibson (stocktaker), Alfred Holmes (tinsmith), Jack Irvine (assistant production manager), R McIntyre (moulder), Victor Pacitti (labourer), Tom Turnbull (patternmaker) and Will Turner (from Mitchell, Russell & Co).

Of this platoon Smith & Wellstood told its customers: "For the protection of the works in the event of invasion, we have from among our own employees a very well-manned and equipped detachment of the Home Guard." After all, it made commercial sense to be patriotic, though this claim was slightly exaggerated as the numbers of the rank and file had to be swelled by men from the nearby Chattan Foundry of Mitchell, Russel & Co. There was also a section from the Bonnybridge power station, an important supplier of electricity to the Carron Works. The protection of the Columbian Works was extended to a wider area than just the foundry premises. The Forth and Clyde

Aerial photograph of Smith & Wellstood's Columbian Stove Works at Bonnybridge looking south-west. The Forth and Clyde Canal is in the foreground, with the Canal Station branch railway on the right.

Canal lay along the north side and formed an obvious barrier in that direction. A flame-barrel trap was set up for anyone approaching through the pend and the bridge was neatly covered by fire from a machine gun from the upper storeys of the foundry's office block. To the south-east a natural hillock, known as Elf Hill, lay astride the Antonine Wall and was fronted to the south by St Helen's Loch. Trenches were dug around the hill top and were manned during exercises. The location of the defences to the south and west are not known, but we cannot help speculating that the twelfth century motte at Seabegs was utilised.

At Camelon G Wortley, the manager of the Gothic Foundry owned by R & A Main, set up an LDV unit at his works. Initially these men too stood guard at the works' gates, but also expanded their area of influence as noted in the section on stop lines. Another Camelon foundry, the Forth & Clyde & Sunnyside, shared the defence of Camelon Bridge with a section from the Rosebank Distillery. They started by placing a night guard at the entrance to their own works, which came as a surprise to some of their work colleagues. One dark night two of the firm's employees, Colin Sharp and Charlie Smith, were called upon to do firewatching duties. They duly arrived, after a dram or

On Guard

The canal Bridge at Bonnybridge overlooked by the offices of Smith & Wellstood. A crowd has gathered to watch a miniature submarine pass through, 1952.

three in a Camelon tavern, and as they approached the foundry they heard a familiar voice shout out "Halt, who goes there?" The body that belonged to the voice was standing with its back against the building and could not be seen. The two men wondered what was happening and failed to answer. The challenge rang out again and still they were perplexed. Then, from the darkness emerged Tommy Arthur in LDV uniform with his bayoneted rifle extended towards them. They recognised him instantly, as they all knew each other from the work in the foundry. They were therefore taken aback when Tommy shouted to his previously unobserved companion, "Corporal Smith, arrest these men!" Nothing happened. The order was repeated and still there was no response. Upon investigation they found Corporal Smith lying on the ground sound asleep – he had been drinking. The three men carried the unresponsive body into the foundry, where a bed was found for him in the HG's rest room and he was left to sleep it off. Smith (not his real name) was a moulder at the foundry, but also the son of one of the managers and it turned out that his drinking was tolerated. Anyway, later that night there was a knock on the office door where the firewatchers stayed and Colin was told that he was wanted. He met Corporal Smith and was offered some whisky, which he was happy to accept and the two men had a quick dram. However, the same

R and A Main Platoon at the Gothic Foundry, 1941. Commanded by Captain Wortley. On the extreme right of the back row is Jack Winchole, with his late father 3rd from the left in the front row. Tom Spence is 2nd from left, front row. Front row: ——, Tom Spence, Winchole, ——, ——, ——, ——, ——, ——, ——
2nd row: ——, John Winchole, Alex Denison, Peter Cole, Walter Logan, Cpt Wortley, David Cattanach, Andrew Auchterlonie, John Cochrane, Alex Maxwell, David Cheape, — 3rd row: Michael Dunn, John Orman, ——, Alex Harrison, Jim Jardine, — back row: —, —, Duncan Cram, —, —, Mr Hill (engineer), —, Leslie Hill (son of the engineer), —, —, Ronald Walton, Jack Winchole.

happened at 3am, and then at 6am, and Colin decided that he could not keep up. He was later directed into the Carron HG and found that this was not typical behaviour.

In Bo'ness Ballantine's New Grange Foundry provided a handful of men for one of the platoons, along with men from Thomson & Balfour's sawmill. Bob Smith, the manager of Thomson & Balfour, became a sergeant in this platoon, but had to retire due to pressure of work. The men from the works who had joined with him had to continue until stand down. The bulk of the men in Bo'ness came from the coal mines and the configuration of the town meant that it was more sensible to defend its outskirts than the individual works. At the core of the town was the dock complex, which as we have seen was guarded too.

The chemical industry in the Falkirk district was vital to the war effort and naturally gave rise to its own units of the HG. These were more restricted in nature and size than those connected with the iron foundries, as the amount

Aerial view of the Scottish Tar Distillery at Limewharf, Tamfourhill, looking east, c1960. The Antonine Wall occupies the tree belt to the right.

of manpower available was much lower. Either the industrial activities were less labour intensive, or there were a far higher proportion of women workers at play. At Nobel's detonator works in Westquarter, for example, there was a lot of dexterous work and there were over a thousand women employed, but under a hundred men. Consequently, the protection of the Westquarter Works was the responsibility of a small security force assisted by the police, reinforced when necessary by the Brightons and Redding HG platoons. The Limewharf Chemical Works run by Scottish Tar Distillers handled large quantities of bulk material and was able to muster a small HG unit. These men met in the stables of Wallside House, the manager's home, which was conveniently situated at the top of Lime Road, the only vehicular way into the works. The main duty of the unit was the defence of the works, made easier by the topography. To the north was the Forth and Clyde Canal with the wharf that gave the works its name. Almost parallel with this, to the south, was the Antonine Wall with its 12 foot deep ditch. To the west was a small burn and eastward the site narrowed at Lime Road.

In Grangemouth the ICI plant was still known locally as Scottish Dyes. The work's platoon was able to make use of the firm's relatively new recreation centre at the walled garden to Kerse House. The big house itself was in ruins, but was used by the platoon for exercises and inevitably ended the war far more ruinous. The platoon kept watch over the works at night. Dealing with poisonous chemicals at work the platoon was particularly concerned about such materials. Coming off night watch they paraded at about 6.30am for training exercises under an instructor called Alec Findlay. Alec always started each morning with a lecture lasting 20 minutes. Unfortunately, after a night's duty, this tended to induce sleep in some of the men and he took great delight in roaring "Gas Alert! Gas Alert!" At which they had to don their gas masks and listen to the final part of the lecture with them on.

Ian Munn wearing his father's ARP anti-gas cape. 1939.

Nodal Points

At nodal points, such as Falkirk and Slamannan, it was essential to have men on duty at all times so that a rapid response could be made to any developing situation. Each night, from June 1940 until December 1944, there were at least two men on guard at the Slamannan HG HQ. They stood outside the door with unloaded rifles. By and large this was a mundane task, with little to relieve the tedium. One night Charlie Finlay and his fellow HG watched the night sky from the Hall as a German plane got caught in the beam of a searchlight. A night fighter homed in on it and before long the enemy plane was spiralling to the ground, followed all the way by the beam of light until it passed beyond the horizon in the direction of Bathgate. The guardsmen had been elated by the spectacle and cheered all the time. The silence of the night sky pierced by the probing lights seemed even quieter after that.

Early in the evening the men on their rest period would pass their time by playing cards or games such as table tennis and guard duty soon slotted into the routine of village life. The wives of two of the guardsmen helped at McCabe's chip shop nearby in Main Street. So, when the shop closed for the night any left-overs were taken to the Welfare Hall for the HG to polish off. In the morning as they went off duty they would call in at the bakery next to Rosemount School for fresh rolls on their way home. It all seemed so normal and run of the mill.

9. V.Ps.

See Appx D.

These are establishments, installations, etc., which by virtue of their importance and/or their location constitute probable objectives for sabotage or enemy attack.

(a) They are classified from 1-4 according to their estimated importance.

(b) Companies are responsible for the protection of any V.Ps. within their Area not otherwise guarded. All V.P. guards will come under Bn. control on "Action Stations".

(c) Each V.P. is allotted a serial number as shown in Appx. D for reference. This number will be used exclusively for security purposes, in referring to the V.P., whenever communications are liable to interception.

Appendix D.

Classification of V.Ps.

V.P. 1   Those important enough to have guard detachments of service personnel at all times.

V.P. 2   Those at which protection is offered:

(a) Against sabotage by service police of various kinds or by personnel employed there (garrison).

(b) Against airborne attack by garrison Field Force Formations or after mustering by the Home Guard.

V.P. 3   Those guarded by civil police.

V.P. 4   No special military protection but guarded continuously by watchmen and/or H.G.

V.P. 5   Guarded by H.G. only on or after "STAND TO".

Priority V.P. 2.
Location & map ref. description anti-sabotage protection anti-airborne protection
Westerglen 67/365992   BBC Stn.C.M.P (V.P.) After "A.S" 2nd Stg. Bn. H.G.
Almond Junc. 459983 R.N. Amm. Siding C.M.P. (V.P.)
do

Priority V.P. 4.
Telephone Ex. Falkirk	3802	Imperial communications.
Garage Falkirk	3801	Post office store.
Carron Coy.	381045	Private factory.
R and A. Mains	362027	do
Falkirk Corpn Gas Wks		
Nobels South Drum	330995	Explosives store.

Defence Scheme 24.12.42.

CHAPTER FIVE

More Weapons

Grenades

Despite the fact that millions of cast iron hand grenade cases were made by foundries in the Falkirk district, it was 1942 before grenades and anti-tank mines were made available to the local HG in sufficient numbers for them to become an effective part of their arsenal. The standard grenade of the British Army was the No. 36M, which was only too familiar to the veterans of the First Word War as its design went back to 1918. They knew it as the 'Mills Bomb' (after its inventor) and were positively jubilant when it was issued to the HG. Two Mills grenades in their pockets gave them a wonderful sense of confidence.

These old hands became the instructors for the new recruits. They started by throwing tennis balls or fist-sized weights (the Mills bomb weighed 1lb 11oz) in order to get accustomed to the over-arm throwing action. In Grangemouth the men formed up in two lines, about 6 yards apart, and threw these substitute grenades to each other. Inevitably one of them got hit on the head – but at least that demonstrated the accuracy of the throw. They were taught that accuracy was of greater importance than distance. These were close-up weapons and a distance of 30 yards was considered fairly good. To encourage accuracy the game of grenade throwing was incorporated into sports days. There were two games. One involved lobbing the dummy grenade into a circle marked out on the ground. In the other the grenade had to be thrown within a corridor cordoned off with two ropes, and the longest throw won. Some men were naturals. Jimmy Meek, the blacksmith in Slamannan, was one. Using his well-practised hammer arm he was unusual in achieving both accuracy and distance. The longest throw at the Callendar Park sports meeting in 1942 was achieved by Marcus Rogers, who won 40 cigarettes as a prize. He says that he gave them away, as he did not smoke. He must have been a popular winner.

Once a satisfactory swing and a reasonable standard of accuracy had been attained, practice continued with dummy grenades, which looked like regular grenades but without any explosive content. Using these, the men were taught how to pull the pin whilst keeping the striker lever depressed and then throwing it. This was done by numbers. On the command 'ONE', they would grip the grenade in one hand and put a finger of the other hand through the ring of the safety pin. On the second count they would pull the pin out and keep the spring clip depressed, stretching the arm out ready for throwing. Finally, on 'THREE', they released the catch, threw the grenade and took cover whilst counting to five. As well as throwing them from the cover of a wall, tree or whatever, they also threw from a lying posture. This, of course, could be executed in the grounds of various HQ buildings or even school fields. Having mastered this art many went on to use live hand grenades in practice, which meant an outing to the range.

Some of the shooting ranges also catered for grenade throwing. The preferred range was Greenhill where the regular army instructors took charge of such sessions. Sunday was the usual day. Some platoons, however, made their own arrangements. The men from Slamannan knew the ideal spot for this sort of thing on the wilds of Darnrigg Moss. Here they could stand in the trenches dug for the extraction of peat and take cover once they had hurled their explosive charges. Indeed they had previously used this site to test out their home-made Molotov cocktails. The platoon later got permission to use a nearby ruin for their target practice. All that remained of the building near Cowan's Farm (Darnrigg Farm) were the outer walls. About 25yds away was the low embankment of a disused railway line that had once served one of the many coal pits in the area. This provided cover for the men to hide behind once they had thrown the grenades. It was quite a long throw and some of the platoon could not reach the old dwelling, whereas John Meek would ask which part of the building he was to place his grenade in.

Complete No. 36M hand grenade with no explosive charge, used by the Falkirk HG for training purposes.

Some of the Falkirk platoons, including that of the Post Office, used the sand holes at Bell's Meadow for grenade practice. The platoons at Laurieston, Brightons and the surrounding area went to a disused brickworks beside the

Gardrum Burn for theirs. Here they had plenty of open space, which was unfit for other purposes and which provided walls for cover and for use as targets. Hugh Baird of the Brightons platoon remembered collecting the grenades from the Drill Hall in Falkirk and being taught to prime them. He also remembered that during one live practice 'Big Jock' Spears threw his grenade straight up in the air. It went high, but it was immediately obvious to the watching guardsmen that it was going to come down quite close to the spot from which it had been so hopefully despatched. Hugh watched in disbelief as it went up and the next moment he found himself standing ankle-deep in water. His sense of self preservation had carried him into the burn and safety. All the other men had scattered in all directions and amazingly no one was injured. But what a fright they all had! For Hugh it was probably the most dangerous thrill of his life and one not to be forgotten. Practice grenades had a 7 second fuse, which would have been reduced to 4 seconds if used in anger.

Robert McNab of the Redding HG, like most other guardsmen, knew that "the most important thing was to drop the grenade outside the trench" when live grenades were being used. His platoon used trenches dug in the grounds of Weedingshall House, though most of the time this was with dummies. The Larbert and Stenhousemuir platoons set up a barricade in Torwood, which provided them with a safe place from which to lob grenades. Members of the platoons were alarmed at the number of occasions when the dummy grenades were dropped after the pins had been removed. When it came to throwing live grenades a regular member of the A and S H from Stirling was usually present. This was also the case with the Falkirk Power Station platoon who dug a pit near the sewage works beside the River Carron at Bainsford from which they threw their grenades into the marshy ground. One of the men threw his grenade and hit the front of the pit. To his horror it bounced back, but the officer from the A and S H simply picked it up and threw it over the side. Just in time – for it exploded in mid air.

Falkirk	Bellsmeadow	NS 893 798
Bo'ness	South of Linlithgow	
Slamannan	Darnrigg Moss	NS 878 751
Grangemouth	Kerse House	NS 915 816
Denny	Near Dales Bridge	NS 816 829
Larbert	Torwood	NS 83 84
Brightons	Old brickworks	NS 924 768
Falkirk/Bainsford	Langlees	NS 892 826

The Denny platoons used land next to their rifle range beside the River Carron for their live grenade practice. Some of the Falkirk platoons were also able to use this site, amongst them the platoon from Falkirk Iron Works. Harry Rogers went with that platoon and an old soldier from the First World War demonstrated the method to be used. He then led each man in turn to one of the two dug-outs and they got to throw grenades, remembering to duck behind the protective bank of earth after having done so. The target was an old boiler and a sandbagged observation post with a viewing slit allowed the platoon sergeant, Tom Lindsay, to monitor the results. Unfortunately, it was on this same course that Jimmy Kerr of the Denny platoon had an accident with his grenade and badly injured his hand, losing its use.

Lt-Col. Cadell of the West Lothian Battalion had some land not far south of Linlithgow where he allowed the Bo'ness platoons to practise throwing live grenades on weekends. One of the youngest members of the platoon thought that the location was quite exotic, as it was the farthest he had ever been away from home. He enjoyed the lorry drive down and because all the road signs had been removed was soon lost in the myriad of narrow country lanes. One day the Lt-Col. was speaking to a platoon sergeant as the training took place. Then one of the men threw a grenade that failed to explode. The Lt-Col. looked at the sergeant and told him that it was his duty to deal with it. The sergeant, rather slowly, crept forward and placed a small explosive charge next to the potentially lethal grenade. On his return to the trench it was detonated using the long fuse wire that he had attached.

Such incidents were only too common. During an exercise with the regular troops stationed around Bonnybridge another grenade failed to go off. As it was in an area used by the general populace it could not be left for long. Lt. Tom Aitken of the HG described what happened next: "A soldier had to slide up to it like a snake, attach some gelignite, insert a fuse, creep away and then safely start the controlled explosion. Not a task for the faint-hearted!"

It was unusual to use live grenades on exercises and hessian bags full of chalk powder (often referred to as flour) were the normal projectile on such occasions. On impact they would cover the target,

Zinc alloy fragments from the centre piece of a hand grenade, found by metal detectorists near Kinnaird House

More Weapons 133

be it a vehicle or a person, with some of the white dust. It was therefore with no particular misgivings that Lt. John Monfries of the Brightons platoon lent his grocery van for use as a mock tank or armoured vehicle during an exercise where they were to defend Torphichen Bridge. His platoon lay in ambush and targeted the vehicle with the substitute grenades. Unbeknown to Lt. Monfries, there had been a slight problem with this ammunition and it was found that there was not enough chalk whitening. Unperturbed the guardsmen simply added some soft earth to the contents. Then, some rather mischievously put small stones in as well. When the van was bombarded with 'grenades', it got rather battered.

The hand grenades were stored in wooden boxes in the armouries next to the rifles. The fuses for priming them were always kept separate, usually in round tins, and it was a simple and quick job to set them in place. At Slamannan, for example, the grenades were kept in the Welfare Hall, but the fuses were housed in the magazine out back.

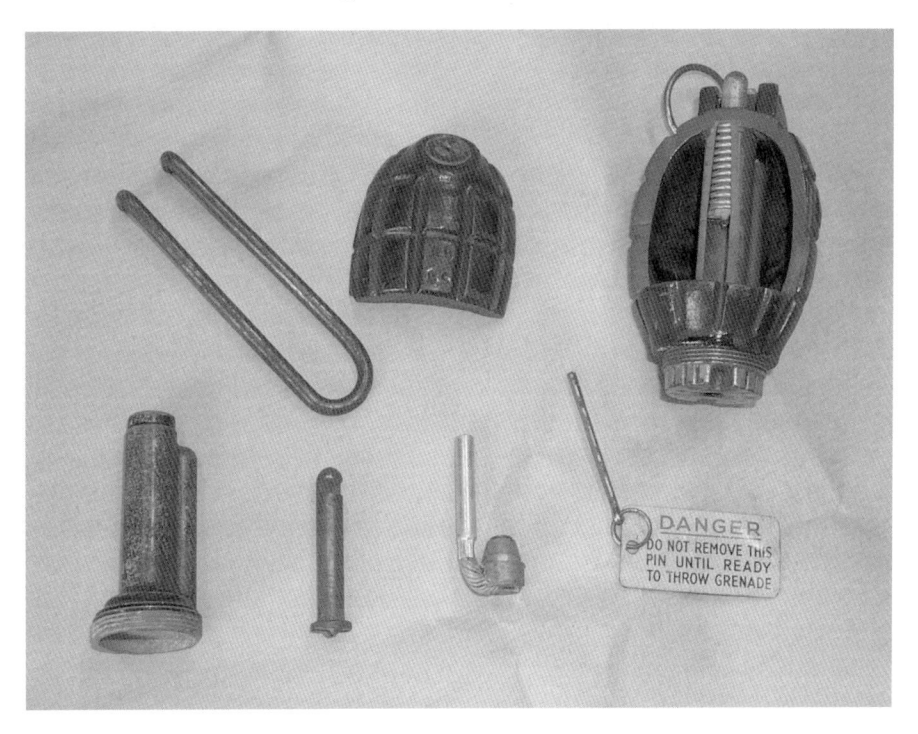

The main components of a hand grenade are shown here. The cut-away grenade, steel striker, retaining pin with warning notice, curved fuse and centre piece were used to demonstrate how to prime the grenade. These were used by the Falkirk HG.

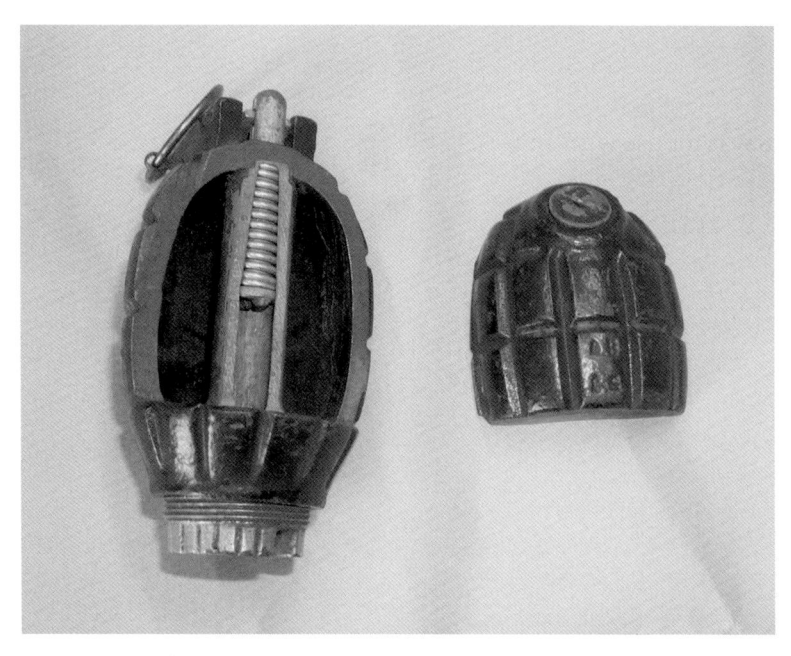

A type 36M hand grenade with a section of the outer cast iron casing cut away in order to show the internal workings. Used by the Falkirk HG for demonstration purposes.

Metal cones from shaped charges of Type 68 anti-tank grenades fired from EY rifles. These were found by metal detectorists in the grounds of Kinnaird House.

The Mills Bomb (No. 36M) was only one of seven different types of grenade issued to the 3rd Stg HG Bn. The No. 68 was for use with an EY rifle and is discussed in that section. The No. 69 had a black plastic casing, instead of cast iron, and an impact fuse, so that its effect was primarily blast and shock. Its principal use was therefore in house-to-house fighting, where it would be followed up with a burst from a sub-machine gun. Some of the HG officers were sent on courses to learn the associated tactics, but for most of the local men it meant a trip to Thornbridge near Laurieston. Here there were two rows of tenements known locally as McKillop's Buildings. They had been built for the employees of the adjacent foundry in 1899, but by 1939 were considered uninhabitable and a closing order was applied. Tenants were accommodated elsewhere and the buildings fell into disrepair, exacerbated by the pilfering of material. The last tenant was re-housed in March 1942 and the buildings were requisitioned by the Army. Part of the usage they made of them was to train the West Kent Regiment, then encamped in the Lower Park at Laurieston, in house-to-house fighting. At the same time they instructed the HG in such fighting, using live grenades, until the buildings were derequisitioned at the end of September 1942 and completely demolished over the following months. Thereafter, house-to-house fighting meant the use of chalk bags for the local HG.

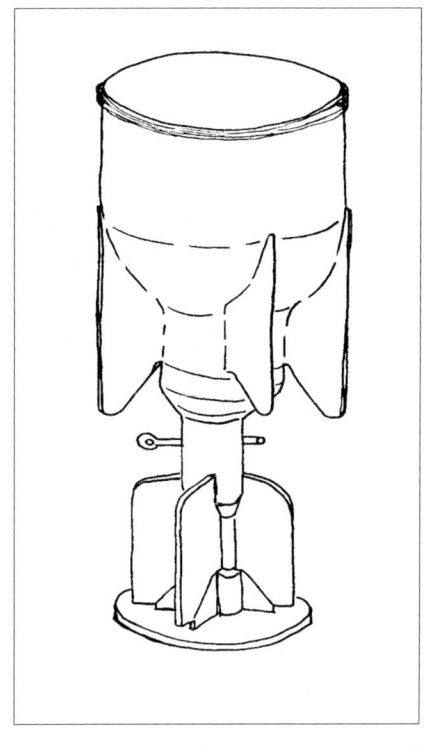

Shaped charge of a Type 68 anti-tank grenades. The fins and the cup-shaped section are the parts found by metal detectorists.

The No. 73 grenade did not have the finesse of the 36M, 68 or 69. It was essentially a lump of gelignite in a biscuit tin, and therefore became known as the 'Woolworth' or 'Thermos Bomb'. It was rather heavy and consequently packed quite a punch, making it suitable for use against tanks, but only at close range. Nonetheless, its early distribution in 1941 to the HG gave them a great morale boost.

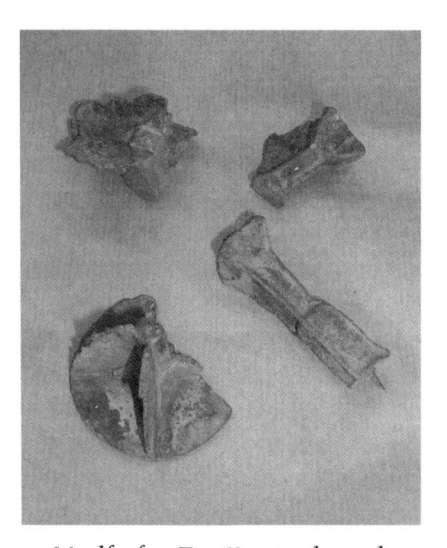

Metal fins from Type 68 anti-tank grenades found by metal detectorists at Kinnaird House.

Perhaps the most famous of the grenades provided for use by the HG was the No. 74, known as the "Sticky Bomb". This consisted of a spherical plastic flask filled with nitro-glycerine. Attached to this was a handle containing a spring-driven striker, fuse and detonator, operated by a lever similar to that on the Mills Bomb. The outer surface of the flask was covered in stockinet material and coated with a clinging adhesive so that the bomb could be attached to its target, be it a tank or a building. Two thin metal hemi-spheres, spring-loaded to fly apart when a pin was released, were closed over the flask and secured to the handle so that it could be stored or carried without sticking to the guardsman. Although it could be thrown, it was far better to place it in position on the tank, calling for considerable courage.

Even exercises involving the use of dummy No. 74s seem dangerous in retrospect. William Sharp, along with other members of the Falkirk Power Station platoon, got to practise attaching duds to moving tanks – well actually a Bren Gun Carrier from Stirling. They lay on the road in front of the vehicle and as it passed over them they removed the outer skin and pushed the body of the sticky bomb onto its weak underside. As they did so the plastic casing (glass in earlier models) smashed with what the man attaching it thought was a deafening cracking noise. The 'tank' crew never heard it above the sound of the engine. The man on the floor then rolled away sideways and only five seconds after he had broken the flask it would have exploded - had it been the real thing. The platoon was shown the devastating impact of a live bomb at the Greenhill Range. John Grierson of the Stenhousemuir platoon was also impressed when he saw one demonstrated at Torwood by a commissioned officer. A giant flame shot into the air. The officer instructed them to go for the back of the tank after it had passed and pointed out that ideally a cluster of such bombs should be used. The tank tracks were another weak point.

Like the Mills Bomb the No. 75 grenade was called after its inventor, in this case Hawkins. The Hawkins grenade was actually a small anti-tank mine detonated by two 'crush igniters', requiring the tank to drive over it. Generally

More Weapons

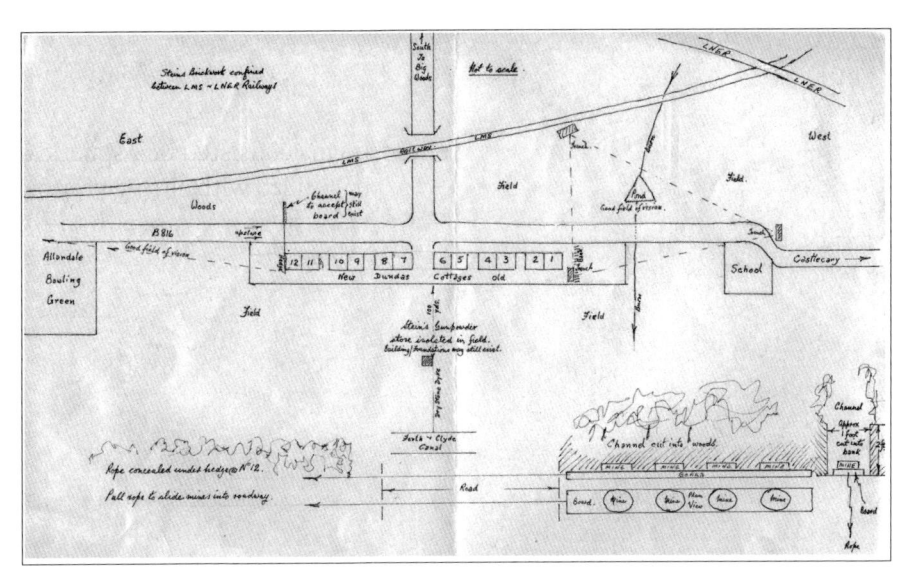

Sketch of the HG positions at Allandale by James Scobbie showing the anti-tank trap.

the Hawkins was buried in some suitable place, but one recommended practice was to tie a number together at intervals on a long string and place them at the roadside, suitably concealed by grass or straw. The end of the string led across the road to an operator hidden in a slit trench. On the approach of the tank, he waited until it was so close that both he and the mines would be below the tank crew's line of vision, and then rapidly pulled on the string to drag the line of Hawkins grenades across the tank's path. He then ducked into his trench to await the bang.

One such anti-tank trap was established at Allandale and was designed for use against tanks travelling westwards from that village towards Castlecary. It lay at the east side of a group of dwellings known as Dundas Cottages and is described by James Scobbie, who as a boy acted as a messenger for the Castlecary Brickworks platoon:

> The excavation of a channel opposite No. 12 Dundas to accept a long board capable of being pulled into the roadway earned it our childhood title as the anti-tank trap. We never saw any mines, but a system was in readiness to place mines on the board and pull the assembly by rope from the concealment of No. 12's hedge into the roadway. As an alternative, another board could be spiked with protruding nails to puncture the tyres of any passing vehicle. These devices would easily be manufactured in Stein's workshops. In both scenarios any vehicle passing westbound would have to negotiate an upslope and momentarily lose sight of the road surface in the vicinity of the trap.

Castlecary Brickworks looking south-east with Dundas Cottages at the bottom of the picture, 1933.

Another anti-tank minefield was proposed at Belmont on the eastern approach into Falkirk town centre (NS 891 800).

The home-made Molotov cocktails, such as those described in Chapter 3, in use by the Bo'ness and Slamannan platoons, were very volatile and likely to spontaneously combust. By the end of 1941 their retention was forbidden by standing orders. In their place the government issued the No. 76 incendiary grenade. The grenade body was simply a half-pint glass bottle, and the filling was a mixture of phosphorus, benzene, water and other chemicals, together with a strip of crude rubber. The rubber softened and partly dissolved during storage to give an adhesive quality to the mixture. When thrown the bottle broke, exposing the phosphorus to the air and causing the contents to ignite spontaneously. For this reason it was commonly known as the SIP grenade, which stood for Self Igniting Phosphorus. It was simple to make and the government spread its manufacture throughout the country so that if an invasion did occur its production could be ramped up in the locality most needed. By August 1941 over six million had been made and distributed, so that it was the first universal weapon of the HG. They were usually buried in boxes against the day when they would be needed. However, in 1940/41 it was not only the HG that was short of weapons and many SIP grenades were supplied to regular units of the army and air force. Being buried, they were often forgotten about when these units moved on. One of the caches was discovered in June 2003 at Muiravonside Country Park when a JCB was digging a new drainage trench. The mechanical arm broke the seals on some of the bottles causing them to erupt into flames. Upon examination it was found that immediately below the surface a small steel plate had been laid, warning of explosives. A foot below this was the box containing 24 SIP grenades. They were dealt with by a bomb disposal squad. They were probably put there by 'E' Company of the A and S H who occupied Muiravonside House in 1941. A similar stash was discovered in 1967 on what had been the southern perimeter of the airfield at Grangemouth when a bulldozer was preparing the site of Bowhouse Primary School and a third lot of nine bottles was disturbed during the digging of a sewer trench across Bellsmeadow, Falkirk.

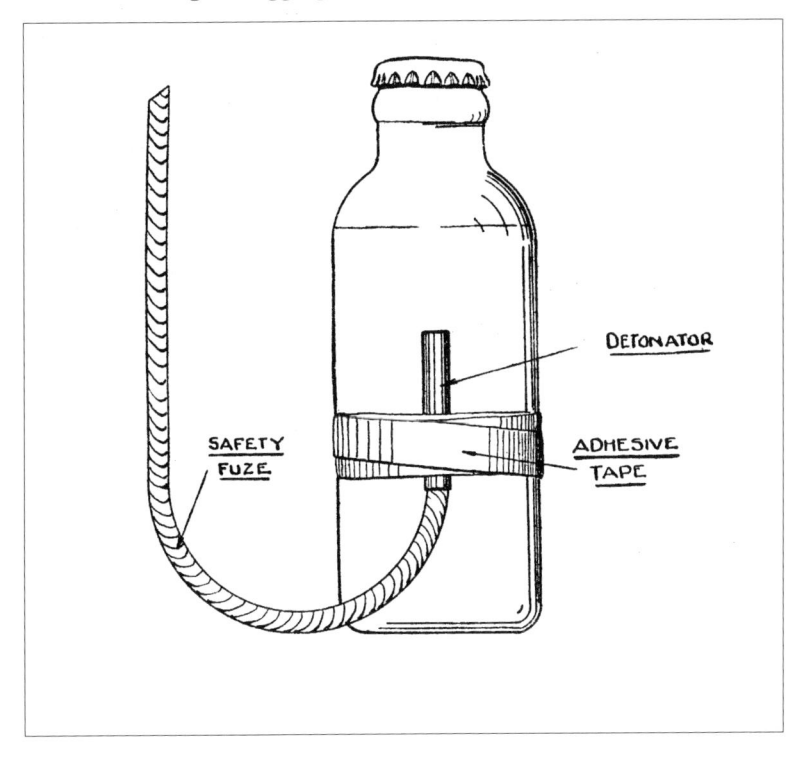

The SIP Grenade (from Home Guard Instruction, No. 51).

Optimistic instructions produced in 1941 suggested that "Six of these bottles breaking on a tank one after the other should cause sufficient heat and smoke to develop all over the tank to bring the crew out." Part of the idea was to burn the oxygen up around the tank and suffocate the crew, in which they echoed the flame barrels (for which see Chapter 3).

Grenade	Dec 1940	Dec 1941	Dec 1944
36M (Mills bomb)	700	—	4,500
68 (rifle)	—	—	1,200
69 (blast)	—	—	200
73 (Woolworth)	—	—	250
74 (sticky bomb)	—	—	160
75 (Hawkins)	—	—	2,000
76 (SIP)	180	120	6,000 nil
77	—	—	306

Grenades in the stores of the 3rd Stg HG Bn

Machine guns

Around the middle of 1942 the 3rd Stg HG Bn was issued with a Lewis medium machine gun, a Vickers medium machine gun and some Thompson sub-machine guns. Initially they were kept at the police station in Stenhousemuir and each platoon was given an opportunity to handle them. To demonstrate the automatic weapons at the Greenhill Range a rating came through from Rosyth. The HG had been practising stripping the Lewis guns down and assembling them and through constant practice they were pleased to have achieved a best time of two minutes. The naval man put on a blindfold and did it in one minute! In all, the 3rd Stg HG Bn came to have eight British (.303) Lewis machine guns and thirteen US (.300) machine guns.

As well as providing a great boost to morale the machine guns were useful in absorbing some of the HG's manpower at a time when there were still insufficient rifles to go round. At Stenhousemuir John Gillespie was assigned to the Lewis gun along with two assistants. It had been found that John could hit the targets, whereas the other two, being strong giants of men, could usefully get the gun to where it was needed. This dedicated crew learned how to work efficiently together as a team. The Lewis gun had a double cylindrical 'pan' magazine on top and John learned how to check the bullets and to load it in the dark – just in case. The magazines always seemed to contain a few dodgy bullets, which were misshaped or too long, and these were taken out before it was used. So the magazine ended up with, say, 47 rounds instead of 50. This was found to be useful because it not only reduced the chances of the gun

More Weapons

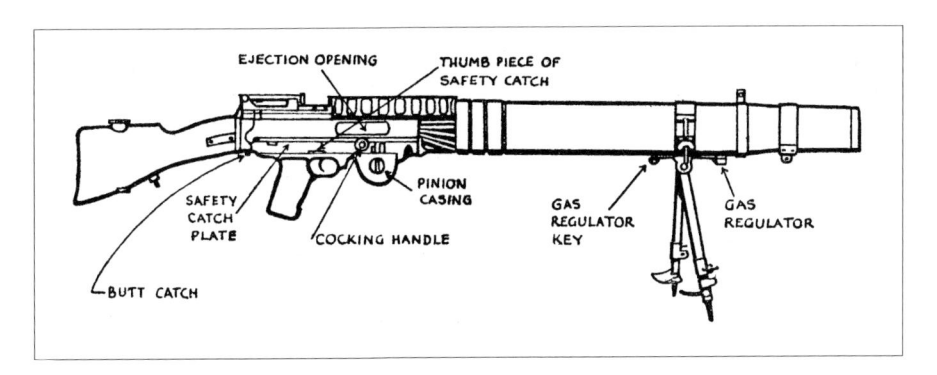

A Lewis light machine gun (from Small Arms Manual, Lt-Col. Barlow & Major Johnson, Nov 1942)

jamming, but also reduced its tendency to overheat. The Lewis gun was air-cooled. If the gun was used when the barrel was too hot it wore out much quicker. Another way around this problem was to change the barrel every so often and plenty of spares were kept in readiness. Changing the barrel was easy, as it had a Body Locking Pin, known in the jargon as the BLP, or to the HG as the 'Lady's Delight'.

When the Lewis gun allocated to the Falkirk Iron Works platoon arrived at the unit's base, James Isdale happened to be on duty and so was chosen to operate it. He became the gunner and had a crewman to help with the reloading. Both men lugged it around on exercises. Live firing took place at the Greenhill Range and there they solved the problem of the barrel overheating by pouring water over it. By contrast, the Slamannan platoon seems to have struggled with their Lewis gun and it is reported that overheating caused it to jam on several occasions.

Jim Isdale was also on duty the first night of the Clydebank Blitz. The sound of the German planes passing directly overhead on their way to the target was deafening to the men desperate to have a go at the enemy. It seemed to the guardsmen that the planes must be low enough for them to be able to take a shot at them. Accordingly, Jim tied a rope to his Lewis gun and then climbed up the firewatching tower that had been erected in the ironworks. Once at the top he hauled the gun up at the end of the rope and then looked for the droning planes. Only then did he realise that they were actually flying too high to be seen clearly and were evidently out of the range of his weapon.

The arrival of the Lewis guns was usually gratefully welcomed, and such appeared to be the case at Shieldhill. The HG there took great pride in their new machine, and waited patiently for the ammunition pans. It eventually emerged that these had been delivered to the HG section at California, just

Photograph of Laurieston HG platoon at Howlet Haugh, Callendar Park, Falkirk. A Lewis machine gun is laid out on its stand in the centre and several of the men have sheathed bayonets suspended from their belts. This picture appeared in the Falkirk Herald on 3rd January 1942. Front row: Alison; Jim Robinson; Jackie Morrison (brother of Watt); Sandy Cunningham (paratrooper at Arnheim). Seated row: Cpl Charlie Hartley (Falkirk Iron Co); Sgt McBride (WWI veteran of France); Sgt Sharpe (sniper with the Laurieston rifle club); Lt Douglas Haston; Sgt Wilson?; Sgt A D Keir (WWI veteran); Cpl Watt Morrison (bugler with the Boys' Brigade, sounded the Last Post at ceremonies in Grandsable Cemetery). Standing left: L/Cpl Jimmy Hunter (golfer); L/Cpl Webster 3rd row: Fleming; Ian Grant; A Barclay; Robert Stirling; Charlie Dunn, Thomson Porteous; Donald McGregor (killed in Canada), Archie Provan; L/Cpl T McLeod; Cpl Robertson. Back row: John West (killed at El Alamein); —; —; Peter or Alfie Liddle; George Erskine; Alex Tidy.

handed over met with a rebuttal and a demand for the Shieldhill men to hand over the gun. There followed a stand-off and after some negotiating it was finally agreed that if the enemy paratroops landed south of the Polmont Burn, then the gun would be delivered to California, and if they landed to the north the ammunition would be reunited with the gun at Shieldhill. What would have happened if parachutists had landed on both sides at the same time can only be imagined!

The Vickers medium machine gun arrived some months later than the Lewis gun. It too was of First World War vintage, but was water-cooled and far more reliable. It was altogether a more substantial beast, weighing in at

More Weapons 143

Shieldhill Home Guard Platoon (2nd Stirlingshire Battalion) in front of Miner's Welfare Hall. 1943. John Jamieson. Note the piper on the left.

43lb with its water cooling jacket, and took a four man team. It was intended principally as a defensive weapon and once set up on its tripod was not expected to be moved often. It received a mixed reception from the First World War veterans at Falkirk. Many remembered its devastating fire against the serried ranks of the enemy and its presence showed that the HG meant business. Others were rather reticent about joining the Vickers' crew. These men knew from experience that such machine guns attracted the greatest attention of the enemy. Actually, it appears that most of the so-called Vickers machine guns used in the Falkirk area were in reality Browning M1917s, the US equivalent. Six of these are recorded as having been in the arsenal of the 3rd Stg HG Bn at stand down, but no Vickers guns appear. Live shooting of the Browning machine guns was limited to the larger ranges, such as that at Greenhill. The only exception to this seems to have been when the Grangemouth Company used theirs to "knock hell out of the buildings" at Thornbridge (known as McKillop's Buildings).

In 1941 the three battalions in the Falkirk district were issued with Thompson sub-machine guns bought from America and already familiar to the public from their appearance in gangster movies. Having been developed

The Blackbraes & California HG, c1943. The men are wearing full uniforms with service badges, arm flashes and webbing ammunition bags. Back row: William Strang, ——, Daniel Liddle, John Liddle, Sandy Pryde, ——, Simon Marshall, Robert Heeps, John White. Middle row: Watson Smith, Sandy Ross, Tom McIntyre, John White, David Anderson, William White, Alex Liddle, David Williamson. Front row: ——, George Thomson, Jim Heeps, William Heeps, John Munnoch, William Walker, George Drysdale, John Heeps, Roberts Anderson.

and improved since they first appeared in production in 1921, these weapons were reliable, but expensive. They weighed 10lb 2oz and could fire 800 .45ins round per minute. The 'tommy' gun, as it was known, was hard to direct at a target at 500yds, but at 100yds could cut a person in half in seconds.

At Denny they practised with the tommy gun on their rifle range near Dales Bridge using the old railway embankment to absorb the spent bullets. Peter Graham remembered that the guns had a tendency to lift from left to right when being used with live ammunition and they had to be held down. The Camelon platoon based at the Gothic Foundry used a sand pit on the west side of the railway near the Three Bridges for its firing practice, shooting towards the Drove Loan. Here Ronald Walton confirmed Peter's observation. As he fired, the gun rose and bullets shot over the pit greatly distressing the man with the red flag near the main road!

The 3rd Stg HG Bn was sent 33 tommy guns in 1941, but all across the country these were subsequently withdrawn for use by commandos and the regular forces.

More Weapons

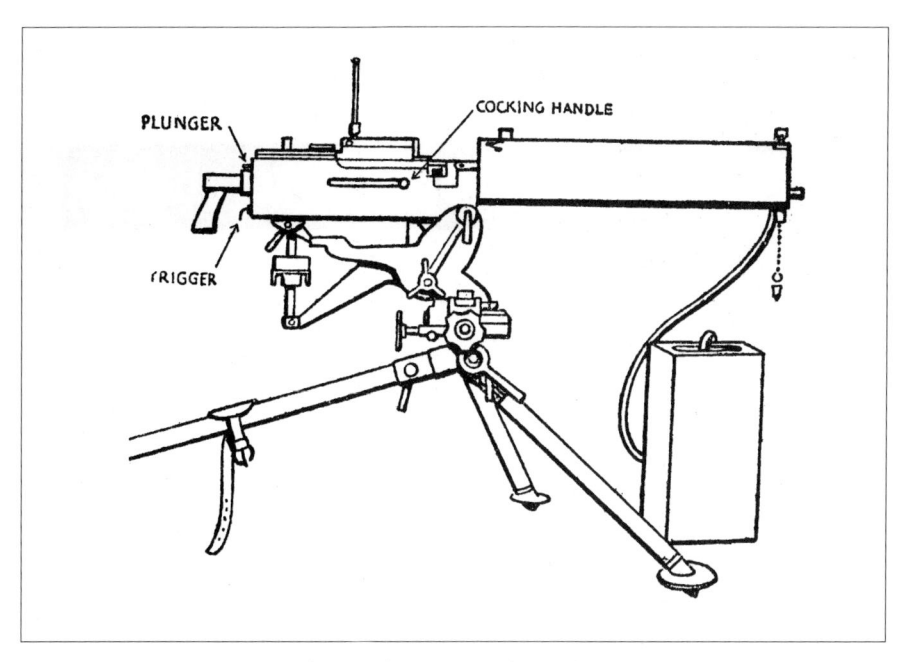

A Browning medium machine gun (from Small Arms Manual, Lt-Col. Barlow & Major Johnson, Nov 1942).

Meanwhile, the British Government got its armament experts to design a simpler sub-machine gun that could be manufactured in large quantities using unsophisticated machinery at low cost. This was quite a challenge and it was January 1941 before trials of the N.O.T.40/1 were carried out. Its performance was so good that it started coming off the production line in June 1941, entering service as the Sten gun. It was made in such large numbers that by the beginning of 1942 most of the immediate demand from the regular forces had been met. The Mark 2 version did away with the wooden

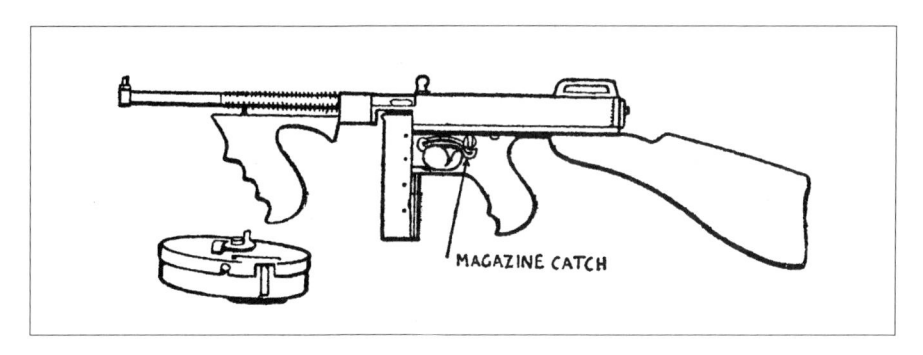

A Thompson machine gun (from Small Arms Manual, Lt-Col. Barlow & Major Johnson, Nov 1942)

components and was said to cost a mere £2.17.4 per gun to produce. Not surprisingly it was issued to the HG in the spring and summer of 1942. By July one in six Home Guardsmen in Britain was in possession of a Sten gun and this increased to one in four by the end of September. The all-metal gun had a crude appearance and was soon dubbed the 'Woolworth Gun' or the 'Gas Lighter'. Despite its appearance, it was very effective and one Edinburgh HG noted: "The day our platoon was issued with Sten guns I knew we were going to win the war. At last, I thought, we've ditched the fine British craftsmanship nonsense."

In the Falkirk district the Sten guns were issued first to the senior NCOs, such as sergeants, before trickling their way down to lance-corporals. A few privates did get to handle them eventually. Sgt. William Reid of the Larbert platoon was one of the first to receive his. He took it home and learned how to strip it down and reassemble it. It was not long before his young nephew could also do it. As acting-sergeant in the Falkirk Power Station platoon William Sharp was given a Sten gun and his rifle was passed on to another

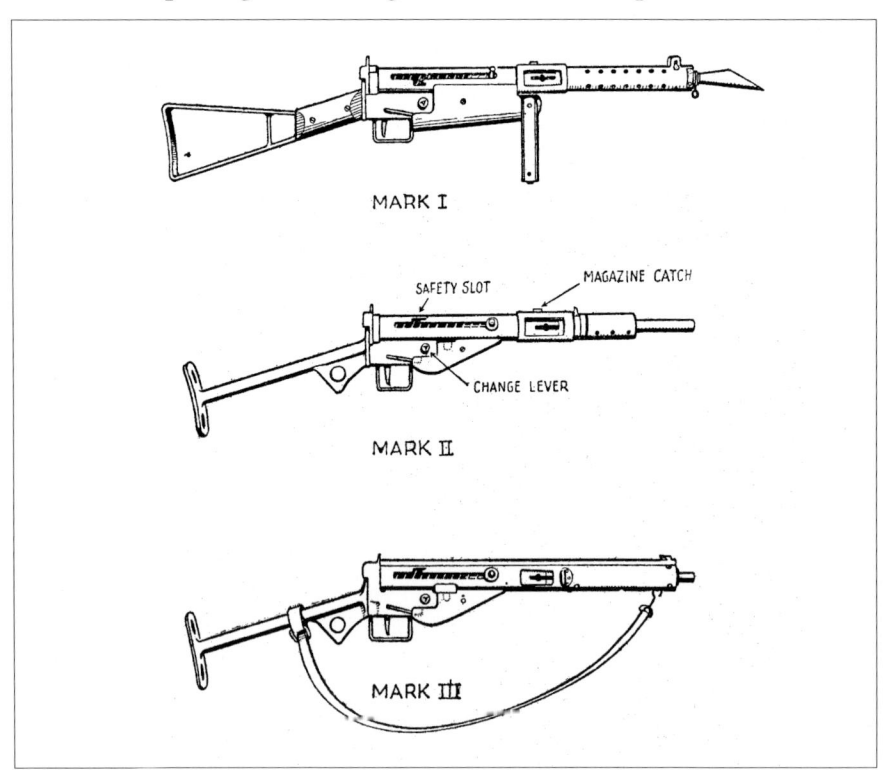

Sten sub-machine guns (from Small Arms Manual, Lt-Col. Barlow & Major Johnson, Nov 1942).

member. He started by firing his new weapon without the magazine of 32 9mm rounds attached and soon learned that if the little finger on his left hand was in the wrong position it was badly hurt. With live ammunition passing through this would have been serious and the Sten gun got a reputation as 'the pinkie-masher'. After instruction he was allowed to walk to about 50yds from the targets and fire short bursts of ammunition. It was hard to aim, but he became accustomed to its feel and before long he was able to use it to devastating effect at close range.

William lived in Abbotsford Street in Bainsford and was often on duty at the Ministry of Defence depot in Lochgreen Road on the opposite side of Falkirk. He found that the easiest, and hence quickest, way to get there from his home was to cut through to the towpath of the Forth and Clyde Canal and follow this to Lock 16, thence along the Union Canal towpath to the Slamannan Road and up to Lochgreen Road. One night he was late and was rushing to catch up when, in the black-out, he missed his footing and fell into the Union Canal. His Sten gun was slung over his shoulder by a strap and his first thought was to take it off his back. He grabbed hold of it and as he struggled to bring it round he accidentally depressed the trigger. The magazine was always kept half full and it was then that he discovered that Sten guns can indeed fire under water, though at a much reduced velocity as though in slow motion. He managed to drag himself and the weapon out of the canal and dried out in front of the fire at the depot. Quite a few remarks were passed, but he did not get into serious trouble from the authorities for the incident.

Up the Braes at Slamannan Cpl. Wilf Berwick had the first Sten gun. Sgt-Major Robins of the A and S H used to travel to Slamannan from Falkirk to train the men how to use it. He would bring with him a Bren gun and they learnt how to strip both guns in case they jammed. On weekends selected men went to Stirling Castle to improve their skills.

William Sharp also remembered a Bren gun being brought from Stirling by the A and S H for demonstration purposes. Some of the officers got to try it out. The gunner lay on the ground with his body in line with the gun and to change the direction of fire he had to realign his body. Consequently they only fired in short bursts of five or so rounds. Even so, William was most impressed when he fired a short burst at a brick and it completely disintegrated. The Bren gun had a greater destructive power than the Sten because it had a much higher muzzle velocity and used .303in projectiles compared to the 9mm of the Sten. No Bren guns were issued to the HG in the district, but had the need arisen they would have been supplied from Stirling. 461 Sten guns were supplied to the 3rd Stg HG Bn alone.

A section of the Slamannan Home Guard with the trophy that they had just won at a competition exercise around Craigieburn and Bantaskine, 1943. The section was led by Sgt Rudy Kerr, who is on the front right. To his left Sgt Jim Storrar is holding a Sten gun and the four men in the middle row have rifles. For the exercise steel helmets were worn. These are seen here covered with netting, to which camouflage was attached. Front: Sgt Jim Storrar (grocer, later joined army), Sgt Robert Kerr (miner). Middle row: Jimmy Meek (farrier), Jock Chalmers (miner), Tom Tripney (miner), Tom Gardner (miner). Back row: Cpl William Millar, Barney Schoneville (plasterer), Alex Gardiner (miner).

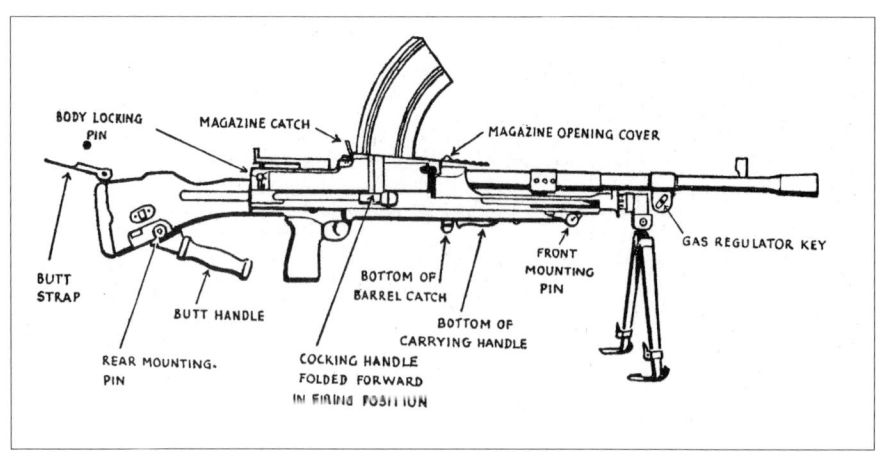

The Bren light-machine gun (from Small Arms Manual, Lt-Col. Barlow & Major Johnson, Nov 1942)

Craigieburn

With the arrival of anti-tank weapons, sub-machine guns and automatic rifles, extra field practice was demanded and so the 2nd Stg HG Bn sought permission from Mr Forbes, the owner of Callendar Estate, to use some fields to the south-west of Falkirk as a training ground. Forbes kindly agreed to the use of an area beside Craigieburn Farm. This was ideal, for not only was it a central location, but the terrain varied from woodland to pasture, bog and moorland. It also bordered onto South Bantaskine Estate, which was then occupied by the Polish Army. After further negotiations, this time with the Stirlingshire Education Committee, they also received restricted permission to use part of the adjacent school at Auchengean for weekend accommodation.

> Captain of C Company, 2nd Stirlingshire Battalion HG, Falkirk, requested permission to use Auchengean School for weekend courses of instruction for officers and non-commissioned officers of the Company. This would mean 20 or less men every second or third weekend from 5pm on Saturdays to 6pm on Sundays. The OC of the 2nd Stirlingshire Battalion HG requested the use of this school as Camp Headquarters in connection with HG weekend camps from the end of May until September for about 70 men. The camps would be open from 2pm on Saturdays until 6.30 pm on Sundays and the sleeping accommodation available at the school would be supplemented by tents pitched in a nearby field. All blanket and equipment would be stored on the premises. (Stirling County Education Committee May 1942)

The bulk of the men on weekend courses stayed in the farm buildings on the Saturday night, with the officers in the school. The accommodation at the farm was pretty Spartan and was supposed to toughen the men up. They

Auchengean School is now a private house.

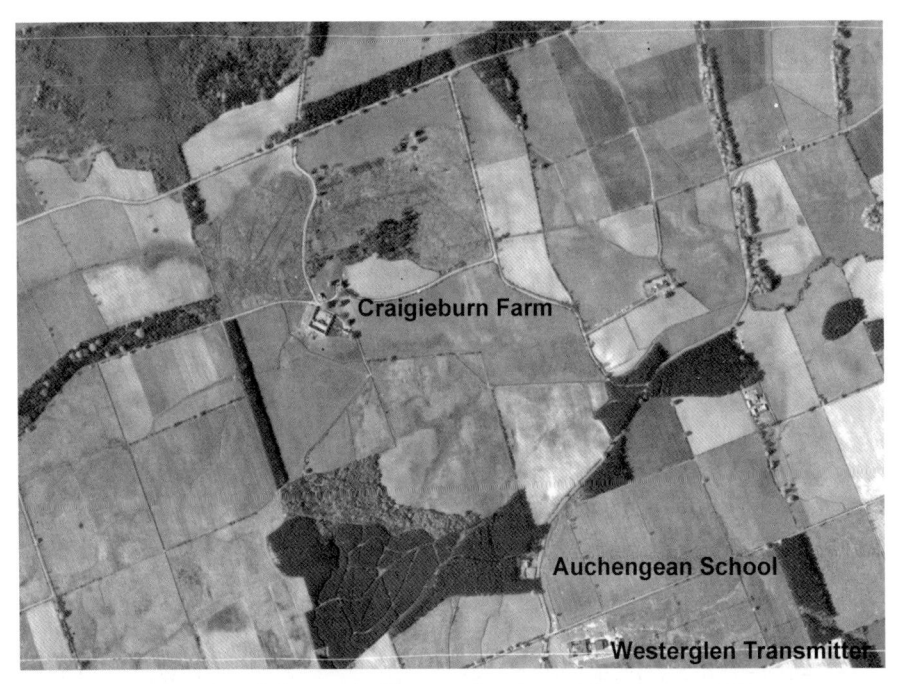

Vertical aerial photograph of the Craigieburn Farm HG exercise area, 1950.

slept, if they were lucky, on palliasses, which they had first to stuff with fresh straw. Each man was issued with a single blanket. Some platoons went a bit further and brought their own bell tents. In either case the latrine was simply a hole in the ground, freshly dug, surrounded by a canvas tent. The dining room was a large marquee. The platoon's cooks got hands-on experience of field catering for the unit. The cook for the Falkirk Ironworks platoon was Mr Elder, who was the head slaughterman at the Kerse Road slaughter house. He always seemed to conjure up good grub. Milk, for breakfast, could be got at the farm's dairy and was untreated.

The availability of this facility provided opportunities for cross battalion activities. In an unusual example of cross border cooperation the Bo'ness HG was invited to use the facilities. Alex McIntosh was not in the HG but he could play the bagpipes and one day he was asked by Sergeant McKinnon to accompany the Bo'ness Company to the training ground for a weekend. He was to entertain the men at night and wake them up in the morning. He knew a few of the men and agreed. What he did not expect was to sleep on a straw palliass on the floor in one of the four Nissen huts, with no heating. In the morning the men stole eggs from the farm. Among the manoeuvres that the men had to do was crossing fields by crawling on the ground.

Northover Projector

In the early days of the HG the chronic shortage of rifles was detrimental to the morale of the men. They rightly felt that they would be cannon fodder should an invasion occur. This view seemed to be backed up by the fact that their principal anti-tank weapon at the time was the SIP grenade, which was essentially a glorified Molotov cocktail and could only be used at close range. Major H Northover, an officer in the HG, came up with a solution that answered both of these problems. On his own initiative he designed a simple line-of-sight weapon to fire SIP grenades at distances of 100-200yds, requiring a three-man crew. It was easy to manufacture and cost a little under £10 each. Orders were placed for enough of these Northover Projectors to equip the HG throughout Britain on a scale of one per platoon and by August 1941 over 8,000 were in service. This is what the 3rd Stg HG Bn had to say about them:

> Bearing in mind the value of demonstration before issue, officers and NCOs were taken to the No 2 War Office School at Kinnaird House to see the Northover Projector demonstrated. Some officers were fortunate enough to see the demonstration carried out by the inventor himself, Major Northover, who succeeded in putting across a splendid demonstration in a most humorous fashion. So much so that complete confidence was instilled into the men regarding the possibilities of the weapon. We now had artillery to meet tanks or motorised infantry. How could the Hun dare to invade Stirlingshire? The gradual issue of new weapons, Tommy Guns, Sten Guns, Browning Machine Guns and Smith Guns always renewed this feeling of confidence and pride in the men.

Each platoon in the Falkirk district received a Northover Projector. John Grierson described the one that belonged to the Stenhousemuir platoon:

> This was a 6ft long cast iron drainpipe with a sheet of pressed steel at one end for the breach block. It stood on a heavy tripod; one leg of which always stuck out backwards. There was a wee stool. The breach plate was like a door with a handle like that on bike brakes. A wee cap was placed in and the breach closed. The 'bomb' was loaded down the pipe or muzzle. It had a ring instead of fins at the bottom end. Few people in the platoon were brave enough to use it and it languished in the store. Most of them were associated with foundries and knew that if the charge failed to work correctly it would shatter the cast iron creating a grenade that would injure those nearest to it.

In fact it was only the tripod mount that was cast iron and which often broke if accidentally dropped on a hard surface. The tube was of mild steel which, although not of a high grade, could cope with the rather feeble discharge pressure. This was produced with the aid of a toy pistol cap and a small black

A Northover Projector and three-man crew at Cardiff in October 1941

powder charge. Far more dangerous was the tendency for the glass bottle forming the body of the SIP grenade to break when it was dropped down the muzzle of the Projector, or when the charge exploded. When this happened the gun and its operators were liable to burst into flames. To overcome this problem stronger bottles were provided, which could still be hand thrown. In order to distinguish these from the older and weaker bottles that had red crown caps, the new ones were given green caps. Edward Sheehan recalled the confusion in the Bo'ness HG over which colour to use in their Northover Projectors when they first came to try them out at the old quarry beside the golf course on Erngath Hill. They sorted it out in the traditional method of trial and error! Subsequent trials of the "anti-tank pipe" were conducted at Lt-Col. Cadell's place south of Linlithgow. When fired from the Projector a cardboard ring was slipped over the bottle neck. This was a tight fit in the weapon's barrel and slowed its descent when loading and also prevented the bottle from sliding out when using the weapon at angles of depression. All in all the Northover Projector was rather a Heath Robinson contraption.

Pikes

By mid 1941 it was only too apparent that the supply of firearms to the HG would not meet demand for some considerable time. As an interim measure Winston Churchill ordered the production of a million simple hand-held weapons consisting of a 3ft 6ins length of 2ins metal piping weighing 5lb with 17ins surplus sword bayonet blades spot-welded onto one end – the infamous pike. These arrived in the Falkirk district towards the end of 1941 and were immediately shoved into the backs of the battalion stores. Here they remained hidden until collected for scrap just a few years later. 108 pikes languished in the Larbert stores. Despite the Prime Minister's assertion that "a man thus armed may easily acquire a rifle for himself," the local HG officers begged to differ and most of their men never even knew that they had arrived. A reaction, it should be added, common throughout Britain. Pikes might have been acceptable in Britain's darkest hours when the LDV was formed, but not in late 1941.

The issuing of the pike by the War Office was an unmitigated public relations disaster. It was exacerbated the following year by the arrival of rubber truncheons, which could at least be used for policing duties or for civil disorder. These too were quietly withdrawn.

Spigot Mortar

After the disappointment of the crude appearance of the Northover Projector the HG were rather sceptical when its successor was announced to be the rather medieval sounding 'Blacker Bombard'. Invented this time by a Territorial Army officer, Lt-Col. L Blacker, it had already been rejected by the War Office in favour of the standard 2ins mortar in 1939. It was, however, capable of use as an anti-tank weapon and was considerably cheaper than the equivalent 2-pounder gun. With Churchill's backing it was put into production in 1942 on a projected scale of one per company. In the event, it proved so popular that they were issued in large numbers and the 2nd Stg HG Bn had 20 by December 1942, the 3rd Stg HG Bn with 17 platoons possessed 31 before it stood down.

The Blacker Bombard soon took on the less archaic title of Spigot Mortar and was certainly more imposing than the Northover. It packed a significant punch in the form of a 20lb anti-tank bomb or a 14lb anti-personnel bomb. These projectiles had tear drop shaped bodies with fins at the rear to give stability in flight and to ensure that, when used as a mortar, the bombs nosed over at the tops of their trajectories to descend nose first so that the impact

A Spigot Mortar demonstrated by members of a HG Travelling Wing, Saxmundham, Suffolk, July 1941.

fuse there detonated on contact with the target. Propulsion was by means of a heavy cartridge lodged in the tail. When it was placed in the smooth barrel-like 29mm tube of the Spigot Mortar the operator was able to release a heavily sprung steel rod (the spigot) at the base to strike the cartridge, which fired and the evolved gas blew the bomb out towards the target.

    The short tube or barrel was normally mounted on four horizontal tubular legs at the ends of which were metal spikes that had to be driven into the ground to absorb some of the 20 tons per square inch of pressure on firing. On the opposite side of the mounting from the barrel was a curved shield behind which two of the operators lay. William Sharp of the Falkirk Power Station platoon remembered this:

The operator lay at the end of the weapon behind a shield and looked through a small slit near the top. The upper side of the slit was padded with foam and the operator put his forehead against it to sight. There were two hand grips, one of which had the trigger lever. When fired the gun had a hefty recoil and the foam banged the operator's head. I learned to aim the gun and then put my head back before firing. I only ever fired duds – mortars with cement in rather than explosives. The platoon was, however, given a demonstration with a live round. At 250yds it exploded with a loud roar and my God was it powerful!

Weighing in at 360lb it had to be dismantled in order to be moved, but this did not stop a five-man crew from the Grangemouth HG from carrying one up the Denny Hills for practice. Again it was the deafening impact of the bomb that most impressed James Buckie – not least because as they watched it explode only about 100 yards away, they saw a large part of the fins returning towards them and were forced to run out of its way.

Aiming the Spigot Mortar was rather crude. Looking through the slot in the shield William Wilson could see the sights, which he likened to a small garden rake laid on its back. With this he was supposed to estimate the speed of a tank. He was not filled with confidence. By contrast, the Spigot Mortar belonging to the Falkirk Iron Works platoon was the pride and joy of Hugh Nichol into whose possession it had been entrusted. He did not like other people touching it, even though he had to share it with the other four crewmen. At the Craigieburn exercise ground he got to experience it working. A dummy mortar was fired at a sheet of steel placed part of the way up the hill towards

Slamannan High Street looking towards the Cross and the Avonbridge Road. The weapons pit was in front of the house to the right of the telephone kiosk.

Auchengean School. Hugh was really pleased to get a shot, but he was extremely chuffed when it hit the target.

The relative lack of mobility of these weapons caused the HG to rethink its tactics. If properly sited and well concealed a Spigot Mortar could score a direct hit with its first shot – which might well be its only shot. Consequently such sites were pre-selected and concrete plinths were erected at them to allow for quick emplacement, dispensing with the awkward legs. One such weapon pit was set up late in 1943 by the Slamannan HG in the grounds of the house opposite the war memorial, next to the post office. Here it commanded Station Road and Avonbridge Road, as well as the area of the Cross. Latterly the mortar was left permanently on its mount in the pit (NS 8563 7310). The Shieldhill platoon placed it behind a stone wall at the crossroads on the top of the brae (NS 8964 7673).

Smith Gun

The third and final piece of sub-artillery produced specifically for the HG was the Smith gun, also named after its inventor, this time a retired major. William Smith was the managing director of a civil engineering firm that manufactured toys and this may account for the gun's unorthodox practicality. It consisted of a short 3ins smooth-bore barrel mounted on a two-wheeled carriage. The wheels were distinctive in that they were 3ft in diameter and made of sheet steel in a shallow cone shape with the edges turned over to provide the rim. In use the crew had to tip it over onto its side so that the lower wheel provided the firing platform and the upper wheel became a shield. It was linked by a tow bar to a small carriage where the ammunition was stored in cylinders placed around the axle. Together they could be readily towed by the average car and gave the HG its first 'real' field gun. However, the muzzle velocity was quite low and at ranges over 300yds its accuracy was dubious.

The weight of the gun and its accompanying carriage meant that its transport was best restricted to the roads. This did not deter the Grangemouth HG from taking one up to the top of Denny Muir. The company had two Smith guns, which were kept in the Talbot Street Drill Hall, and eight men were detailed to their use. All of them were present when they manhandled the gun up the moor across the rough terrain – and they were all needed. The rim of the wheels was relatively thin and they kept sinking into the soft ground at the numerous small burns. On such occasions it had to be pulled by the muzzle as well as pushed by the wheels and from behind. Finally they got to their destination, which may not have exactly been the one that they had

More Weapons

Winston Churchill at a demonstration of the Smith Gun in June 1941. (IWM)

plotted on the map at the outset, and set the gun up. When everything was ready the bicycle-grip type lever was operated and the gun lifted off the ground with a suitably loud bang. Then they had simply to retrace their steps. Going down hill was more difficult than they had anticipated. The gun took on added momentum and they soon learned to zigzag down the slopes like sheep. At a particularly wide burn they took a run at the dip, only for the central shield to dig into the soft mud and into Arthur Middle's leg, bringing the whole show to a shuddering jolting stop. Eventually they made their way home and made sure that this particular experiment was not repeated. Such experiences were repeated by the Bo'ness HG, which spent a weekend with its Smith guns in the Bathgate Hills. The Denny HG did not bother with the hills, but restricted its activities with the Smith gun to the lower lying ground – at Castlecary and the golf course at Denny.

On solid ground the Grangemouth HG became very proficient with the Smith gun and drilled to a high standard. In the Drill Hall they were able to bring the Smith gun into action in 14 seconds, or so it is said, and demonstrated this to the other platoons. On the third anniversary of the HG, in May 1943, a Smith gun team from the Falkirk Battalion HQ showed how slick an operation it was when they competently handled the hefty two-piece weapon in front of a gathering of the general public.

Although not mentioned in the list of arms and equipment of the 3rd Stg HG Bn, it is known that 'A' Company (Denny) had been allocated two, as was

Manhandling a Smith Gun across rough ground (from Home Guard Instruction, No. 51, 1943).

'D' Company (Grangemouth). It would therefore seem that the item appearing on the battalion list as '3"OSB' was not the 3ins mortar (ie Ordnance Smooth-Bore) as we might expect, but the Smith gun, which also conforms to that description. The Battalion had eight of these, two for each of the four companies. The 2nd Stg HG Bn probably had a similar proportion of two per company. One of these, belonging to 'B' Company, was kept at the arsenal in the Falkirk Iron Works. It used Smith guns on exercises against the regular army and France Penman saw the HG defending the bridge over the River Carron with its Smith guns placed at Mungal Mill Farm.

Mortars

The old soldiers in the Grangemouth Company of the HG had experience of mortars in the trenches and were so eager to practice that they used drainpipes and empty food tins to simulate the real thing. Shouting bang impressed no one, but some of the Grangemouth men had experience in the International Brigade and were quite capable of turning this look-alike into the real thing.

It was some considerable time before the HG in this area was provided with mortars. Again these devices required specialist crews and training. Some companies were able to get enough practice to gain a reasonable degree of competence. 'E' Company even provided a public demonstration in May 1943 at Brockville Park, attacking a mock tank. The platoon based at the Burgh Stables in High Station Road made these mock tanks out of wood and canvas. Some of them were dismantled and reassembled at the Greenhill Range, where they were destroyed during exercises.

The Castlecary Brickworks platoon carefully excavated three trenches to cover the western approaches to Dundas Cottages, between Castlecary School and Allandale. The clay dug from them was removed, rather than piled in a heap, so that there would be no obvious sign of any disturbed earth. The trenches were designed to take mortars and had an unobstructed field of fire across the main road (see illustration on page 137). They were filled in again after the war.

Other platoons seem to have temporarily shelved their mortars to concentrate on the existing weapons. Some of Carron's mortars were stored in a back room in the hut in Church Street that they used. The main room was used by the Scouts of the 54th Stirlingshire Troop, who were told not to touch them – thereby increasing their natural curiosity.

Anti-tank rifles

In November 1937 the Boys anti-tank rifle went into production for the British Army. At the time the average tank armour was only 15mm thick, so that the 0.55in calibre steel-cored bullet that left the Boys Rifle at a velocity of 3250ft/sec. stood a good chance of penetrating it at a range of 250 yards. By the start of the war the front armour plating had been thickened and the rifle was far from effective. Its use then depended upon hitting the tank at closer range, preferably at a weaker point in its armour, from a concealed position. All of which seemed more appropriate to the HG. Consequently, when better alternatives such as the PIAT appeared, the Boys Rifles were transferred to the HG. The 3rd Stg HG Bn received five.

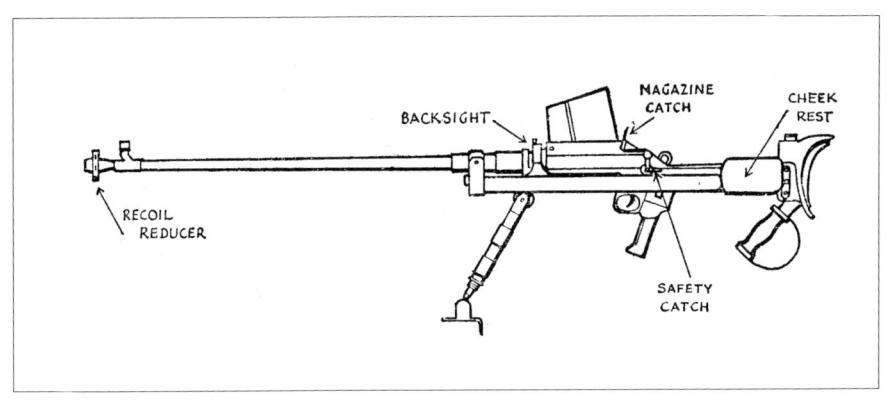

The Boys anti-tank rifle (from Small Arms Manual, Lt-Col. Barlow & Major Johnson, Nov 1942)

Anti-aircraft guns

The list of weapons for the 3rd Stg HG Bn includes nine Hispano AA. These were 20mm anti-aircraft guns, which must have been strategically sited throughout the battalion area and not kept in stores. The site of one, or perhaps two, of these guns was at Higgins Neuk, guarding the southern approaches to the Kincardine Bridge. The small platoon at Airth took over responsibility for the bridge some time towards the end of 1943.

Several more probably lay in the hands of 'D' Company to protect the airfield at Grangemouth. The RAF's own AA flight of five officers and 43 men under F/Lt Hilditch moved down to the London area late in 1943, leaving a gap in the RAF station's defences. It may have been at this time that new AA stances of concrete were built on the north side of the Bo'ness Road and at Northpark in Old Polmont. These would have been manned by the Grangemouth and Polmont HGs. At the RNA depot at Bandeath the platoon was reformed into an AA unit. A third possible site for the 3rd Battalion was at Denny and several civilians report having seen large guns in the grounds of the Drill Hall at the end of the war. One of these would have been from the battery located to the north of the river Carron near Middle Barnego. In mid 1944 the 2nd Battalion too was reorganising to take under its aegis a light AA battery, but this did not materialise.

Shells found by a metal detectorist at Higgins Neuk at the site of the AA battery.

Explosives

Although the local HG was not issued with explosives other than grenades, many of the men were familiar with handling such material from their work in the mines. A generous supply of dynamite for the Castlecary Clay Mine was kept in a brick-built magazine 100 yards north of Allandale and was available to the Castlecary Brickworks platoon. Some of the men actually kept the gelignite under their beds at home! Without a detonator it was safe enough.

That such stores were easily accessed was generally well known. During HG exercises in Torwood it was common practice for the miners to bring some along to add an air of authenticity. One man in particular, a shot-blaster at the Plean Pit, delighted in this role.

Slowly the use of explosives was formally introduced into the HG, with selected officers attending training courses. At first these were held in the base barracks of the regular army at Stirling or Dreghorn. Then for a sort time they were on the curriculum at the No. 2 War Office HG School, which opened at Kinnaird House, Larbert, in April 1941. However, at this early stage in the war the only anticipated use of explosives by the local units was in conjunction with the regular army and a number of clandestine meetings were held to inspect local bridges to formulate methods to destroy them in the event of an invasion. This was to be a last resort, as it was recognised that the bridges would be needed for any counter offensive.

In the two Stirlingshire battalions six men went through enhanced training so that they could act as instructors for the area. John Robinson of the Grangemouth Dockyard Company was one. He remembered that on one occasion an explosives expert was sent to Grangemouth to give them instruction in the use of plastic explosives. They met at the ruins of Kerse House in the recreation grounds of ICI. The expert

John Robinson with fellow instructors of the Grangemouth HG at Torwood, 1942. Bob Lindsay (banker in Falkirk Clydesdale Bank) in charge of battalion, Harry Sanderson of Falkirk KOSB, John Robinson, ——, shot blaster from Plean, ——.

produced a metal disc containing the explosive substance and then slapped it with considerable force against the walls of the building to attach it. Accustomed to more sensitive materials, the six men dived for cover in great fear and horror. The expert calmly walked over to them, took cover, and detonated the charge. Carronbank House (NS 897 817), to the east of Bankside, was also used to practise demolition techniques.

As they became more proficient and supplies more plentiful, the tactics involved in the use of explosives changed and information was cascaded down the ranks. Even if the officers were to use the explosives, the men needed to know their roles and to experience the types of blast created. So it was that in 1944 members of the Manuel Brickworks platoon were taken by bus to Dreghorn Barracks. One of the demonstrations was to create a large crater, which a tank would then drive into. As it drove out again it would reveal its soft under belly for the men to attack. The crater was duly created – what a spectacle! Then the tank drove into it, and got stuck. Apparently it was there several weeks later when the men paid another training visit to the site.

For most of the HG the closest experience of an explosion was provided by thunderflashes. By 1943 these were readily available and were used on exercises to get the men accustomed to the sounds of battle. Although essentially simply small detonators, these devices still had to be treated with some care. John Robinson demonstrated this to those using them by placing one under a cardboard box. The force of the miniature explosion was sufficient to hurl the box 40ft into the air. Some officers took the accustomisation further than others. One Saturday night, for example, the Grangemouth HG was called out and told that there was something afoot. They reported with great anticipation to the Drill Hall, where an officer threw a thunderflash into the middle of the hall to see how they would react. In the confined space the men were somewhat deafened and reacted by complaining. They were then formed into line and after the parade the officer asked all the NCOs to step forward. Jimmy Macdonald took one step forward, but it was obvious from his attire that he was not an NCO. The officer looked at the dishevelled man, walked up to him and asked in a loud voice "Are you an NCO?" Jimmy put his hand up to his ear to indicate his temporary loss of hearing and replied, "Oh, I thought you said So and Sos!"

Accidents occurred when the HG handled explosives. Lt W Hannah from Bathgate was the bombing officer for the 1st West Lothian HG Bn. In July 1943 he was awarded a Certificate for Gallantry for a "bombing incident" at Bathgate. He had previously been involved in a similar incident at Bo'ness, when he sustained serious injuries. Unfortunately the report does not clarify what form the incident took.

Gas

Although the HG was never issued with poisonous gas canisters, they had to have training in how to recognise the various types of gas and in the use of their gas masks (properly known as respirators). Selected officers were sent on gas training courses and upon their return passed the information on.

Each man was issued with a service respirator. These had a heavy canister containing charcoal fitted by way of a corrugated tube to the face mask. In the ready position the canister was carried in a small haversack on the chest.

William Sharp recalled that when on drill the Falkirk Power Station platoon would every now and then be ordered by the sergeant to put the gas masks on. The sergeant then walked up and down the line, stopping at an individual and asking if it was on properly. He then grabbed the tube tightly in his hand and watched as the wearer choked. If he did not choke it was a sign that the mask was not on correctly.

To try them under test conditions the platoon was sent to the HG HQ at Stirling, where about 20 of the men were put into a sealed steel room. The respirators were put on tightly, followed by the steel helmets, and then tear gas was released into the room. After about five minutes or so a voice came over the loudspeaker ordering them to remove their masks. Some of them tried to hold their

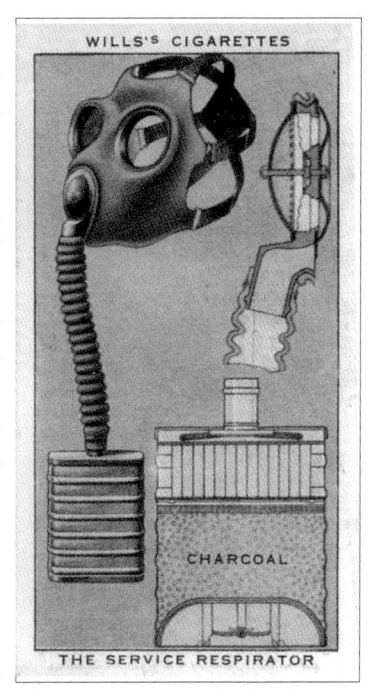

The service respirator gave longer protection than its civilian counterpart. The weight of the charcoal filter canister is carried in a haversack placed over the wearer's chest. (Wills cigarette card no. 31).

Two mobile gas vans used for testing respirators. The white canopies are airlocks to prevent the gas escaping when the doors are open. The picture shows a training session at Hendon Police College in 1939. (Wills cigarette card no. 38).

breaths, but this made it worse for them when they finally gasped, drawing the air deeper into their lungs. Eventually the door was opened and they were allowed out. At other locations in the Falkirk district the men were tapped on the head as they emerged coughing and spluttering from the room with their eyes streaming – just to remind them that the helmet too had to be worn correctly.

The Slamannan platoon was sent into a darkened tent full of gas, especially erected at Craigieburn. Putting on their service gas mask they entered by one door and had to fumble around until they found the exit door. They were only too pleased to whip the masks off to gulp in the fresh air.

Occasionally the HG held joint exercises with the ARP authorities using tear gas in public areas, such as busy streets with shops. These events were advertised in local newspapers well in advance so that the civilians using these areas would bring their gas masks and join in to make the exercise more 'realistic'.

Home Guardsmen and air raid wardens at the entrance to a gas exercise area in Lumley Street, Grangemouth.

More Weapons

Full List of the Arms & equipment of 3rd Stg HG Batallion

	Dec 1940	Dec 1941	Dec 1944
Rifles .300	757	— —	666
Rifles .300 EY	— —	— —	110
Rifles .303	83	— —	54
Boys A/T	— —	— —	5
Bayonet. STDs (pikes)	— —	108	nil
9mm M/G	— —	— —	460
Northover projectors	— —	15	15
Spigot mortars	— —	— —	31
3" OSB	— —	— —	8
Truncheons (rubber) 1942	— —	— —	100 nil
Browning M/G	— —	— —	6
BA rifle	20	— —	20
TS M/G	— —	33	nil
Mines A/T	— —	168	166
Grenades 36M	700	— —	4,500
Grenades 68.	— —	— —	1,200
69.	— —	— —	200
73.	— —	— —	250
74	— —	— —	160
75	— —	— —	2,000
76	180	120	6,000 nil
77	— —	— —	306
Molotovs	400	— —	nil
Flame throwers Harvey	— —	2	nil
Flame throwers HG	— —	1	nil
Flame trap barrels	— —	— —	96
Ammunition .300	52,000	— —	350,000
Lewis M/G .300	— —	— —	13
Lewis M/G .303	— —	— —	8
Hispano AA	— —	— —	9

CHAPTER SIX

Training and Exercise

Training

When it was called to arms in 1940 the LDV or HG attracted a lot of unwanted attention from the local community from which it sprang. This was particularly so amongst the youth of the area who tormented the guardsmen something rotten. The sight of the old men with their armbands and pretend weapons was one that was easy to ridicule, but not so easy to forget. Long after the novelty of the HG had ceased to be the focus of attention it was this image that remained in most minds. This was very fortunate for the HG, as it allowed them to train undisturbed, and in doing so they gained in confidence. The HG remained in the background, almost unnoticed. By the time that they emerged from this relative obscurity they had been fully equipped with uniforms and weapons. They were better trained and organised – so much so that the large-scale parades of the summer of 1943 came as a revelation to many of the public. The following report from the Bo'ness Journal gives some idea of the contemporary feeling, although somewhat exaggerated for propaganda purposes:

> An unforgettable and inspiring ceremony took place at Glebe Park where Major Dalyell of the Binns, the Officer Commanding, addressed the 3rd West Lothian Company and afterwards took the salute as Deputy Lieutenant of the County. Long before the ceremony crowds were thronging the vicinity of Glebe Park and when the three platoons marched in headed by the Federation Pipe Band the townspeople had the opportunity of seeing their own citizen-soldiers. They noticed with confidence their soldierly bearing and fine appearance. That grim summer of 1940, when Mr Eden called for men for the old LDV, as mentioned by Mr Churchill, seemed very distant to a spectator watching these men, and observing the deadly array of weapons which they have mustered, and in whose use they have reached a high degree of efficiency, for the reception of any foreign invaders. It is perhaps not giving away vital information to state that the size of the Company, together with its hard-hitting potentialities, as manifested in the mortars and machine guns, came as a revelation to most. The sight was certainly reassuring and provided

an unmistakable indication of our preparedness to meet any military eventualities on the home front." (Bo'ness Journal 21st May 1943)

With the increase in equipment and proficiency came a change in role. Gradually static observation gave way to a more active search and destroy mission linked to strong points designed to delay enemy movements and infiltration. One platoon in each company was made into a mobile unit. Thus at Bo'ness, for example, one of the three platoons became very well acquainted with the topography and by-ways of the town's perimeter, and with great gusto 'attacked' farm after farm each Sunday until a sure-fire method of dealing with the enemy was evolved.

At the formation of the LDV the officers had little idea how they were going to train the men. They conceived the movement as a resistance force, where every man would do his bit in his own way to slow down the enemy advance. It was soon realised that the LDV had to be formed into an army in its own right, requiring military discipline and training. Ex-soldiers were brought forward to instruct in elementary musketry and drill. The former was somewhat hampered by the lack of weapons and the latter by the scarcity of uniforms.

Regular army instructors were not readily available in the early summer of 1940 and it was only towards the end of the year that the first terse instruction books began to appear. Left to their own devices platoon officers came up with their own training schemes. Some were more enthusiastic than others, introducing physical exercises and elementary field craft. Field craft was an extension of the activities undertaken by such youth movements as the Boy Scouts – camping, field cooking, living off the land, camouflage and concealed movement. Tips on camouflage appeared in the national press and could be achieved at little cost. They involved breaking up the outline by use of attached foliage and varying the tones of the solid mass by use of facial blacking and so on. Practice showed which forms were most effective. Concealed movement involved the use of natural vegetation for cover and a lot of crawling on hands and knees or, if need be, stomachs. Exercises were soon held to show how men could traverse apparently open ground without being seen – though before the issue of uniforms crawling in mud was far from popular. By and large the men stuck to wooded areas. In 1940 the Manuel Brickworks platoon started a series of fortnightly exercises in Haining Wood adjacent to the works. Their concealed movement, made more difficult by the sound of cracking twigs, led to the discovery of several courting couples. In such an isolated community it was inevitable that the couples lived in Whitecross and were also employed at the brickworks. This led to much leg-pulling at work the following day. Before long the wood was empty.

Kinnaird House looking north-east in 1990

The HG battalions became affiliated with the local regiment, which started to take a hand in their basic training. Stirling Castle and Dreghorn Barracks provided shooting practice and officers attended courses on tactics and weaponry. Slowly the proficiency of the HG officers was enhanced and certificates issued to reflect this. In January 1941, for example, Sgt. Sam Martin from Bridgeness, a member of No. 13 platoon West Lothian HG Bn, completed a special instructors' course at Glencorse Barracks and in April was appointed as a full-time sergeant-instructor for the battalion. This involved a lot of travelling to Bathgate.

The 28th April 1941 saw the first course commence at the newly opened No. 2 GHQ School at Kinnaird House, Larbert. The course was for newly appointed adjutants/quartermasters. This school was specifically set up to train HG from the whole of central Scotland, including men from Glasgow and Edinburgh, and was known as No. 2 War Office Home Guard School. One of the subjects taught was ambushes and the 3rd Stg HG Bn was asked to provide the demonstration party. This it did from the opening, one day each week, for many months. The men felt honoured to undertake this duty and gained useful experience. It was at Kinnaird House that the officers and NCOs of the battalion were introduced to the Northover Projector by the inventor himself. Other well known visitors included Lt Tuner Lesham RA, who on 26th March 1942 lectured at Kinnaird House on 'Paratroops in Crete'. This led to a redeployment of the local HG to defend Grangemouth Airfield.

Les Barnes was a driver with the School of Artillery at Woolwich in 1941. Late that summer, at the age of 23 years, he was posted to Larbert. It was a long train journey north over night and he was tired and hungry when he arrived at Kinnaird House. He was shown to his billet – one of the wooden huts under the cover of some large trees near the house. After a sleep he was

Larbert Station looking north with the Station Hotel to the left

advised to go to the Salvation Army canteen in Stenhousemuir Main Street for a good feed. With some fellow members of the School he set off, but in King Street they were ambushed by some locals who invited them to a 21st birthday party. It was here that he met his future wife for the first time.

Part of Les' job was to pick up new batches of HG officers from Larbert Station in the army lorry and drive them to the House. When the train was delayed – and wartime schedules were always speculative – he had to wait in the Station Hotel, making it quite a worthwhile job! Some of the HG men he met came from as far south as Carlisle. He then helped to teach the arrivals how to use weapons and artillery from an Enfield rifle up to a 4.5ins gun; the latter using dummy shells. Discipline was strict and the trainees also stayed in wooden huts on the estate. The House was used for classrooms to impart the theoretical aspects of the weapons and tactics. It also accommodated some of the officers and administration. There were about 15 officers and 5 drivers attached to the School and they considered themselves to be an elite unit.

William Sharp remembered attending Kinnaird House for what he called 'over-night games'. The men slept in the outbuildings on palliasses, known as 'hat biscuits', with a single blanket, to get them accustomed to battle conditions. The day started at 4.30 am with the sound of a bugle. During the day the sections attacked each other, yelling and screaming.

Despite the use of live ammunition, there was no sentry at the entrance to the estate and it was not unusual to have to chase local boys wandering around. One of the things that the boys were looking for were the base plugs from exploded hand grenades. These thick metal discs had embossed lettering on them giving the codes for when and where they were manufactured and the

Training and Exercise

Base plugs from hand grenades found in the grounds of Kinnaird House. Each has lettering on, making them collectable to the boys of Stenhousemuir and Larbert.

type of variant they were. This made them highly collectable and in the days before Pokemon cards, with football cards unavailable, the base plugs were eagerly swapped and widely traded.

The School was at Kinnaird House for a little over a year when it was transferred into a set of travelling wings to coach the HG personnel in every part of the country, including the Hebrides. Writing shortly after its closure, late in 1942, Alexander Keith related the following story of the School and its HG occupants:

> At one time the school was located in a mansion that had – in what might be called happier times – been part of a lunatic asylum. The Commandant, an Englishman, took special pains to point this fact out to the students at the beginning of each course. A few remnants of the earlier population of the building still clung to its neighbourhood, and wandered about the grounds, unperturbed by the detonations of sub-artillery and the racket of the whole canon of grenades. At one course, held during the worst of the great snowstorm of 1942, the students were returning from a sortie, ploughing their way, silent and weary, in the wake of their spry Instructor of Tactics, through a foot of snow, and hoping the canteen would contain enough to rectify the balance in frames not as young as they once were. As they neared the house they passed a small group of erstwhile patients. One of these, with a pitying glance at the column of speechless trainees, remarked to his companions, "Stupid b————s." When the course closed the students had been unable to make up their minds whether the man was daft or fey. (A G Street, 1943, From Dusk till Dawn, p.110-111)

Other specialist schools were opened and closed as required. In May 1942 two officers of the Bo'ness HG completed a course in street fighting in the south-east of Scotland. Upon their return they passed the techniques on to their men, giving rise to the following report in the *Bo'ness Journal*:

> Residents in Castleloan and other districts who have been intrigued and not a little mystified by unusual happenings in their midst following the visits of a platoon of the local Home Guard, such as the spectacle of soldiers apparently flying over high walls impelled by their own volition, have been witnessing the latest ideas in training. Climbing up the face of tall tenements by way *of* spoil-pipes or by the use of ropes and scaling high garden walls by means of improvised ladders formed by men holding rifles or wooden spars in such a position as to acts as steps, are among special features in the training of the ordinary soldier of today. In all kinds of ways the members of the Forces are being taught to think and act quickly in any circumstances which may arise. These new ideas are being passed on to the Home Guard following a visit to a Street Fighting School in the south-east of Scotland by two officers of the Bo'ness Company; and a representative of the Bo'ness Journal recently had the opportunity of seeing at first hand this special commando training, when along with a party of journalists he visited the school. Hand-to-hand fighting always brings out personal gallantry, quick decisions, and power of leadership, but if mistakes which may prove costly are to be avoided, every soldier must have some knowledge of the best means of dealing with the various situations that may develop in street encounters. It is the aim of the schools to train leaders, men who will be able to put the new ideas into practice, and to find, if possible, new ways of using the various weapons with which they are equipped, so as to meet the special needs of the moment. At the school where the demonstrations in street combats took place there have been men from commandos, from the field forces, and from the young soldier battalions, as well as numbers from the Royal Engineers, RAF Regiment, and the Home Guard. It is strongly emphasised by those in charge of the school that the course is not of the special character. It is training that concerns all ranks and all arms, and the point is made that street fighting is especially a soldier's battle. As one of the officers put it, "the troops can be shown how to avoid

many of the elementary forms of suicide." There will be an enormous difference between the casualty list of a unit which has been trained in street fighting and that of a unit which has received no special instruction, and goes into the fight just hoping to muddle through. The demonstrations took place in an area in which there is a considerable amount of dilapidated property, and it formed an ideal background for the mock battles of the day, in which rifles and anti-tank guns were fired and grenades thrown. It was shown how easily snipers could be hidden from view. In a street which appeared to be almost completely deserted, a whistle was blown, and instantly fire was opened by many men who had been cunningly concealed in cellars, doorways, or at windows. Then the right and wrong methods for the movement of troops in streets were demonstrated. Several ways of climbing high perpendicular walls by means of ropes were put into practice, and the various uses to which the toggle rope can be put were inculcated. It was demonstrated that brick walls could be penetrated by automatic fire by anti-tank rifles and by anti-tank grenades, while heavy doors could be shattered by hand grenades.

(19th June 1942)

By this time too there had been a proliferation of handbooks published on various aspects of HG activities, including the art of camouflage, hand to hand combat, how to set up a firing range, the use of sub-artillery and so on. The most important of these were those dealing with battlecraft and battle drill. These pointed out flaws in earlier tactics and taught how to avoid suicide. As the role of the HG changed, as new weapons became available and experience highlighted earlier errors, these guidebooks went through several editions. Instructions handed down through the official booklets took precedence over those in commercial productions and in November 1943 GHQ Home Forces published 'Home Guard Instruction No. 51 Battlecraft and Battle Drill for the Home Guard: Part IV The Organisation of Home Guard Defence', which became the standard work.

Men were allocated to specific weapons and were eager to learn all they could about them. Instruction manuals showed how to use and maintain the equipment and deal with problems. All the weapons could be stripped down to their basic components and reassembled. Having learned how to strip down and reassemble a weapon proficiently in the light, the next step was to repeat the exercise wearing a blindfold so that it could be done in the dark if need arose.

As well as guidebooks instructional films were produced and shown in the local cinemas. As early as November 1941 the Bonnybridge HG had watched a film in the Drill Hall there depicting the correct methods of platoon attack and defence. In Bo'ness HL Dickson, the manager of the Hippodrome, was a member of the HG and not surprisingly the venue hosted several training films. In March 1942, for example, the HG saw a film on how to handle UXBs (unexploded bombs). Cinemas were actively engaged in the war effort, raising funds for the Red Cross and helping evacuees. Aiding the HG came as just another responsibility and in Falkirk the Regal in Princes Street was placed at their disposal; in Denny it was the Cinema de Luxe. The Larbert HG were able to utilise the facilities at the Co-op Hall, already requisitioned for the regular troops and later taken over by the HG. In October 1942 three films were played here with the exciting titles 'Airborne Invasion', 'Observation & Information Reporting' and 'Shoot to Kill'.

All the while new courses were being put together and attended by the HG officers. In August 1943 Capt William Miller of the Bo'ness HG was reported to have

> brought back from a Commando Course somewhere in the Highlands, many invaluable and very practical lessons in battle, including unarmed combat, bridging, guerrilla warfare and so on. The course was a strenuous one, but full of interest, and results from experience in actual battle. He is now passing this on to his men, along with the lessons from a course on street and house fighting that he attended at Leith some time ago. (Bo'ness Journal)

The travelling wings also visited the area. In January 1944 officers and NCOs of Nos. 1, 3 and 4 Companies of the 1st West Lothian HG Bn were given a course of instruction on 'Battle Practice' at the Gardeners' Hall in Bo'ness by officers of the HG School of Training.

Princes Street, Falkirk, with the Regal Cinema on the right.

Training and Exercise

When possible, theoretical tactics were practised in the field and lessons drawn. First came the basic training in the new tactics and later exercises in which these skills could be tested. Outdoor training was usually conducted on a Sunday, with the weekday evening meeting restricted to theory and drill. However, in Bo'ness during the summer months it was found to be more practical to hold outdoor training in the long summer evenings leaving the weekend free for the miners to attend extra shifts down the mine.

Weekend camps started in the summer of 1941 and carried on in 1942 and 1943. In July 1941 the Bonnybridge HG camped in tents in the hills to the south of the village and this close proximity was typical of the early camps. In 1942 the 2nd Stg HG Bn organised a campsite at Craigieburn on Callendar Estate land. This was used throughout that summer by each company in turn. The 3rd Stg HG Bn utilised three different campsites in order to give each unit an opportunity to spend a weekend in training. One of these sites was adjacent to the scout campsite at the Barrwood. The surrounding terrain provided ideal ground for exercises, as reported in the Scouting history of the site:

> In May 1941 Denny and Stirling agreed to have a battle. Point 503, the highest spot in the Barrwood was the objective. After a terrific bolt clicking of empty rifles at three yards range from behind birch trees, the two sides fraternised beyond the reservoir. The only known casualty was one bayonet deficient. It has never been found. The 15th, who were in camp, had a great time later picking up paper bags and empty bottles.
>
> A far more 'serious' encounter took place in August 1942. Home Guards made a night march from Larbert and Grangemouth through the Barrwood, shadowed (by request) by a party of 17 Patrol Leaders who lay in wait for them in the rain and dark, and then lost them till about 1am, when a few thunder flashes (kindly provided in advance by the OC Home Guard) caused considerable annoyance to the tired Army in bivouacs. The theft of a rifle and some sets of equipment provoked no reprisals – only some highly coloured Army language the following morning when the articles were retrieved at the muzzle of a Sten gun. (History of Barrwood)

It should be added that the bivouacs were home made shelters using branches and waterproof sheets, camouflaged with foliage.

Andrew Bain remembered the incident:

> One weekend at Barrwood, a few of us were gathered together, to be told by Sir Ian that he would like us to take part in a Home Guard exercise by acting as a guerrilla group that would test the preparedness of the part-time soldiers. The plan apparently was for the Home Guard to get into a chosen position over the weekend, along a route that would pass near Barrwood, and for us to find them, identify them,

General view of the Scout camp at Barrwood with a pond in the foreground.

and harass them. Playing our part with understandable adolescent enthusiasm, conviction and vigour, we spread out at night, with black faces and in dark clothes, upon our search, and three of us were lucky enough to find the exhausted Home Guard, all fast asleep, without posted sentries, and with their weapons carefully strung out along a wire fence. Unable to believe what we had found, we held a whispered consultation about what we should do, before lifting some of the weapons and making a hasty retreat, leaving the thrown thunder flashes to shock the platoon into a more wakeful state. Next morning, the still irate commander was all for punishing these insolent boys, until Sit Ian reminded him that, had we been real soldiers, his men would not have survived their sloppy fieldwork.

Another of the campsites favoured by the 3rd Stg HG Bn was at Torwood. William Wilson of Larbert recalled: "on one occasion I remember Peter Swan, a local coalman, was one of the acting cooks and the pans for the porridge and the tea were switched to speed up heating, unfortunately one of the pans had already been salted – so we had salted tea!" On bank holiday weekends the HG would arrive at Torwood on the Friday and get back at 6.30 pm the following Monday. Emphasis was on fitness and infantry exercises such as crossing ditches on flimsy bridges, vaulting hedges, climbing walls and the like; only the younger men did the hedges. When it came to thick hedges the method of crossing them was to throw a blanket over it upon which the first man lay. His companions then climbed over him. They also learned how to use vital military equipment, such as the potato peeler! Their portable canteens consisted of a giant blowlamp placed under a metal grill supported on bricks – great for eggs and bacon.

Training and Exercise

One weekend camp held by the 3rd Stg HG Bn was laid on as a commando course. Only men under 35 years of age were allowed to attend and numbers were limited to 40. At dusk on the Saturday a picture was painted to them of the enemy overrunning a lonely part of the countryside. A map reference as to where to bivouac was given, and also three reference points of positions held by an 'enemy' which must be attacked and captured on Sunday. None of the HG partaking in the exercise had made a reconnaissance of the ground. At dawn they proceeded to attack the first enemy point. This necessitated the crossing of the River Carron at a rather dangerous place. No bridging materials were issued and the attacking party was compelled to improvise materials. The crossing was successfully accomplished and all three 'enemy' positions were captured. Training was also received in crossing rivers using a single rope for the feet and a second as a handrail. The ropes were suspended from trees or any suitable anchor points and at Carron one was left in place for some considerable time so that it could be used over and over again.

Dan Niven (right) of the SEC HG in Larbert and David Thomson of the ATC, March 1942. Dan was a member of the 'gang' that found the HG in the Barr Wood.

Some of the successful Scout patrol at the salute of the flag at Barrwood, 1943.

There was little regularity about the training pattern over the first two years. Companies had to find their instructors from within their own personnel, and with the lack of equipment and up-to-date teaching, little progress was possible. Guard duties and demands for work parties made heavy calls, and training was largely confined to patrols, squad drill and elementary musketry. In 1941 it was observed that standards in the various platoons of 3rd Stg HG Bn differed considerably, and from 1st January 1942 the monthly programmes were issued from Battalion HQ at Larbert Church Hall. Permanent Staff Instructors (PSIs) had been appointed towards the end of 1941 and over the following year their presence greatly improved the performance of all the platoons in the Falkirk district. The PSIs, with increasing assistance of instructors from the regular army, were able to lay on a series of demonstrations that brought new scope for instructional activity and this was eagerly taken advantage of. The 2nd Stg HG Bn specialised in tank ambushes, attaining a high standard of proficiency.

Progress in the widely scattered rural platoons of the 1st West Lothian HG Bn was even more sporadic.

> Certain field exercises were attempted from time to time but the state of the training was not yet such as allowed of well-organised movements of troops in open country. There was a marked reluctance to train by Sections rather than by Platoons. This was due partly to lack of sufficient leaders and partly to the shift system among the miners, which militated against regular attendance of the same men at each parade. Many of the NCOs from the last War proved ineffective except for the teaching of drill and elementary musketry that they were prone to teach parrot fashion. This had a considerable bearing on the standard of efficiency reached by most of the Platoons as it was later very difficult to displace these NCOs, although some of the younger men without previous training proved to be more efficient. There was a noticeable absence of any trained instructors from regular army units. This continued to be the case during the whole history of the LDV and HG in West Lothian owing to the absence of regular units in the County Area. On the few occasions on which regular NCOs were available for any length of time, it was noticeable that they made a considerable difference both to the keenness shown and the results obtained. At no time, especially in the early days, was it found easy to employ the more talented HG officers or NCOs as instructors away from their immediate locality. What the men would learn from their own immediate leaders or from regular NCOs (when available), they would not willingly learn from someone from the next village. (National Library of Scotland)

The advent of Battle Drill at the beginning of 1943 brought the greatest influence for advancement and revolutionised the training standard. Battle platoons were trained with greater gusto, and the standard of mobility and patrols and night movement made the HG quite a formidable force to be reckoned with. As the march of events changed the outlook in the European theatre and the risk of invasion receded, mobility and weapon proficiency, with emphasis on the training of sniper screens, were developed. More progress was made towards service standards in the last year before stand down than in the previous three.

The value of competition in stepping up training was realised early on, and a healthy competitive spirit between platoons and companies was maintained throughout, in all forms of weapons training and battle drill. To encourage this, trophies were provided by the officers and friends of the HG.

The government encouraged youth groups to teach subjects that would be useful once the teenagers were old enough to join the armed forces – such as map reading, navigation and signalling. Air Scouts, Sea Scouts and Sea Rangers were established in the area and soon the government set up its own organisation of army cadets. These were affiliated to the local HG companies and many of their instructors were Home Guardsmen. Much to the annoyance of the Scouts any boy joining the Army Cadets was given a free uniform. When old enough they graduated into the HG proper, and then into the forces.

Grangemouth Army Cadets. June 1944. Front row: Ian —, Sam Bishop, 2nd Lt A Howie, 2nd Lt M Thomson, Capt A Grant, 2nd Lt J Bryce, 2nd Lt J Grant, Jock Grant, Alex Chalem, Jock Duncan. 2nd row: —, —, Bill Wallace, Ian Stein, Davie Inglis, —, Danny Chisholm, Danny Evans, —. 3rd row: back row: —, —, —, Duke Pitcaithly, —, —, —, Kid Leckie, —, —, Maurice Fleming.

*Photograph of Carronshore Army Cadets at Carronshore Old School.
Front row: —, —, Peter Wright, —, Andrew Allan, —, —.*

Exercises

Practical field exercises were arranged by the HG to test their training strategies under more realistic conditions than the lecture room or meeting hall. These exercises introduced elements of surprise and chance for those taking part and greatly increased their knowledge and ability to react to developing circumstances. It pointed out the many weaknesses in tactics and circumstances, allowing these to be improved upon each time.

The scale and complexity of field exercises tended to increase with time. To begin with it was not possible to coordinate large bodies of men, and exercises started at platoon level with one section pitted against another. Each section would wear different coloured armbands, usually either red or blue. Before long companies were testing each other's reflexes and on Sunday 15th September 1940 the 3rd Stg HG Bn staged its first large battalion-wide tactical exercise. Appropriately enough this was an 'attack' on Grangemouth Aerodrome. For this exercise 'B' and 'D' Companies acted as defenders, with 'A' and 'C' Companies as the enemy. The spirit of the HG at the time may be assessed by the code words used. The enemy adopted 'Coming' and the defenders 'Welcome'. Details of the exercise are sadly not available, but lessons were learnt on all aspects. For example, the Battalion noted that:

From this exercise the CO decided that to gain full benefit from such exercises umpiring must be of a much higher standard. The CO therefore instructed the IO Captain McKinlay, to train suitable personnel as umpires. Capt McKinlay attended a Field Force Umpire's Course for 7 days, and upon his return, he held umpiring courses within the Battalion, with the result that there was a marked improvement in the control and efficiency of future exercises.

Thereafter company tactical exercises were held each month, some of which were nocturnal, and battalion exercises every three months. Although these posed various scenarios, the airfield remained the focus of many and was repeatedly attacked. One of the early daytime exercises in 1941 involved the use of Johnny Robertson's motor bike (for which see the section on transport). The Stenhousemuir platoon was part of the attacking force and the Grangemouth platoons once again tried to keep them out. The Stenhousemuir men were keen to put on a good show and over the weeks before the scheduled date of the exercise they reconnoitred the area looking for weak spots in the defences. John Grierson was part of the party that made a reconnaissance trip to Jinkabouts, from where they could clearly see the ground crews working on the Spitfires. On the day of the exercise he was the gunner with Johnny

A group of officers and non-commissioned officers of the local HG who took part in manoeuvres in the Falkirk area in September 1941. They are wearing coloured armbands to distinguish umpires and the opponents of the two teams. (Falkirk Herald 4th Oct 1941).

Robertson and carefully strapped himself into the side car. Very early that morning, before anyone was up and about, they took up their appointed position in Dundas Street. They did not have radio communications with the rest of the company and so they waited patiently until the designated time and then started the motor. They sped along the Bo'ness Road in the direction of the airfield. By starting their run from within the town the Grangemouth HG was taken by surprise and, "coming out of nowhere", they pelted the men at the main gate with bags of whitening – the standard missile on exercises. Swinging the motor bike around they retraced their steps before the guard had any chance to recover and disappeared into the side streets. They were in and out so quickly that they received no return fire and the umpires declared the attack a great success with no casualties for the motorbike crew. The noise and mayhem of the incident drew a lot of attention as the defenders organised their counter attack. Meanwhile, the real advance on the airfield by the main body of the Stenhousemuir platoon commenced from the south-west.

Exercise 'Daffodil' was staged on 9th May 1942 to test the HG defence of the town and the western approaches to the airfield. 140 men of the RAF Regiment and two platoons from the station rifle squadron attacked the three Grangemouth HG platoons. The townscape was natural fighting terrain for the lightly armed defenders and they evidently acquitted themselves well.

Further exercises were held in which the Grangemouth, Polmont and Redding HG platoons were asked to make a frontal assault on the airfield itself. The HG officers were unhappy about staging this form of attack in broad daylight, particularly as the defenders knew in advance the day of the exercise. Very quickly half of the HG were 'wiped out' and the RAF was able to launch a successful counter attack. This hurt the pride of the HG and for several weeks thereafter Bobby McCowan, the Redding HG platoon commander, and a handful of his men dug trenches towards the airfield perimeter at Northfoot. The luxuriant vegetation, composed chiefly of nettles, hid their approach. Then, when all was ready, he took 44 men into the airfield and captured the command centre – much to the embarrassment of the RAF.

> My father was a sergeant in the Grangemouth Home Guard. Their proudest achievement was when they took the aerodrome by a surprise night attack. Their faces were all blacked up. They went in from the Polmont end, making their way through fields. They arrested the guards and took the control tower. Boy, were they chuffed! The RAF commanders were not and the shit hit the fan. It even got into the newspapers. (Betty Haslam)

As the defence strategy for the airfield evolved the Brightons platoon became part of the outer line of defence that stretched from Polmont Hill to Mumrills

Beancross village looking towards the pit bing at Kinneil in October 1951. The main road ran from left to right through the small settlement.

and also included the platoons from Maddiston, Redding, Laurieston and High Bonnybridge. The Brightons platoon prepared defensive positions at Beancross on either side of the main Polmont to Airth road. A gun platform was formed from a sandy mound on the south side of Mumrills Brae, overlooking the hamlet, and it was this that Hugh Baird and his team occupied during an exercise against another HG platoon. The mound was slightly hollowed out so that they had a degree of protection and could not be seen from the main road. They were in position when the 'enemy' arrived in vans and cars. The small convoy stopped in the hamlet below Hugh's post and its occupants disembarked, but as they evidently suspected trouble from the direction of the hill they hid on the other side of their vehicles. Hidden from Hugh's view a battle royal then took place when the second gun position occupied by the Brightons platoon opened up on them. They seemed to pelt each other with the flour bags for some time. Then, according to Hugh, it was time to go home.

It was not only the airfield at Grangemouth that provided an important strategic target, so too did the dock complex. The defence strategy of the Grangemouth HG was therefore, in the first instance, to engage the enemy at the river crossings and the perimeter of the urban area. They would then put up a stubborn resistance, falling back when necessary to secondary posts.

Grangemouth Railway Station from Station Brae.

Falkirk HG was challenged to penetrate this defensive barrier and take control of the Report Centre in the heart of the town. On the day of the exercise the Grangemouth HG had a large turnout, determined to beat their rivals – the two neighbouring towns had been competitors for decades. Very early that morning members of the Grangemouth HG carefully took up their pre-arranged defensive positions and check points on the roads into the town. Anyone entering the controlled zone was asked to show their ID cards. Road blocks at Earl's Gates and the Bo'ness Road were supplemented by a lone guard at Beancross. Normally local people were able to walk along the side of the Grange Burn or 'Ditches' unchallenged, but not that day. Even the towpath of the Forth and Clyde Canal came under scrutiny and any vessel on that waterway was to be challenged. The Falkirk HG had its own timetable to follow, which did not involve an early start. They were able to have a leisurely breakfast before assembling at Grahamston. Here they marched to Grahamston Station, where they caught a scheduled train that delivered them into the centre of Grangemouth – the town was theirs!

The Falkirk men were not always successful. On another occasion the Falkirk Ironworks platoon was attacking Grangemouth by way of Middlefield. They crawled across the field south of the Forth and Clyde Canal and warily approached the railway embankment that led from the canal bridge at Orchardhall to Fouldubs depot. This obstacle provided them with a problem as anyone passing over the top of it would be silhouetted against the skyline. Then a woman was spotted pushing a pram up the lane to the farm. The officer in charge of the Falkirk platoon asked her if she had seen any sign of the Grangemouth platoon and was told that they were lying in ambush on the other side of the embankment just a little way along it. He thanked her and relayed the information to his men. He now formulated a plan. If they crawled through a water culvert under the railway embankment they would emerge behind the Grangemouth men and could take them in the rear. His men looked at the culvert. Yes, it was large enough to crawl through – but it had 20ins or so of water in the bottom. "It's only a game!" the officer was told, and the plan was rejected. They tried to outflank the obstacle and inevitably were captured by the Portonians who had the advantage of the terrain. On yet another occasion 'Wild' young Jim Grant took 40 men hostage on the north side of the canal bank by outflanking them.

The HG officers were often more enthusiastic than their men and this stretched their powers of persuasion. Sgt. Will Kirkland (known to the street children as 'Major K') was in charge of the Denny HG platoon on a day exercise, which led them down to the River Carron near Dales Bridge. Corn stooks stood in the fields leading to the river and these were used to cover their approach. There was no way across the river itself, which was relatively low that late in the summer. Kirkland walked into the water holding his rifle above his head in both hands and the rest were ordered to follow. This they did somewhat reluctantly, except for Jimmy Forsyth. He made his way along the river bank to Dales Bridge and joined the main group later.

Attacks by one platoon on another became a regular feature of Sunday exercises. William Sharp was asked to lead his section of the Falkirk Power Station platoon against a defended position held by another platoon beside Woodend Farm to the south of Callendar Wood. This was one of the perimeter strong points for the town of Falkirk and commanded good views to the south and east. For the purposes of the exercise William and his men were dropped off in the vicinity of Westquarter to simulate an attack from the east. He realised that a direct approach would have dire consequences and instead led his men through Laurieston and under the railway bridge into Callendar Wood. They made their way through the wood until they could see Woodend Farm from the north. Crawling on their bellies they got to within 25yds of the strongpoint before throwing their bags of whitening. The first that the enemy platoon knew of their presence was when the bags burst, covering them with chalk. They were rather annoyed, not least because it meant that they had to have their uniforms washed. William's section suffered no casualties.

On such exercises the men were instructed not to fix bayonets – just in case anyone got carried away with the play acting or the inter-unit rivalry became too personal. Canvas bags of whitening were used instead of explosives and sparklers for incendiary bombs. Normally the rifles were empty and it was curious to see men facing each other with their weapons clicking as the bolts slid home. It was left to the umpires to decide how effective this had been. Occasionally blank rounds were used to accustom the men to the noise, though these could cause burns if used too close because the wadding was hot. Thunderflashes, or what some civilians called 'crackerjack fireworks', were also used. Other weapons were improvised, as when the Falkirk Power Station was attacked. The unarmed workers there assisted their colleagues by throwing oily rags at the aggressors and turned the hosepipe onto them.

Civilians also got caught up with the spirit of the occasion and joined in. There were, for example, a couple of weekend exercises in Denny involving the whole of the ARP services and the HG. 'Enemy paratroops' were to land and attack important establishments. In due course a small contingent of the regular army crossed the Forth and Clyde Canal and approached from Longcroft. They entered the outskirts of Denny along Paris Avenue, where they were seen by two special constables. These constables were in their 70s and did not want to get involved in what they saw as a comical farce, and so they went to seek shelter in the fire station until the whole affair was over. However, when they mentioned the enemy advance to the station master he considered that the honour of Denny was at stake and immediately advocated action. He ordered his men to lay out some hoses from the water hydrant to the railway embankment that separated the fire station in Dryburgh Avenue from Paris Avenue. As the six enemy soldiers crawled over the ridge and down his side, the firemen opened up the nozzles and played the water on them. The soldiers were completely drenched and soon surrendered. There was much moaning, but they made an amusing sight as they were marched to the police station in Broad Street by the two septuagenarian constables.

Such incidents were hard for the umpires to police, as they often went unseen. One man that they always saw was a member of the Railway HG at High Bonnybridge. He had asthma and made sure that he was 'shot' very early in any exercise. For the fitter and younger members of the HG it often came as a disappointment to find themselves written off at an early stage. Willie Scott was an ARP messenger and on exercises he could be attached to the wardens or the HG. On one rather promising exercise he was serving with a member of the HG, but within five minutes they were both given tickets to say that they had been killed. So the two of them just slunk off home. It was preferable to 'die' than to be captured. The 'dead' could at least walk home, telling the many questioners that they had been shot and were "out of the game". Though, of course, they got some ribbing both at home and at work. Those who were captured suffered the indignity of gibes from the enemy and a long period of inactivity when they had better things to do with their 'free' time. The umpires also declared men to be injured so that they could receive first aid treatment on the spot. During one exercise on the hill between the town and golf course of Bo'ness a particularly corpulent member of the Bo'ness HG was labelled as a non-ambulant casualty. The umpire told his two companions that he required urgent treatment at the hospital in the town and they would have to carry him. They looked at the victim and then at the umpire, wondering if the latter would accompany them all the way back or if there was a chance of a miracle cure in transit. Then one of them lifted his rifle and 'shot' the wounded man dead – no need to carry him any more.

Wood clearing exercises were common, as it was thought that enemy paratroops would lie in them at night. The Brightons platoon did so many exercises in Ercall Woods that Hugh Baird knew the area like the back of his hand. "If the enemy had landed there we would have saved the day," he said. "Anywhere else and we were in trouble!"

After 1942 the exercises often involved the regular army, providing testing situations for both bodies. The KOSBs, West Yorks and Polish Army were all billeted in the Falkirk district and took part. "One big exercise involved the Polish Army. We were to defend Fairley's Farm on the Bellsdyke Road against invading Poles who came on foot and in Bren carriers. Blank cartridges and thunderflashes were used and we were, needless to say, overrun." (J Wilson)

2nd Lt John Robinson, 1944.

For the 3rd Stg HG Bn exercises with the regular army frequently meant operating in the area north of Stirling, around Sheriffmuir. John Robinson was one of the instructors who acted as an umpire. On these occasions he would stay in Stirling Castle on the Saturday night so that he was ready for the exercise on the following day. On one of the exercises it lashed down with rain. The instructors waited in the wood near the Abbey Craig for the men to find the spot from the grid reference that they had been given. As they waited they held a groundsheet over their heads to keep of the worst of the rain. After a few hours they returned to the castle, only to find that the men had not even set out. They had decided that it was too wet to play.

The weather could even be too hot. On another Sunday Colin Sharp and some of his colleagues in the Carron platoon were taken by army truck to a drop off place in Sheriffmuir. They were to represent a unit of German paratroopers that had landed in the Ochils and were told to make their way to the railway beside the Wallace Monument at the Abbey Craig to blow it up. The section was issued with rifles and blank cartridges, as well as a lot of heavy 'explosives' equipment. It was a hot sweltering day and the going underfoot was firm and dry. The section commander decided to take a circuitous route to avoid detection by the other HG units who would be out looking for them. They started to walk down a valley that took them off the direct course and the men knew it was going to be a long day. Then Colin developed an insatiable urge to pull the trigger of his rifle to experience what it felt like – he had never had an opportunity before. The hollow report echoed around the valley and spread a certain amount of panic amongst his fellows. The officer approached and Colin readily acknowledged his guilt. He was severely reprimanded – it was not to happen again. They set off once more on the long march. Eventually they descended to the large loch on the Airthrey Estate (now Stirling University). The officer, a fit man, slid down the bank to the loch shore and ordered his men to follow. They were already greatly fatigued by carrying the heavy equipment in the heat. Big Bobby McGill barrelled down the slope, gathering momentum as he went, and would have gone into the water had not his descent been arrested by a large branch lying on the ground. Others followed with varying degrees of success. When it came to Jock McArthur's turn he refused, saying that he would rather go to prison then tumble down the hill. It was agreed to leave him behind and finally Colin made his descent. The band of rather tired and not so merry men then skirted around the edge of the loch and eventually found their way to the Wallace Monument. Now they had to leave the higher ground and make for the railway and as they did so a local HG platoon opened fire on them and there was confusion. By this time they were suffering from heat exhaustion and were well and truly knackered. When Jock Braidwood was told by the umpire that he had been killed, he irately retorted "Bugger that! I'm here to blow the railway up." Shortly afterwards he and the rest of the squad reported the total destruction of the railway network and they were able to relax. They were resting when they saw Jock McArthur happily waving to them from a vehicle – he had been captured by the loch and was happy to accept a lift. Charlie Smith was so debilitated by the day's exercise that he had to take a week off work!

Training and Exercise

Colin became accustomed to playing the part of the German invader, though he was not always available. One Saturday night the HG sent a runner round to his home, but Colin had been drinking and decided to ignore the knocking and shouting. The next day he reported as required for the Sunday duty. The commanding officer was there and Colin went up to him. "Airchie," (pronounced Ayrshire) he said, "what was all the fuss about last night?" "Less of the Airchie!" came the reply, "It's Captain McCallum to you!" They had been looking for men to form a surprise party of 'Germans' to pretend to blow up the Larbert Viaduct.

By the middle of 1944 the war was going well for Britain and her allies and after four years hard slog the HG was beginning to take things easier. The men still realised that guard duty was important, but they had less truck with exercises. The Command too seemed less willing to pay the men subsistence for mere exercises, especially for ones that they had not instigated. It was with this background that a rather unusual branch of the armed forces asked for assistance with a training exercise at rather short notice at the beginning of May 1944. The dates set for the exercise, 11-15th May, were significant, just three weeks before D-Day, but the HG did not know that at the time. Nor did they realise that the force of commandos that had made the request was one of the elite units – 'C' Squadron of the 1st S.A.S. Regiment. HG battalion commanders failed to pass the information on to company level and when some company commanders found out about the exercise through the police, who were cooperating fully, they were told not to participate.

The exercise involved small parties of 3-6 commandos, who were to attempt to get from Edinburgh to Glasgow without being detected, 'blowing up' designated targets on the way. The targets included canal, road and railway bridges, stations, crossroads and pylons. Most of the local targets were in West Lothian around Livingston and Winchburgh, but the route took many through the southern part of Falkirk district. Fortunately the Slamannan and Avonbridge HG platoons did get to hear about the exercise and the men were keen to prove their abilities. They were warned by their officers that the commandos were a tough lot.

At noon on 13th May the Avonbridge HG succeeded in arresting L/Sgt Goldie and his three companions on the road just west of the village. They were marched back to the platoon HQ and subsequently allowed to continue the exercise. Then at 5.15pm the same day a party of five commandos under Cpl Jones was spotted in a wood to the south of Avonbridge. Messages were promptly despatched, but the HG section sent to investigate advanced along the road. This meant that they were easily heard and readily ambushed by the commandos. Although the ambush was successful it was probably the means of the commandos undoing. As news of their being in the vicinity circulated the area was swamped with children and dogs, with the result that the men's cover was broken. The remainder of the HG soon had them in captivity and then had to escort them some distance out of the village before they could release them away from the prying eyes of the gangs of youths. The official report dryly states, "Dogs & children troublesome."

Meanwhile the Slamannan HG was on the alert. The officers decided that they would watch all the roads, especially the minor ones. Ian Arthur, the village doctor's son, was one of the youngest members of the platoon and was on duty one night. He was sent out to Lochrigend Road to lie in wait. His helmet was covered with camouflage netting from which twigs and other vegetation protruded and he lay beside the roadside hedge for cover. As he waited he noticed that whenever he moved so did part of the hedge on the other side. Out there on his own he became a little anxious and it was some time before he realised that his camouflage had caught in the hedge and was causing the movement. After several hours he decided that he had had enough and went home to bed. He never heard any more about the commandos.

The Slamannan Army Cadets met in the Primary School under the command of Rudy Kerr, the commanding officer of the Slamannan HG platoon. One of their favourite exercises was the art of concealed movement when half the group would be given the task of moving from point A to point B, and the other half had to find them – the classic game of hide and seek and a smaller scale version of what the SAS was doing. On 14th May 1944 the cadets held their most memorable exercise. The group that was to lie in hiding included Matthew Penman and they started to the south of Balquhatstone Mains, crossed the Slamannan Railway and found cover in the woods south of Balquhatstone House. Proceeding slowly along a ditch they heard a twig snap ahead of them. Frozen still for a moment, they realised that they were not alone – unknown animals were evidently close by. Even more slowly and very cautiously a few crept towards the source of the noise. To their immense surprise four British commandos came into view. They had been told about the exercise, but this was still unexpected. Two boys were promptly despatched to inform Rudy Kerr. Shortly after they had left, the remaining boys were discovered and captured by the commandos. A quick interrogation followed and the boys were sent packing so that the commandos could get under way again. In the meantime the Slamannan HG had acted with amazing promptness and had approached the party undetected. They soon had them captive and marched their prizes back to the village. It was all done in good

Training and Exercise

The Slamannan Home Guard with the trophy that one of its sections won at Bantaskine, 1943. Front row: Barney Schonville (plasterer/slater), Jim Storar, Rudy Kerr (miner), George Watt (schoolmaster), Wilfred Berwick (miner), David Simpson, Jock Jamieson (miner). Second row: Jim Lynn, Hector Maxwell, Joe Gardner, Scott, Andrew Chalmers, C Simpson, Tam Tripney, Alex Gardner (miner), Willie Millar (miner). Third row: George Connell, A Scott, —, Johny Drysdale, Tom Connell, C Sneddon, Geordie Walker, A Tulloch Back row: —, Andrew Penman, Jimmy Meek (blacksmith), S McLintock, Robert McLintock, Chris Jamieson or Geordie Walker?, Hughie Lambie, Tam Wilson

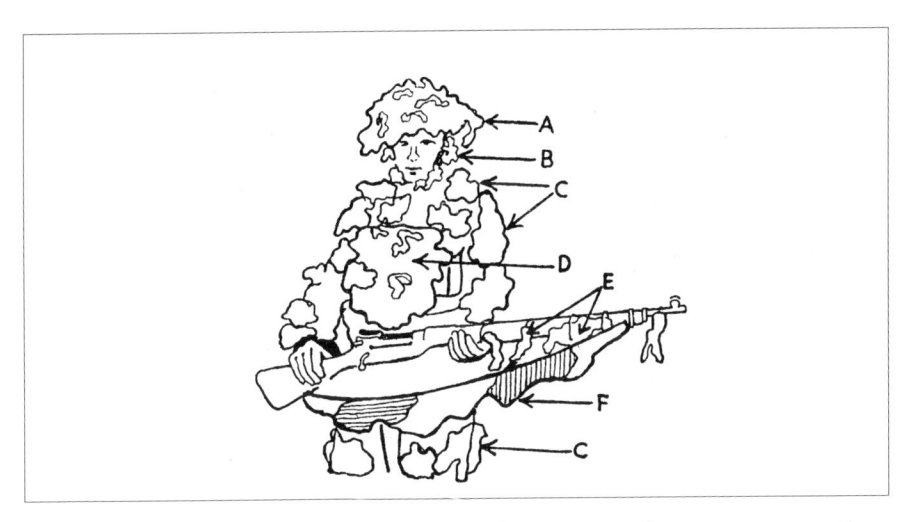

Use of camouflage to break up the outline of the body (from Home Guard Instruction, No. 51, 1943).

spirit and the four enemy soldiers chatted with the HG as they walked home. There was no telephone in the Welfare Hall and so news of the capture was communicated to Company HQ using the public telephone box at the Cross. It was just after 5.30 pm. (See Appendix 3 for the contemporary report.)

Whereas the local boys at Avonbridge and Slamannan had been an advantage to the HG on these occasions, this was not always the case. Just as in training, the boys followed them everywhere, exposing their positions to the enemy troops. If they hid in a close at, say, the Garrison waiting to ambush the enemy as they came over Grahamston Bridge, the lads would be there talking to them. Should the HG be fighting the regulars the boys would be giving away the deployments of those troops. Should, however, the enemy be another HG platoon the boys were just as likely to 'help' the enemy.

In the early days of the LDV at Denny the men carried wooden poles on their field exercises at Thorneydyke Quarry. As usual one set of men would 'attack' another, followed around by the young boys. That summer there was a particularly good crop of a yellow flower which, when uprooted, had a large ball root to which the earth clung at the end of a long stem. The boys found these ideal for throwing at the guardsmen until eventually the children replaced the Germans as the enemy. The guardsmen threw thunderflashes at them, only to find that the children actually enjoyed this even more. The HG soon tired of this asymmetric warfare and informed the police of the children's annoying practice. One day shortly thereafter the LDV chased the children straight into the arms of the waiting police. Stern words and cautions followed, parents were visited, and that was the end of that game.

The larger scale exercises required the use of transport, which was in part provided by the Camelon platoon based at the Walter Alexander bus depot in Brown Street. This platoon also provided transport for platoons beyond the Falkirk district, travelling as far afield as Kippen or Aberdour. The drivers had to remain with the vehicles and always took a nice picnic with them, and at Aberdour they were treated to an ice cream. Hugh Baird of the Brightons platoon was a car driver and often got the job of chauffeuring the Company's officers around on exercises – much cushier than crawling through the mud!

Communications, as we have seen, were rather primitive, relying upon the public telephone kiosks and messenger boys. It is not surprising then that exercises were often over before all the participants were aware of the fact. An example of this occurred when the Falkirk Ironworks platoon were about to bombard a Bren gun carrier with chalk as it crossed the bridge over the river at Carron Ironworks (See chapter 7). One railway worker with the Polmont LNER platoon was almost late for work because he had stayed out all night on

Two mobile canteens donated to the WVS in East Stirlingshire and made available to the HG during exercises.

an exercise that had finished at least six hours before. Another member of the same platoon made the mistake of climbing a tree to get a better sniping position, only to find that no one knew that he was there and therefore did not inform him that the exercise was over. Hours up the tree had made him stiff and it was with great difficulty that he got into work.

The number and variety of these training exercises was immense and no complete record now exists. Some idea may be gleaned from the examples in Appendix 3, which gives details of those reported in local newspapers.

CHAPTER SEVEN

Defence in Depth

Stop Lines

The early road blocks were designed to stop infiltration and thus sabotage, but as the HG became better equipped their role changed from one of observation to one of delay. The HG realised that they were incapable of halting a German invasion, but if they could slow down its progress from any beachhead, it would give the regular army a better chance of pushing the invader back into the sea. As a result a number of road blocks of a semi-permanent nature were set up on important arterial roads where it might be possible to cause such a delay. As with the temporary road blocks, these started with improvised barriers. On the main road to Stirling, just north of Denny (at NS 8425 8049), the Denny HG tied a thick wire rope obtained from a local colliery to an oak tree on the road side. Here it was left until needed. Then, on exercises or during invasion alerts, the wire rope was carried across the road and tied to another tree there. At this point the road ran through a slight cutting and lay on a bend so that the trap and the surprise were complete. As at Thorneydyke Quarry there was a 'pillbox' or check point nearby, this time set a little back on the rise in the field to the east of the road. In this position it was not silhouetted against the skyline. It was also manned as a regular check point and the men waited in the post many a night. The local children soon discovered it and thought it great fun to go up to the post and cut the sandbags, allowing the sand to trickle out.

At Falkirk the main stop line was the Forth and Clyde Canal. The bridges at Bainsford and Camelon were both guarded, the former by the Falkirk Iron Works platoon whose HQ was almost adjacent, and the latter by the platoons based at the Rosebank Distillery and the Forth, Clyde and Sunnyside Works. These were swing bridges and could be jammed in the open position, denying their use to the enemy. As we saw in chapter two, the Grangemouth HG mounted guard at the Kerse Bridge over the River Carron, better known as the

'Pay Brig'. From here they could keep a wary eye on the canal bridge at Dalgrain. Arrangements were also made to destroy other bridges along the canal, such as that at Lock 16. As tactics became refined, it was realised that even with the bridges at Bainsford and Camelon open the enemy would soon bridge the short spans that remained. So explosives were attached to the two bridges, which were only to be detonated by senior officers of the HG. The ideal time to do so was when there was an enemy vehicle on the structure, the debris from which would cause a further blockage. To make this work it was necessary to strengthen the road blocks at the ends of the bridges to slow these vehicles down. The form of obstacle used was that known as 'hairpins'. These were H-section steel girders, 6-8ft in length, bent into a V-shape, which could be fitted into previously prepared sockets in the roadway. Each needed three or four men to lift it into position and they were therefore kept stacked nearby in readiness. Ordinarily the sockets were covered with metal plates and went mostly unnoticed. In close support of these positions, commanders sited their fire trenches, from which to bombard the halted transport.

Rivers also provided secondary stop lines and the guard at the Pay Brig has already been mentioned. Here the roadway had been narrowed into a single lane to slow the traffic down. And two men were on duty between dusk and dawn. Those men on their rest period at this post had the luxury of a house at 9 Devon Street. This was a new building, partially complete, which the HG initially requisitioned from the Grangemouth Town Council in July 1940.

Kerse Bridge over the River Carron with the houses of Devon Street in the background.

The old toll house on the Bo'ness Road at the west end of the bridge over the River Avon. This was used as a guard post by the HG.

When, the following month, it was discovered that they did not actually have the power to requisition any buildings the commanding officer came to an agreement with the council and they continued to use it until January 1942. The house had a commanding view of the bridge.

The next river bridge to the west was Carron Bridge. Here too giant hairpins were left beside the road, with concrete blocks attached to the ends that did not fit into the road sockets. The bridge was defended by Smith guns and grenades during exercises with the regular army. Harry Rodgers of the Falkirk Iron Works platoon remembered being at the bridge late on the day of one exercise, along with five colleagues. When they heard a Bren gun carrier coming towards them past the Carron Iron Works they arranged their ambush at the southern end of the bridge. Harry and some of the others sproggled themselves on the parapet, hidden by the large capstones set on small pillars. The vehicle advanced steadily without noticing them. The defenders flexed ready to throw their bags of whitening at it, when the soldier on top suddenly noticed them and frantically waved and shouted. The manner of his gestures told the HG that there was something wrong – the exercise had already finished and they had not been aware of it!

The road bridges over the River Avon were subject to similar checks. The five principal bridges were, and still are, those at Grangemouth, Linlithgow Bridge, Muiravonside, Slamannan and Avonbridge. At the first of these, on the Bo'ness Road, the Grangemouth HG shared the responsibility with the RAF from the nearby airfield. Indeed, one RAF man said that he had guarded the bridge from below with nothing more than a pike! The HG were able to utilise a hut next to the old tollhouse on the west side of the bridge, secure in the knowledge that there was a concrete pillbox just 100yds further along the road (the Hospital Road Pillbox). At Muiravonside the Torphichen Bridge crosses the Avon Gorge at a high level and gave the defenders a great advantage. Exercises were often held here (see the section on hand grenades in chapter 5), usually with the attackers coming from the south. The assumption was that the German paratroops would land on the moors and, having regrouped, would make their way north to capture the airfield at Grangemouth or the docks at Grangemouth and Bo'ness. For the men at the bridge at Slamannan, this presented a minor dilemma. The village lay to the south of the river and would have to be abandoned – a sacrifice they knew was for the common good. Unperturbed, they dug a series of slit trenches beside the road north to Falkirk on the Dyke Brae. From here they had a good field of fire onto the bridge. The trenches were about 4ft long and occasionally had to be re-dug due to silting, but at least they did not fill with water. The officers were aware that this was to be merely a temporary holding position to slow the enemy down, as here the river could easily be forded by paratroopers in the summer months. It is not known what precautions were taken at Avonbridge or Linlithgow Bridge – but for sure there were some.

Perhaps the most important road bridge in the Falkirk district was the Kincardine Bridge over the Forth Estuary, which had only been completed in 1936. It was the lowest crossing of the Forth for road users, the next bridge being over ten miles away by road at Stirling. Central government had recognised its significance from the beginning and before the war it was designated as a Vulnerable Point. On the eve of the declaration of war a police guard was mounted on it. With the threat of invasion very real, two concrete pillboxes were placed on the margins of the approach road, narrowing the access route and providing the basis for a road block. These were manned by the regular army, along with a nearby Anti-Aircraft unit. As more and more of these troops were drawn abroad the guard at the bridge was supplemented by members of the HG from Airth. By the beginning of 1944 the HG had taken over and a small detachment could be seen just before dusk forming up at Airth Castle. They marched down the approach road to take up the night duty in the pillboxes. Before long a special section of the Airth HG was trained to man the AA guns near the Keith Arms – a popular duty!

Defence in Depth 199

Looking from inside the north-eastern machine gun post towards the Kincardine Bridge.

A machine gun post at the end of the wall bounding the road to the old ferry at Higgen's Neuk. The view is taken looking back to the farm (demolished in 2006) with the Kincardine Bridge behind the photographer.

The Kincardine Bridge.

Another VP that the HG helped to guard was the airfield at Grangemouth. About 50yds down the Bo'ness Road, between the main gate to the airfield and the town proper, was a semi-permanent road block with huge concrete wing walls encroaching onto the carriageway. This, of course, was not the only obstacle to an approach of the air strip and the defence of the airfield is discussed elsewhere.

Nodal Points

The evolution from check points on roads thrown up willy-nilly by roving local patrols to inspect cards and identify and intercept Fifth Columnists and spies, to semi-permanent road blocks constructed by engineers and designed to retard or even stall an enemy invasion, was a natural one. The pace of change varied throughout the country. By the end of June 1940 nearly all HG units were mounting ad hoc road blocks with little central coordination or overall embracing strategy. Over the following year such an overview was supplied and the main arterial roads were covered. It was still essential for the men at each road block to report the arrival of enemy forces so that GHQ Home Forces was able to properly assess the nature of the invading force. Its size, composition and direction of movement helped central command to mount a suitable response using the regular army. The men at the road blocks were trained to put up a good fight before retiring before superior manpower.

The disposition of the road blocks was determined by the lines of communication and inevitably influenced the next stage in strategic thinking. A casual look at the road blocks erected in West Lothian clearly shows the importance of Linlithgow. It was ringed by a set of such guard posts, reflecting its nodal position in the road network of the area, a situation similar to that of Falkirk to the west. Despite the opening up of the Eastern Front in June 1941, GHQ Home Forces remained obsessed with the fear of an imminent invasion. As more and more regular troops were being transferred to other theatres of the war it was essential for the role of the HG to be further modified to fill the gap. Instead of just observing and harassing the enemy and then retarding them at the many stop lines, it was decided that the HG would establish 'nodal points' or strongholds to create a defence in depth that would hold out and delay the enemy even further. These were defensive positions built around settlements and important road junctions. Now when the HG was faced with superior force they would retreat to these nodal points and fight it out until overwhelmed. The men were expected to sacrifice their lives to give time for a counter attack to be properly coordinated and indeed most knew this and were prepared, in theory, to do so as long as they could take a few of the enemy with them.

At Falkirk new road blocks were put in place to create a perimeter defence from which the men would fall back to set positions nearer to the town centre. This included a number of flame-barrel traps and pre-arranged ambush sites where the men were trained to lie in wait behind walls, banks or hedges that had previously been reconnoitred. To the south-east of the town the outer perimeter was extended to the top of the hill behind Callendar Wood. A strongpoint was constructed adjacent to Woodend Farm. Further along the ridge to the west road blocks had already been staged on Lochgreen Road using tractors and then cuddies, later supplemented with flame barrel traps. It must be assumed that similar measures had been arranged on the road to Slamannan near the hospital. After delaying the enemy at these locations the HG, unable to hold such an extensive perimeter, would continue to fall back. Lochgreen Road joins the Slamannan Road and descends the hill towards the town centre, crossing over the Union Canal on the way. Although it crossed the canal at the end of a long tunnel this provided the HG with another opportunity to delay and confuse an advancing foe. To the north of the road the land drops away dramatically into the cutting for the tunnel mouth, and to the south the huge bing of the Policy Pit dominated the landscape, impeding

During excavations in the grounds of Rosehall House a pattern of circular spade marks was found (front right). This is the bottom of a pit dug by the HG for a Browning machine gun. Located next to Pleasance lane, it covered the southern approach to the town centre.

easy cross-country access. An enemy might waste much time trying to circumvent a road block at this point. As fortune would have it, the entrance gate to the house next to the canal had a tall stone boundary wall that projected out across the footpath. By cutting out two gun loops in this wall the HG had a commanding view of the Slamannan Road. Sub-artillery could be used from the entrance gateway.

On the urban fringe it made sense to utilise the upper storeys of houses that overlooked the open countryside. The starkest example of this occurred at Windsor Road on the western side of Falkirk. In September 1942 the council tenants of numbers 31 and 72 (see page 205), then the last houses on either side of the road, were informed "by the military authorities that these houses may be required for the purpose of civil defence. The OC 2nd Stirlingshire Battalion Home Guard stated that it was not proposed to carry out any defence works at the houses at present, but they might have to utilise them in an emergency." In any street fighting the HG had the advantage of home ground. The patrols fully acquainted themselves with all the nooks and crannies of the towns and discussed what features in the landscape could be used to provide the best defence in depth.

The enemy advancing from the north would be delayed at the River Carron, and at Bainsford Bridge, but another road block was needed at the town itself to turn it into a strong point. The site was well chosen and lay just south of Grahamston Railway Bridge. Once again sockets were placed in the road to take the giant steel hairpins. When not in use they were stored around the corner near the end of McFarlane Crescent (see page 204). Piled up, one on top of another, they made ideal 'forts' for the children of the area to play in. When needed they had to be man-handled into position and any vehicle approaching from the north would not see them until the last minute due to

Defence in Depth

Slamannan Road looking down hill towards Falkirk. On the left a garden wall containing a letter box juts out across the footpath. Behind it the tall trees indicate the position of the Union Canal.

The letterbox has a small hole to either side of it – rifle loops. These are chamfered so that they are larger on the inside. They are both lined with cement.

the small incline created by the bridge crossing the railway line. Any tank stopping on the crest of the bridge would give just the slightest glimpse of its soft underbelly – a suitable target for a Spigot mortar or Smith gun. Any further on and it was vulnerable to attack from the upper storeys of the surrounding buildings. This was typical of the new road blocks, which combined obstacles with semi-artillery or mines to form a tank trap.

The principal of defence in depth was extended to the outlying villages. To the west of Falkirk lies Camelon with platoons based at the Gothic Foundry, Rosebank Distillery and the Forth, Clyde & Sunnyside Foundry. The latter two platoons shared the guard of the canal bridge, but the first platoon guarded the entrance into the village 1.25 miles to the west. At this point a large railway embankment provided an obvious defensive line. Here the

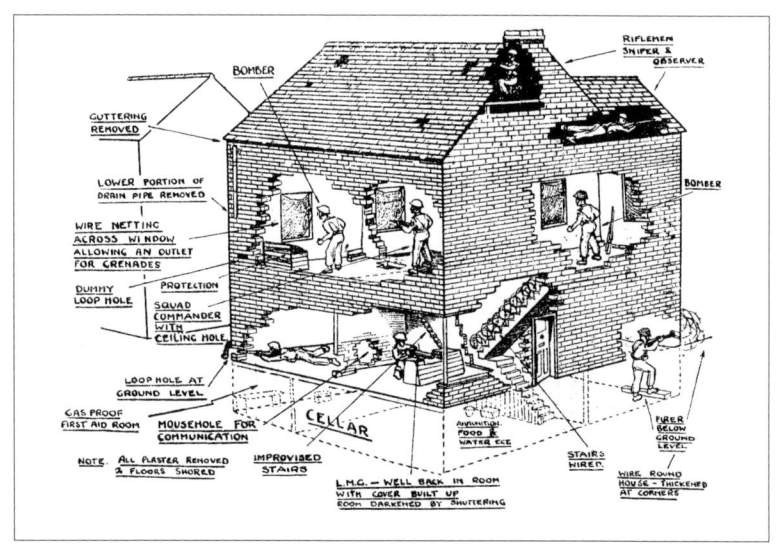

General layout of a defended house taken from Home Guard Instruction, No. 51 Battlecraft and Battle drill for the Home Guard.

Grahamston Bridge, c.1920. This view taken looking down Vicar Street to Grahams Road gives a good impression of the hump in the road at the railway bridge. MacFarlane Crescent is on the right. The tram system was dismantled in 1936.

Defence in Depth

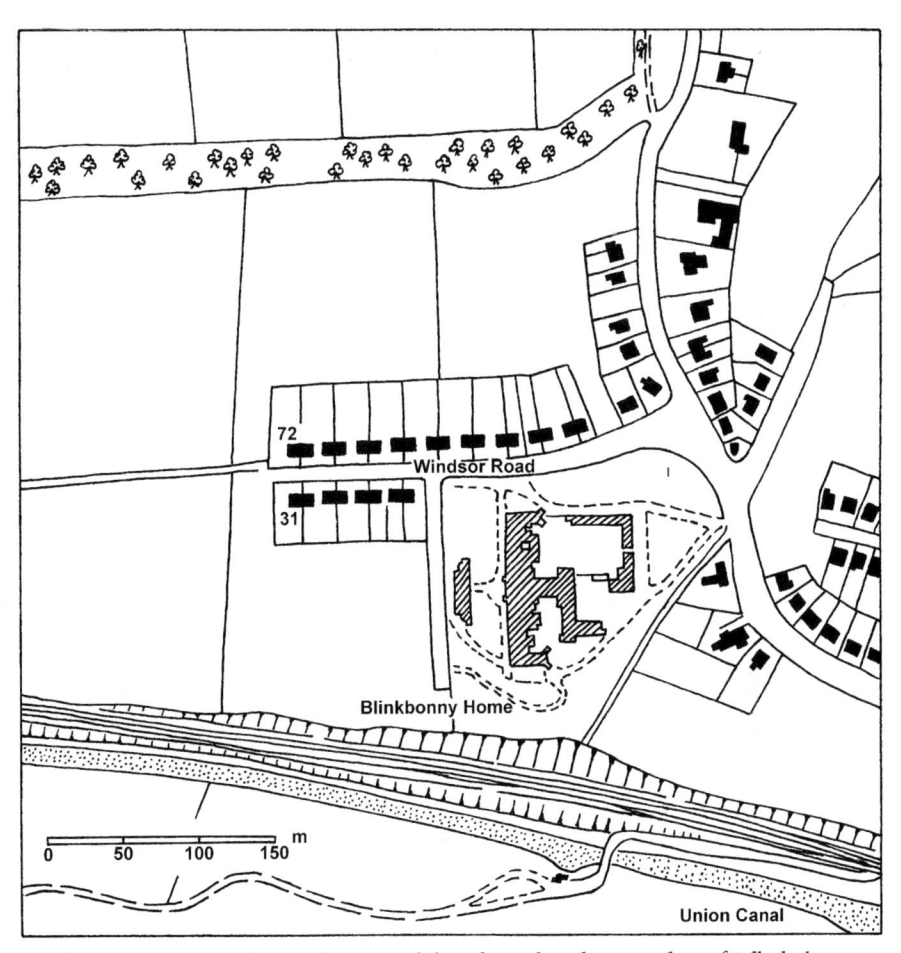

At the time of the war Windsor Road terminated abruptly, marking the western limit of Falkirk's housing schemes. To the south were the Edinburgh/Glasgow Railway and the Union Canal.

road dipped a little to pass under three railway bridges, giving the area the name of the 'Three Bridges' (see page 206). A brick wall conveniently overlooked the road at the bridges and behind this the Camelon HG lay in wait. On one exercise the HG from Bonnybridge were tasked with invading. Unfortunately the realism was marred by the way in which the general public just carried on their normal everyday business and by the arrival of spectators. The latter were keen to observe the turn of events and consisted of those with nothing better to do, such as children and even a tramp. Once past the defending forces the children dispersed to get a better view, but the tramp threw off his dishevelled coat and revealed himself to be one of the opposing force.

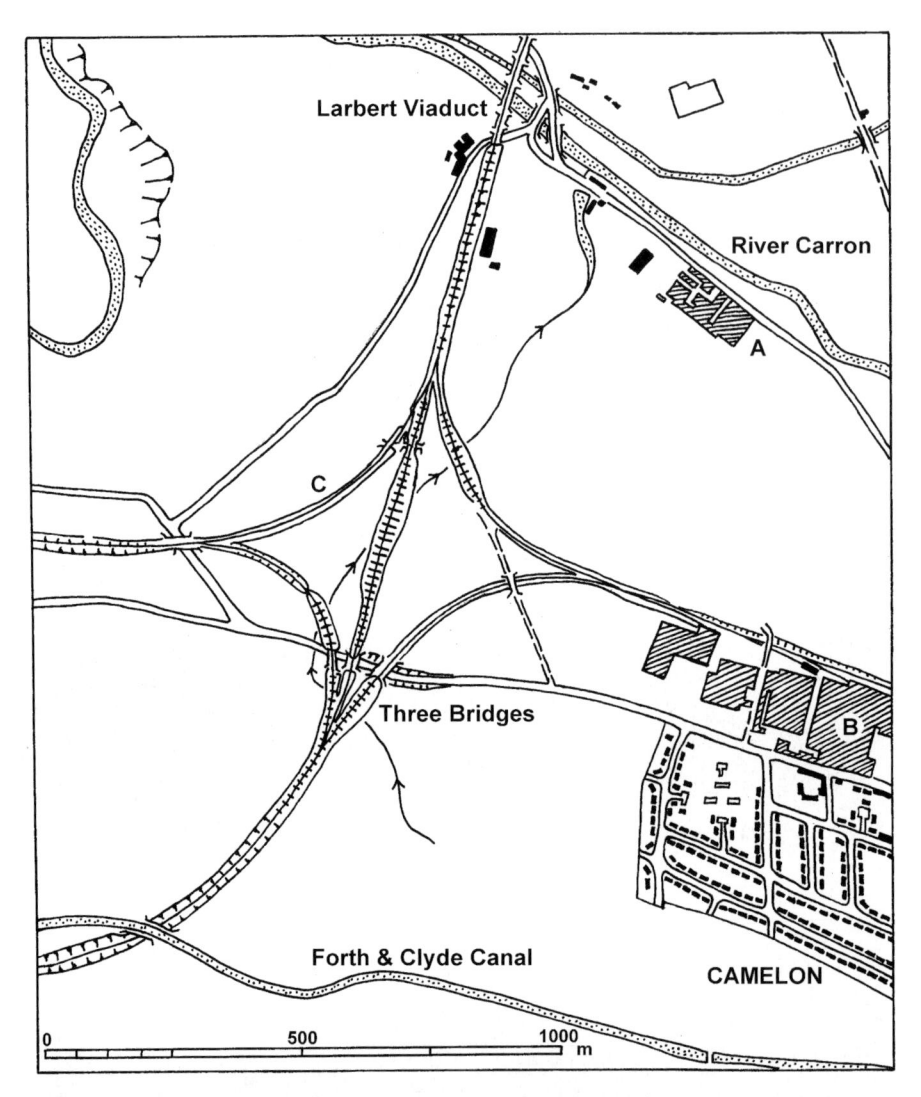

Map showing the area to the west of Camelon known as the Three Bridges. Alexander's bus depot is denoted by 'A'; the Main's Gothic Foundry by 'B'; and the place where the Royal train used to stop overnight by 'C'.

To the east of Falkirk the main road passes through the village of Laurieston and here the natural outer line of defence was the valley of the Westquarter Burn, with the railway embankment at the Skew Bridge as a fall back position. Set back from the road, but overlooking the causeway across the valley from the east side was Carhowden House belonging to the Stirlingshire Education Committee. It had been requisitioned by the Military following Dunkirk and in early 1942 the local HG was able to make use of it. In April or May that year the OC 2nd Stg HG Bn gave instructions for nine of the trees in the grounds to be cut down to improve a machine gun post that was being set up. However he did not have the owner's permission and in July the Education Committee made a claim for compensation for two elms, two oaks and five saplings.

The villages up on the Braes all made some provision for a limited defence and Slamannan was designated the second nodal point in the Falkirk district. The slit trenches overlooking the bridge on the River Avon have already been mentioned, as has the weapons pit opposite the war memorial. Now the Slamannan HG hired a contractor to cut a gun loop or two in the boundary wall of the bowling club facing up Station Road, the main road to the south. Another two were cut in the manse wall facing up the road to Falkirk to the north. At the west end of the village, at Brownrig, was a searchlight battery of ten men, and at the east end was the Welfare Hall used by the HG as the platoon HQ. Avonbridge must have made similar arrangements, for in September 1941 the HG there sought permission from the Education Committee to make two loopholes in the north-west corner of the playground

Station Road, Slamannan, looking towards the village. In front of Balquhatstone Church is the bowling green where gun loops were cut in the perimeter wall facing the photographer. The church tower would have made a good lookout.

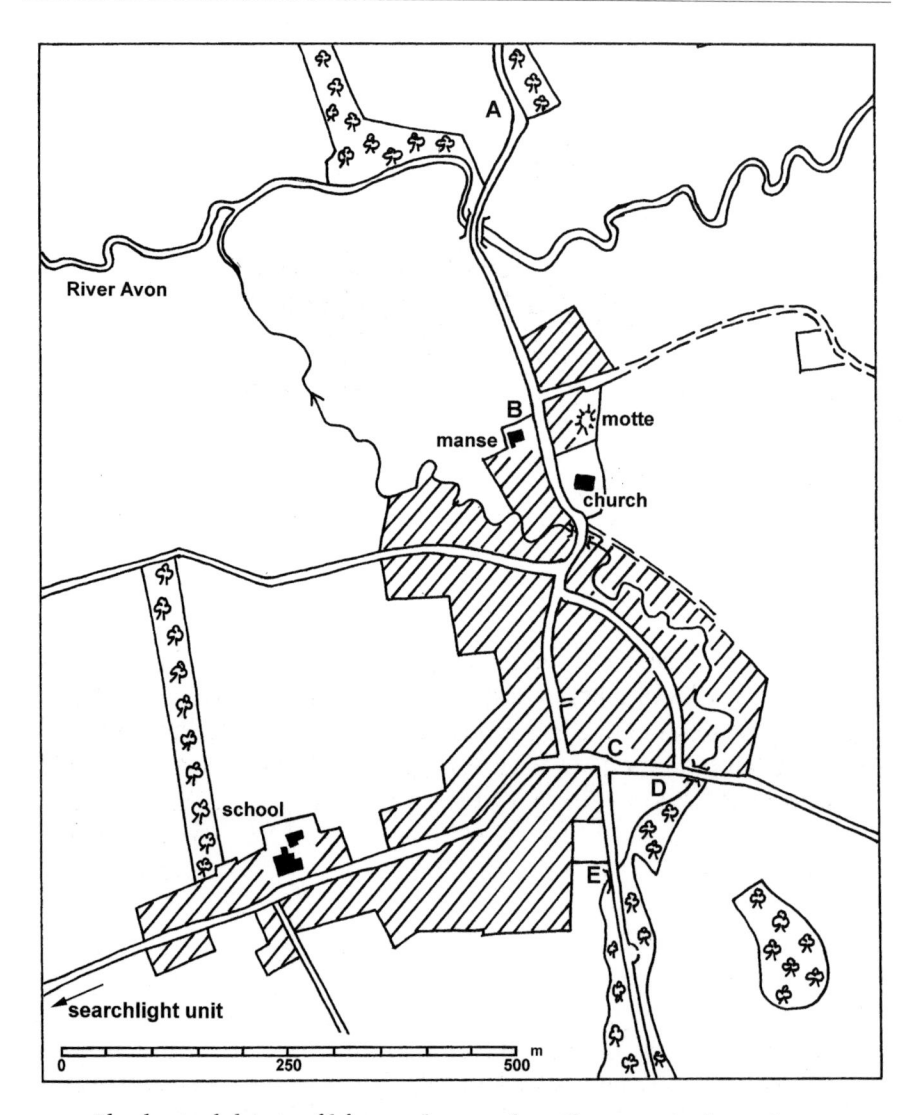

Plan showing the location of defences at the approaches to Slamannan. A – slit trenches on Dyke Brae; B – gun loop in the manse wall; C – weapons pit next to post office; D – Miners' Welfare Institute used as HG HQ; E – gun loop in the bowling green wall.

wall "for defence purposes." This was granted, provided that the wall was restored after the war. The gun post at the Cross Brae in Shieldhill was probably the centre of another unofficial nodal point.

Elsewhere details are even sketchier. The official status of the defensive ring around Smith and Wellstood (described in chapter 4) is uncertain. It is

Use of a Smith Gun at a prepared position (from Home Guard Instruction, No. 51, 1943). HG115

also known, for example, that there were gun posts just north of Larbert Cross and on the Drove Loan in Bonnybridge and that there were a number of flame barrel traps in these areas. The post near Larbert Cross was on the south side of Pretoria Road at its junction with Stirling Road. A strip of unused land here was separated from the footpath by a high wall. It commanded views northwards and was used at a very early stage by the LDV – but did it form part of a later system? Even more puzzling is how the dugouts mentioned in the following account by Findlay Russell fitted in:

> During the war period various exercises were carried out to find the efficiency of the defence. I was in charge at the same place, Dennyloanhead Corner, the only road going to Glasgow via Kilsyth. We were told that 'enemy soldiers' would enter the area with white slashes in their shoulders. The police station was at the other end of the road where the fork heads for Kilsyth and Glasgow. It so happened that the train stopped in Castlecary Glen and the enemy spilled out in all directions. Some came down by Castlecary and commandeered a car and asked to be driven straight to the police station. The poor police inspector who enrolled me into the specials was locked up and handed over to them. I was in charge of the Home Guard and had six of them under me. At that time there was the old railway bridge and just down from the corner I said to one of the Home Guard, "I think that that is some of the enemy talking to Willie Duncan" (the retired farmer who lived directly opposite the school). I made for the phone box to notify headquarters, but my actions were noticed by the enemy and they rushed up and pulled me out of the phone box, cable and all. That was the line dead! They stuck a bayonet between

my legs and said that I was a prisoner from now on. They had learned from Willie Duncan that I was in charge of this section and that my shooting brake was up at the corner. They explained to me that in normal circumstances they would take the keys from me and take my car. As it was only an exercise they would allow me to drive the car on their instructions. I had no option but to agree. Two of the 'enemy' jumped in beside me and we drove to the first dugout, which was the corner of Larbert/Falkirk Road. Of course the men assumed I was arriving with a message and merely waved. Along the side and to the rear they threw in smoke bombs. The two men in the dugout appeared like black and white minstrels. They got a fright (and so did I!). We drove on to the next dugout at Peathill Farm corner. This procedure lasted until all the dugouts in the district had been done. They were all taken back to Dennyloanhead Corner and lined up against the wall as prisoners. Mrs McAlpine had the hotel on the corner and her maid came out early in the morning to sweep the steps. I asked her to get Mrs McAlpine to phone police headquarters to tell them what happened and that we were all held prisoners. Mrs McAlpine came out and shouted over, which 'enemy' heard. They were not pleased at me at being left loose so they commandeered the local newsagent where we were all marched to and locked in until the exercise was over.

In 1942 the HG received vast quantities of barbed wire and used it liberally to augment existing defences. At Denny the Company officers decided that the disused railway line into the Anchor Brickworks provided a weak point in the northern defences of the town. Enemy troops might easily follow the line from Quarter past Ingleston Farm and on to the branch leading into the brickworks, which then crossed the Anchor Burn. Consequently, the men had to lay over 200yds of coiled barbed wire along the branch line from the burn to the main road. This caused great inconvenience to the local children, who had been accustomed to using this track as an escape route when being pursued by someone in authority. Some actually forgot that it was there and ran straight into it!

At the Mungal Foundry such large quantities of barbed wire were used that it formed a significant strongpoint adjacent to the bridge over the River Carron. Trenches were dug within this perimeter so that the HG could man them in time of need.

Protected Areas

On 21st March 1944 the Government made the following announcement:

> For operational reasons, the Secretary of State for War has made eight Orders, under Regulation 13 of the Defence (General) Regulations 1939, declaring certain areas to be Protected Areas. The Orders come into force on the 1st April next. The new Protected Areas consist of a coastal belt some ten miles in depth, extending from the Wash, round the East and South Coasts, to Lands End, and certain smaller Areas on the Firth of Forth.
>
> The general effect of each of the Orders is to prohibit persons who were not, on 1st April 1944, resident in the Protected Area declared by the Order from entering or being in that Area after that date. Certain classes of persons, such as members of the Forces on duty, Members of Parliament, and certain Government servants on duty are altogether exempt for the operation of the Order. Other classes of persons are given general permission by the Orders to enter or be in the Area. The classes of persons covered by this general permission are as follows:
>
> (A) Persons engaged or employed on necessary business which cannot be deferred and which they cannot transact or carry on otherwise than by entering the Protected Area.
> (B) Persons visiting their parents, parents-in-law, persons in loco parentis, husbands or wives; provided that the person to be visited was ordinarily resident in the Protected Area on 1st April 1944.
> (C) Parents or persons in loco parentis visiting their children or wards in the Area if under the age of 16 years.
> (D) Persons visiting near relatives in the Protected Area who are seriously ill.
> (E) Patients going to or being in a hospital or nursing home within the Protected Area and tubercular patients going to or being in a sanatorium within the Protected Area.
> (F) Persons passing through the Protected Area by train or public service vehicle without breaking their journey in the Protected Area.
> (G) Students or pupils of a university, college or school within the Protected Area.
> (H) Persons taking up residence with a person resident in the Protected Area of whose household they are ordinary members.
> (I) Persons holding a certificate issued by a local authority that they have been rendered homeless as a result of enemy action who enter the Protected Area to reside with relatives or friends therein.
> (J) Members of the Merchant Navy holding Form CRS 52 or Form CRD 53 returning home on leave.
>
> This list may be subject to variation of which public notice will be given in accordance with operational requirements from time to time. Even if a person

comes within one of the permitted classes, the Government hope that he or she will refrain from entering a Protected Area save in cases of real necessity. Individual permits will not be required by persons entitled to enter it. Any person who enters a Protected Area may be required at any time to establish to the satisfaction of the police or Service authorities that he comes within one of the protected classes. A person who fails to do so will not only be required to leave the Area but will be liable to be prosecuted and if convicted of contravening the Order will be liable to a fine of £100 or three months imprisonment or both.

The Protected Area affecting Bo'ness and Grangemouth was as follows:

> Those parts of the counties of Midlothian, West Lothian and Stirling bounded on the east by the western boundary of the City of Edinburgh from the mouth of the River Almond to its intersection with the main Edinburgh-Falkirk road) and on the south by the north side of said road through Linlithgow (but excluding any part of the burgh of Linlithgow) to the crossroads about 1 mile west of Polmont on the west by the east side of the main road (A905) from said crossroads direct to Kincardine Road Bridge.

The order duly came into force at 5am on Saturday 1st April 1944. At first a certain latitude was allowed, but this was soon tightened up. This gave people time to make alternative arrangements. Some housewives, for example, who had been brought up in Grangemouth, but who now resided outside at places such as Polmont and Laurieston, were registered with the shops there.

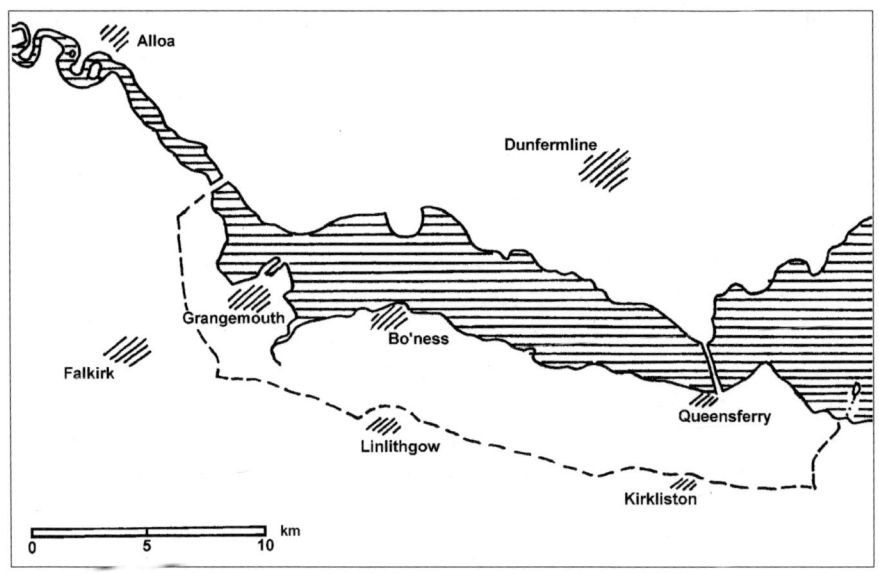

Plan showing the Protected Area on the south shore of the Forth. From this it can be seen why travellers from Falkirk were allowed to take the bus to Edinburgh via Linlithgow, but not by way of Bo'ness

They had to transfer their business elsewhere. There were also people from outside the designated area who looked after relatives in Grangemouth who were elderly rather than ill. They too had to make other provisions.

No physical road blocks were erected, but the road checks were reintroduced. During that first weekend a large number of military police (blue caps) were brought in to help the civil police to check ID cards. Quite a few of the people trying to enter Grangemouth by train or bus were not considered to be on essential business and were turned back. Others, who said that they were employed in the town, but had forgotten their ID cards were also turned away and cautioned. Checks were made on members of the armed forces to make sure that they were actually on duty in the area. Military and county police also arrived in Bo'ness that first Saturday and created havoc when they checked ID cards at the bus stance and the LNER station at Corbiehall. Many of the passengers were from Falkirk making the journey on to Edinburgh and could not show good cause for being in transit through the town. They were turned back and the queues for Edinburgh remained much diminished for the whole time that the Protected Area was in force. Other police were stationed at the old HG road block sites at Walton, the Flints and the Avon Bridge to check upon all the buses arriving at these points. One or two forgetful people were ordered to report to the local police station for leaving their ID cards at home. Work buses carrying women from Linlithgow and Bathgate to the docks in Grangemouth had no trouble.

The consequences for the civilian population of these areas slowly emerged. It was no longer possible for sports fixtures to take place at Grangemouth or Bo'ness if outside teams were involved. Nor could performers of any sort visit the area, be they brass bands or circuses. Even more inconvenience was discovered when it came to marriages. If the person from inside the Protected Area was marrying someone from outside at Grangemouth or Bo'ness, it was

Bobby Miller of the Grangemouth Home Guard.

impossible for the outsider's family to be present at the ceremony. As a result many wedding receptions were held in the Leapark Tearooms on Callendar Road in Falkirk – neutral ground! Young men from Falkirk courting girls from Grangemouth were supposed to kiss them goodnight at the boundary line – that cold and draughty place called Earl's Gates. Children were allowed to visit their parents, and vice versa, but siblings were not allowed to visit one another. In this adversity the people of Grangemouth and Bo'ness suddenly found common cause and a lot of the old animosities between them melted away. Anyone from outside the Protected Area was now called a 'foreigner'.

There were important economic implications too. The hotels and public houses lost business, though the cinemas did slightly better. Shops lost trade and Grangemouth Town Council projected a huge loss on the arrangements that it had made to hold their annual 'Holidays at Home' campaign in Zetland Park. That event had been a tremendous success in the previous two years, attracting people from all over Stirlingshire to spend their holidays there and avoiding wasteful travel. 'Holidays at Home' had been championed by the Government and Grangemouth felt itself to be a victim of its success in advancing it.

By the end of April those infringing the regulations were being prosecuted. In the last full week of that month 60 people were taken to court for entering the restricted area without their ID cards. The first case was that of a lorry driver from Glasgow with an urgent load. Another man was rushing to attend an HG parade! One woman tried to show her ration cards instead. The following week 63 were charged and fined 5s each. A woman who committed the same offence twice within a week was fined 30s. Control was getting tighter and the second week of May saw 133 ID card offences at Grangemouth, some of which were for people for not having signed their cards. One lady attended court on behalf of her son, only to be stopped herself on the way home and found not to have her card. Thereafter fines increased to 10s each. The following week 104 people were fined and this proved to be part of a downward trend as people became accustomed to carrying their ID cards or avoiding the road checks.

After May the blue caps were deployed elsewhere and the HG took over the onerous duty. They were back on the old road checks, but compared to 1940 and 1941 the public were far less tolerant. Back then they had been worried about an invasion; now they failed to see any reason for the disruption to their lives. The HG had a small wooden hut at the Earl's Gates crossroads and one night they stopped a man on his motor bike going to his night shift. His ID card checked out all right and he was told to proceed. The bike would not start and the rider, now a pedestrian, swore and told the guardsmen what he thought of their antics and their parentage as he hurried slowly to work.

The blue caps had been billeted at Muirhead's Sawmill and so they had stopped buses as they passed it. As the drivers and passengers had been accustomed to this, the HG with the local police continued it. Both the HG and police had been issued with capes and helmets, so checks went on no matter what the weather was. On the bus they would quickly check the ID cards, ignoring any children present. Indeed, children were never stopped in the streets and even adults quickly learned that the canal towpath was not subject to checks. Nor was the well-used footpath via Newlands. Clearly the HG was being much looser in its control than it ought to have been. It was struggling to find the manpower to man the checkpoints it did have.

In any case, the scheme was largely a sham. It had been imposed for two main reasons. The first was to obscure shipping movements, as many vessels passed through the Grangemouth Dockyard in preparation for the D-Day landings. Though anyone with binoculars could have seen daylight movements from the hills, many ships left after dark to take up their positions ready for the big day, and indeed the Germans were caught totally unawares. Secondly, the War Office wanted the Germans to know that the area around the Forth was included in the Protected Area because it would mislead them into the belief that the Allied invasion of the Continent would take place further north than it did. Grangemouth and Bo'ness were essentially decoys.

It was because of the need to continue this deception and thus cause the Germans to hold valuable troops in Norway and the north that the ban on entry into the Protected Area was only lifted on Saturday 29th July 1944, long after the initial success of D-Day. The news of this lifting came as a surprise even to the burgh officials at Bo'ness and Grangemouth, who read it in the national newspapers along with everyone else. In lifting the ban the War Office turned Grangemouth into a 'Restricted Area', where people had to carry ID cards, but were not allowed to carry binoculars or telescopes. For a short time the HG continued to assist the police in this duty by undertaking random checks within the area, but even these were soon abandoned. And the 'Holidays at Home' was a quiet success.

Enemy Bombs

The HG's first priority was the defence of the area against invaders. The likely prelude to such an invasion was thought to be a heavy aerial bombardment and so it was essential that the HG did not spread its forces too thinly by helping the ARP services or bomb victims. However, when there was no reason to suspect such a follow-up to a bombing raid, it was recognised that the trained manpower could be valuably deployed. The ambulance or first aid sections would help at the first aid posts and the men in clearing rubble, searching for survivors, directing aid and traffic and so on.

> 12. Co-operation with Civil defence Services.
> (a) BEFORE "ACTION STATIONS". No action by the Home Guard is required in an air raid warning being sounded, but should bombs actually fall on any town or village concerned, will turn out immediately and report to their Ptn, Headquarters, and will be available to assist the Civil Authorities. These Sections will go armed and act under their own Commander. Their duties may include any of the following: (1) Dealing with incendiary bombs. (2) D.R. duties. (3) Roping off and clearing blocked streets. (4) Assisting in the evacuation of area threatened by fire or U.X.Bs.
> (b) AFTER "ACTION STATIONS". Military duty must always come first, but having regard to the local Military situation, up to one third or if urgently necessary a greater proportion will be placed at the disposal of the Civil Defence authorities I required.
>
> Defence Scheme, December 1942

As it happened, few bombs were dropped in the Falkirk district and the ARP authorities took the lead on such occasions. On the first night of the Clydebank Blitz the occupants of Dunipace were guided to the Anchor Brickworks by air raid wardens and members of the HG. Here they were led into an old brick kiln that had been selected for the purpose some time before. It had a strong vaulted roof. However, once in the shelter someone pointed out that there was only one way in and one way out and that if anything happened to it they would all be trapped. This unnerved many of the occupants and, despite protestations from the HG, a lot of them made their way home preferring to shelter under their own stairs.

The large numbers of German planes involved made some suspect that it might be the prelude to an invasion. In Slamannan Tom McCracken was in bed when his father woke him up to tell him that the police had called to get the Home Guard out on duty. Tom had to put his uniform on and pick up his rifle, which he always kept besides his bed. He got the task of guarding the police station (behind Rosemount School). His mate, Tom Gardener, was given a Lewis gun and guarded the post office.

On the night of 5th May 1941 HE bombs fell in a line to the north of Slamannan from Middlerigg Farm to the Dyke Farm. Most of the ARP personnel and HG were asleep in their beds and were woken by the tremendous noise and the blast from the explosion at Dyke Farm. The wardens ran up the hill to the farm and found that the bomb had exploded next to a derelict building to the east of the main Falkirk road, heaving stone and earth onto it. The road at Barebreichs was impassable. Shortly afterwards the HG arrived to assist and were told by one of the wardens on the scene that he had heard several more descending in the vicinity and these must have failed to detonate. The HG and the village NFS (National Fire Service) agreed to join in the search for the unexploded bombs. After several hours fruitless search it was agreed that the warden must have been mistaken. Meanwhile the ARP had forgotten to direct traffic at the road blockage – it was the middle of the night – and in the black-out a police car coming from Falkirk ran straight into the pile of earth. The HG retired to their beds, tired but smug. This air of superiority was dispelled at 8am the next morning when there were two loud bangs in quick succession from Hillend Wood and inspection revealed two large bomb craters.

The search for unexploded bombs in the dark was always going to be problematical and in rural districts, such as Slamannan, somewhat unnecessary. It was far better to wait until daylight, giving the explosive device time to go off unimpeded. All the men knew this, but the officers often had different ideas. When a Dennyloanhead farmer called Wilkie reported having heard something drop at night in a field nearby, Findlay Russell ordered one of the HG to investigate immediately. "What am I looking for?" came the reasonable question. "Anything, a body, an unexploded bomb, part of an aeroplane – whatever's there," he replied. "Not bloody likely!" retorted the HG and he went off home to his bed.

When the two land mines fell near the Russell Pit at High Bonnybridge on the first night of the Clydebank Blitz on 13th March 1941 only one of them exploded. Part of the blast from the explosion caught the parachute of the second mine as it neared the ground, giving it sufficient uplift to slow the mine's descent to a gentle drop and directing it into a watery pit. Its huge size and proximity to the crater made it easy to find, but what should be done with it? Jock Todd, the local policeman, decided to call on the local expert in explosives. He cycled to the nearby home of James Gray, the No. 1 Fireman at the Dykehead Brickworks Clay Mine. Gray was in the High Bonnybridge HG and would, the policeman thought, be able to defuse the mine. After some discussion Gray agreed to take a closer look and the two men approached the mine with extreme caution. Gray carefully examined the exterior and wandered what on earth he was supposed to do. It was then that they heard the ticking noise. Jock was on his bicycle and away before Gray realised that he was alone. Gray looked at the land mine, walked home and took his family to the refuge of Bonnybridge School, where they spent the night. Despite the explosive potential of the device, the silk parachute was soon detached and removed by local residents for the making of clothes over the following months. This removal was executed despite the police guard, which was now augmented by PC James Fotheringham of Longcroft and PWR George Hall. It came as no surprise to the Bomb Disposal team when they arrived early the next morning – they had seen that happen before. What did surprise them was the discovery that James Wilson from High Bonnybridge had already defused the bomb! Wilson had no training in that line of work.

It was conspicuously evident that the HG required its own specialists in bomb disposal, if only to do a better job of guarding these lethal devices. The opportunity for training in the subject occurred when No. 20 Bomb Disposal Unit, comprising one officer and 24 airmen, moved to Grangemouth on 3rd July 1941. This squad, under P/O Gillet, was tasked with neutralising unexploded bombs on RAF property over a considerable area of Scotland. An Auxiliary Bomb Disposal Unit was formed and attached to one of the ICI platoons in Grangemouth. They wore the regular uniforms of the HG, but upon this they bore a badge with crossed bombs. The unit's practical exercises were completely different from those of the regular HG. They were told to dig a deep hole in the grounds of Kerse House and to shore it up with timber from the local woodyards, as if they were searching for an unexploded bomb that had sunk into the soft ground. They took an age to complete the task and finally an expert came to inspect it. He merely glanced at it and said, "Fine. Fill it in." Then the cycle was repeated, hole after deep hole.

If anti-personnel mines were dropped in the area John Buchan of the ICI platoon was trained to line up civilian volunteers and lead them across the affected area. He, of course, being the man who had to deal with them, led from the back! The platoon trained hard to keep up with the latest developments in German bombs, but thankfully no bombs fell in the area after May 1941. In May 1943 the No. 20 Bomb Disposal team moved to the south of England.

Transport

When it was formed, the LDV was not seen as a mobile force and so there was little need for transport. Indeed, the most important transport component of this early period was the bicycle. Messengers, usually teenage boys on bicycles, were used to call out the HG once an alert signal had been received by the CO. They were also used by the troops themselves, with some guardsmen cycling from Standburn to Queensferry during an invasion alert. No one seriously thought that the Germans would use bicycles, but the silent approach of a bicycle in the black-out could be dangerous. One dark night in September 1940 an HG patrol was walking along the road approaching Larbert Cross and failed to detect the looming presence of a tandem. The unsuspecting cyclists collided with the patrol and Sydney Jackson of the HG received head injuries, which necessitated his removal to Falkirk Infirmary.

It was almost axiomatic that officers had to have their own transport. At Slamannan Lt Ewen, the first commanding officer of the platoon, had a motor bike and took upon himself the job of raising the men in an emergency. His platoon sergeant, Tom Menzies, always attributed his 'election' to that rank to the fact that he had access to his father's car. This he used to collect the equipment and uniforms from Falkirk as they trickled in. Later he also conveyed ammunition. Most of the senior officers had their own cars and Lt-Col. Stein even provided a chauffeur to get the movement off the ground by ferrying ex-sergeant-majors around. John Millar, director of the Ford car dealership in Callendar Road, had an old converted Morris 10, which he had suitably painted in a camouflage scheme. When a plane crash-landed at Gardrum Moss he took some of his men to the site in the car to guard it and was thus able to get there before the souvenir hunters.

Each HG company had access to between three and seven cars. Initially this was done on a voluntary informal basis, but as petrol rationing bit and non-essential car use was clamped down on these arrangements were formalised and the vehicles were 'earmarked'. The bureaucrats found a way of siphoning petrol for their own use. For some this meant the difference between keeping the car on the road or laying it up on blocks for the duration. Letting the HG use the car had its hazards, and not only from the heavy army boots or equipment. In March 1944 Eric Joyce applied for planning permission to erect a wooden garage at the south end of Rae Street in Stenhousemuir "As I am at present using my car for Home Guard purposes and would like my garage to be nearer my house" as it was "being ruined by the children where it is at present."

In 1942 battalion HQs were given cars belonging to the War Department for their use. Falkirk had two, which it allocated to the quartermaster and the PSI. Such cars were for use on HG duty only, though there was always a temptation to push this to its extreme. In December 1943 George Burns of Bo'ness was fined £12 and disqualified from driving for a year for misuse of the Bo'ness HG Company's car. He had driven some officers to a conference in Bathgate and did not get back to Bo'ness until 5pm. As he had not eaten since breakfast he used the car to find a place to eat, but everywhere in Bo'ness was closed and he ended up in Blackness, where the inn was usually open. After eating he gave a naval officer and his wife a lift back to Champany. The court decided that the official use of the vehicle had ended at Bo'ness and that the trip to Blackness was therefore not insured and the use of the petrol had been illegal. Giving others a lift when uninsured had simply exacerbated the problem. Whilst the year's driving ban may have deprived the HG of a driver, it also caused George Burns difficulties, as his job was as a van salesman. One wonders who reported him!

For the movement of the guardsmen and their equipment lorries and vans (Load Carrying Vehicles or LCVs) and coaches were earmarked. The lorries and vans were in everyday commercial use and so it was not sensible to earmark the vehicles of long distance hauliers, as these could be outside the district when the hour of crisis arose. In fact in the event of an invasion any vehicle on hand could be requisitioned. The vehicles that were earmarked were those that could be used in the case of an alert, or for any exercises simulating an alert. It is not surprising therefore to find LCVs belonging to firms like Smith & Wellstood, the Falkirk Iron Co, R & A Main and JM Millar Ltd on the list for the 2nd Stg HG Bn. Some of the vehicles, such as Johnson's baker van in Bo'ness, were quite old. Johnson's van had the old-fashioned wire wheels.

Private cars, motor cycles & load carrying vehicles earmarked for use of Home Guard.

"A" Company

Private cars	reg. no.	owner	required at
	WG 1844	J.C. Leith	Bonnybridge
	SX 4252 (G Cert)	D. Keir	do
Motor cycles.			
	WR 4979	J Fleming	Bonnybridge
	WS 9781 (G Cert)	K. Wallace	do

Load carrying vehicles

WG 9376	Smith & Wellstood	Bonnybridge
WG 3351	do	do
BHN 538	P. Stewart	do
WG 2709	J. Struth	do

Two of the above are for Bn. Reserve and will remain at Bn. H.Q. when reserve called in.

'B' Company
Private cars

WG 6793	J Middleton	Falkirk
WG 9407	R. McNair	Falkirk
WG 8064	W. Rattray	do
WG 6822 (G Cert)	R. Wilson	do
US 1244	J. Green	do

Load carrying vehicles

WG 9843	D. McNair & Sons	Falkirk
WG 7028	G. Thomson & Sons	do
WG 6107	Falkirk Iron Co.	do

"C" Company
Private cars

WG 7408	J. Forrester Ltd	Falkirk
YS 242	J.S. Brown	do
WG 7960	J.M. Miller	do
AFS 857 (G Cert)	T.F.S. Menzies	Slamannan

Motor cycles

1 W.D.		
CPK 237	M. Brown	Falkirk

Load carrying vehicles

CRH 966	R. Barr & Sons	Shieldhill
GFS 390	R. White	Slamannan
WG 5826	H. Drysdale	do

'D' Company.
Private cars
    CS 4820 (G Cert)   A. Sharp   Polmont
    WG 5381 (G Cert)   A.E. Thomson   do
    US 4292 (G Cert)   T. Calverley   do
    YS 224   R.M.W. Brown   do
    WG 4907   H. Barlow   do
    WG 6116   D. Haston   do
    WG 9355   R. McCowan   do
    WG 8051 (G Cert)   R. McCowan   do
    US 8725 (G Cert)   Cpl. T. Reid   do
Motor cycles
    RX 8377   D.C. Steel   Polmont
    WG 3668   J. Scott   do
    W 9402 (G Cert)   J. Foster   do
Load carrying vehicles
    WG 8960   J. Smith   Polmont
    WG 5691   R. Barr & Sons   do
    VD 2538   J.M. Millar ltd   do

'E' Company
Private cars.
    WG 6539   H. Armstrong   Falkirk
    WG 6901 (G Cert)   A.L. Alexander   do
Motor cycles
    WG 1150   W. Collins   Falkirk
Load carrying vehicles.
    WG 4107   Callendar Coal Co   Falkirk
    DSP 284   R. Douglas & Sons   do

"F" Company
Private cars.
    WG 5403   H.C. Davie   Falkirk
    WG 9219   G.W. Wortley   do
    WG 8180   E.J. Boston   do
Motor cycles.
    1 W.D.
Load carrying vehicles.
    WG 1326   R. & A. Main Ltd   Falkirk
    WG 6079   G. Thomson & Sons   do

Defence in Depth

> Bn. H.Q.
> Private cars.
>
> | | |
> |---|---|
> | WG 5461 | Col. A. Stein MC. |
> | WG 6099 | Major R.T. Haddow MC. |
> | DNA 918 (G Cert) | Lt. C.W. Mathieson |
> | WG 7022 (G Cert) | Lt. J. Hill |
> | DSG 336 | Lt. C. Palmer |
> | WG 5040 (G Cert) | Lt. A.K. Thomson |
> | W.D. vehicles | Adj/Q.M. (2) P.S.I. (1) |
>
> Motor cycles.
> >   2 W.D. (1 for S.S.A.)
>
> Load carrying vehicles.
> >   2 from "A" Company with Bn. Reserve
> >   5 light trucks (not yet received).
>
> (Appendix K Defence Plan, 24.12.42)

In 1940 some 600 vehicles from the Scottish Motor Transport Group (SMT) of Companies were earmarked throughout Scotland. These included a sizeable number of Walter Alexander's Ltd buses at the depot in Larbert Road, Camelon. Early in 1941 it was decided that this arrangement needed formalising in order to provide training and support for the drivers. Sixteen HG Motor Coach Companies were formed in Scotland and attached to the general service HG battalions for administration and infantry training. The company incorporating the Camelon depot thus came under the 2nd Stg HG Bn. It was connected to the DDST, Scottish Command, for RASC training.

The motor coach company based at the Larbert Road Garage had its most dramatic moment on the night of Friday 14th March 1941. The night before, Clydebank had been hit by wave after wave of German bombers. The area lay in ruins and the inhabitants had little shelter and scant resources. All the HG transport companies in central Scotland were mobilised. Even before they received their orders the men from Falkirk knew where they were going. They had watched until late into the night as aircraft droned over their heads and bright red lights flashed in the sky off to the west. The resulting fires were clearly visible on the far horizon. Everyone expected that the bombers would return, but during the lull that Friday some 2,500 people were evacuated by bus to the Vale of Leven and 1,000 to Helensburgh and Kirkintilloch. Thousands more went off on their own to stay with friends or relatives. As

A selection of baker's vans owned by John Galloway of Grangemouth, 1937. Some of these vehicles were requisitioned by the army during the war and the remainder were available for use by the HG.

night fell the bombers returned. The HG drivers were unable to return for more passengers; instead many worked through the night taking the refugees to onward destinations such as Perth, so that the staging posts would be clear for the morning when the process would be repeated. The landscape that greeted the buses on their arrival that Saturday was one of desolate devastation. Over 200 buses were used to shuttle the homeless. It is estimated that 7,000 went to the Vale of Leven, 3,000 to Coatbridge, Airdrie and Hamilton, 1,500 to Paisley, Bearsden and Milngavie, 2,500 to other parts of Renfrewshire, Lanarkshire and Dumbartonshire. As they patiently boarded the buses the refugees had little inclination of their destinations and indeed the drivers often did not know anything more than their first staging post. After resting overnight in makeshift accommodation in the Vale of Leven large numbers continued their journey to the Central School in Larbert, where they were processed and billeted on local families. Other members of the HG from the Falkirk area volunteered to go to Clydebank to help on the ground. Only the older men, preferably single, were allowed to go and were there for around a week. It was an experience that stayed with them for the rest of their lives. For the exhausted drivers it had been a task with horrific sights and human tragedy, but one that proved their worth.

Defence in Depth

The sixteen Motor Coach Companies operated more or less independently of each other and it was agreed that this would not be conducive to the best use of resources when trying to defend the nation. In order to further coordinate the supply of transport in September 1942 they were formed into one motor coach battalion of sixteen companies, known as No. 1 Scottish Motor Coaches Battalion HG. The new HQ was in Edinburgh and this fixed administration provided greater cohesion. There was also more, much needed, training. The Battalion's main function was to move both regular and HG units as required on 'Action Stations'.

The battalion was remodelled in January 1943 and renamed No. 1 Scottish HG Transport Column. The sixteen companies were reduced to 12, each with an establishment of 60 buses and a larger number of drivers. In fact more buses than this were allocated as a margin of 10% above this number were expected to be off the road at any one time due to maintenance and repair work. Weapons were now issued to each member of the column. By the middle of the year there were 1,850 men with 660 motor buses capable of conveying 20,000 troops. They were able to be fully turned out in 4 hours.

No. 2162 Company was based in Falkirk. It covered the Falkirk area, Kilsyth, Stepps and Milngavie.

Co Commander	Capt R Bruce on formation to 1944
	On Jan 1945 it was Major T McMain
2 i/c Company	Lt W Clark on formation to 1944
	On Jan 1945 it was R Bruce
Platoon commanders	Lt D Bennie on formation to 1945
	Lt M McMain ditto
	Lt J Laidlaw ditto
	Capt Clark in Jan 1945

Lt. Clark was generally out on exercises about once a week. Occasionally, if his wife was out, he would take a rifle or a grenade home to dismantle it in front of his young daughter Elma. She was only a child, but she was meant to inherit the mantle of resistance to the Germans. Even the transport unit of the HG was going to fight to the death!

Buses of the Transport Column were used to convey HGs to the firing range at Lochgreen and on their exercises at Sheriffmuir and elsewhere. On these exercises the transport itself might be 'attacked' by Spitfires from RAF Grangemouth to see how quickly the men debussed.

In June 1944 volunteers from No. 1 Scottish Transport Column moved into northern England with their coaches. This was in the aftermath of D-Day, when most of the transport on the south coast was being used to get troops across to France. Meanwhile, transport units from the Midlands were taking reinforcements from that area to the south coast, and in turn their places were taken by units from the north. This was the last big exercise for the Column and in January 1945 it was stood down. Almost its last act was to take part in the HG stand-down parade in Edinburgh on Sunday 3rd December 1944. HG officers, NCOs and men from Larbert Road, Stirling, Perth, Alloa, Stepps and Milngavie depots were there under the command of Major T S McMain, coordinating officer of 2162-3 Companies of Messrs W Alexander & Sons Ltd.

For the smaller HG contingents lorries rather than buses were used to take the men to the Targets at Greenhill. Again the War Department provided these to battalion HQs. One of the oddest LCVs given to the Stenhousemuir platoon for the duration had a small home-made crane fixed to the back so that it could be used to lift concrete blocks onto a road to close it. Most of the time it lay behind the police station. Most lorries remained in private ownership and in 1943 it was decided to introduce a system similar to that for buses. No. 2 Scottish HG Transport Column was formed, consisting of twelve companies of LCVs, each with a carrying capacity of from 3 to 5 tons. The Column HQ was in Queen Street, Glasgow. 2184 Company (West of Scotland District) had its HQ in Bowling, with 'B' platoon based in Grangemouth with 30 LCVs under Lt William A Mitchell (promoted to the rank of captain in 1944). It was a motley collection of vehicles from the commercial businesses of the area. There was an Aitken's Brewery lorry, some laundry vans and local contractors' vehicles – such as a small lorry belonging to William Mitchell himself. Shortages of manpower were a major problem for the transport column as a whole, as being formed so late in the day most of the drivers were already in the existing HG and Civil Defence units. Transfers were not supposed to be permitted, but there were always ways around such regulations and Bill

---

No. 2 SCOTTISH HOME GUARD TRANSPORT COLUMN
Company 2184   "B" Platoon

Telephone:
Grangemouth 79.

DRILL HALL,
GRANGEMOUTH,

Letterhead used by the platoon of the Transport Column based at Grangemouth's Drill Hall.

Talbot Street, Grangemouth, looking east with the Drill Hall on the right.

Henderson, the butcher, who was already in the HG stayed with his van. In fact, most of the HG drivers were the men who drove the vehicles during the day.

'B' platoon met once a week and went through various exercises and maintenance routines. Training included learning the location and use of petrol points, ammunition refilling points, supply transfer points, mobilisation, drill, mess tin cooking and vehicle parades. Most of the men had a Lee Enfield rifle, but the platoon was also issued with EY rifles, Sten guns and a Boys anti-tank rifle. Grangemouth Drill Hall was used for rifle practice with .22 calibre. Just after D-Day the men were issued with rations in readiness to move to the south of England with their vehicles, where they might be needed to transport supplies in support of the landings should those being used be destroyed by enemy action. In the event the landings went better than expectations and they never went.

Harry Grant joined the transport platoon at Grangemouth because he was keen on motorcycling and was finding it hard to get petrol. He was given an army motorbike and crash helmet and became a dispatch rider, along with William Crabis. Harry was pleased to find that discipline in the unit was rather lax and that it concentrated on the vehicles rather than square bashing.

Rosehall House, Falkirk Pleasance, had been built for the Neilson family, but was requisitioned during the war and used by the Home Guard

On one occasion a visiting brigadier was speaking to Captain Mitchell when one of the drivers, Alex Kerr, arrived. Without saluting Kerr asked, "Where are we off tomorrow Will?" Had it not been for the brigadier no one would have questioned such an approach.

The motor coach platoon of Walter Alexander's garage in Camelon was also allocated some old army motorbikes. The designated riders had a lot of fun taking them on the moor as part of their training. A few of the ordinary HG platoons were also issued with motorcycles. One Portonian learned to ride an RAF bike on the platforms at Grangemouth Station before joining the railway company's own HG platoon. These platoons used the bikes not only to carry messages, but also to reconnoitre their areas when foot patrols ceased. Again the temptation was to use them for personal enjoyment; as they were kept at the homes of the riders there was often a thin line between personal and official use. In July 1941 when Emerson McNeish, a coal miner from Castleloan in Bo'ness, was caught using a motorcycle that was registered and licensed for use with the HG he claimed that he had just repaired it and was giving it a road test.

Lt. Tom Aitken of HQ Company was based at Rosehall House in Falkirk as a Liaison Officer (LO). His main task was to deliver messages between the HG and the regular army units of the 52nd Division stationed between Callander and Dunblane. For this he was given a green Rudge-Whitworth motorcycle, which he kept on the path beside his house in Bonnybridge. The rifle with which he had previously been issued was taken back and he received a service revolver instead that was far easier to carry. Petrol for the bike was obtained from a garage in Laurieston on the presentation of a signed chitty. The mileage of the intended journeys was pretty well calculated in advance and so there was usually little petrol left by the time that he got home. Had there been an unexpected emergency causing his redeployment he would not have got far. Tom was usually given a four-figure grid reference and told to deliver his messages there. He had driven in the area before the war and knew the roads reasonably well and so was never really troubled with the black-out. Soon he became responsible for training HG recruits in map reading and navigation using watches and compasses.

By and large most of the HG motorcycles were used by their owner, who was given a petrol allocation that was strictly for HG services. Johnny

The Carronshore & Bothkennar HG Platoon at the new school building at Carronshore. 1941. Note the prize cup and shield. There is a despatch rider on the left.

Robertson of Stenhousemuir had a sidecar to go with his bike and decided that it would make a suitable gun platform. Being an engineer he manufactured a machine gun mounting for it, together with a scarf ring so that the gunner was not able to shoot either the driver or the bike. The scarf ring was basically a guide rail that stopped the gun from pointing in certain directions. To use it the gunner had to kneel down and so the safety straps had to be modified for that position. However, this was neither safe nor comfortable for long distances and the kneeling position was only taken up when an attack was imminent.

Arthur Coutts had a motorcycle, but found that he was unable to get petrol for it, so in 1942 he lent it to his younger brother, Allan, for use by the Edinburgh HG. It was then officially requisitioned by that unit and Arthur did not see his motorbike again until 1945. Although Allan had ridden it through to Edinburgh, the bureaucrats would not allow him to ride it back and it was delivered to Larbert on the back of an army truck. Arthur subsequently received compensation of three farthings for every gallon of petrol that it had consumed during its HG service, using records meticulously kept by their quartermaster.

In June 1943 the HG organisation was officially allowed to recruit women for specific tasks. The first women Auxiliaries in the Falkirk area were Miss Helen Brough of Falkirk and Mrs McKerron of Grangemouth. Both served with 'D' Company at Grangemouth, which accepted them with open arms as drivers. Despite this early acceptance, the numbers of women officially in the Home Guard Auxiliaries remained very low, probably only around 20 or so in the Falkirk district and only 32,000 nationwide.

Signals

Long distance communication between different parts of the HG was important to coordinate activities, particularly any response to an enemy incursion. As always the HG started by improvising. Semaphore was taught at evening meetings and the men practised sending messages from hill top locations. Often they were joined in this activity by some of the local youth organisations, such as the Scouts and Girl Guides, who might act as messengers during an emergency. At Avonbridge on one occasion the Scouts were practising their semaphore when the police, who thought that they were part of a spy network, arrested them.

Young boys were recruited from the schools as messengers – the only stipulation being that they should provide their own bicycle. The boys were evidently far more enthusiastic to fulfil their duty than their parents and many who volunteered were forbidden to attend. A number of the boys that did turn out subsequently joined the HG and their ranks were slowly depleted. New equipment made their services less vital and after the Clydebank Blitz, in which the casualty rate amongst messengers was unduly high, their use was discontinued.

Most of the HG learned to read and send messages in Morse code on a key over a wire and the best were able to send 20 or so words a minute. They were given Aldis lamps that could be used in the dark. The advantage of these was that telegraph wires were not required, but the message was more easily intercepted. The Post Office platoon and the railway platoons specialised in the use of existing wires and the laying of temporary land lines. The HG was also able to make use of the police and its network of communications. New telephones were installed in schools and various premises used by the HG and ARP services. It was late 1943 however, before the local units were issued with walkie-talkies.

First Aid

Like all the civil defence services the men of the HG were trained in first aid. As well as the usual range of splints and bandages there was information on how to detect and treat poisonous gasses. Theory taught in the classroom was tested during exercises and often the HG pretended to be casualties to be treated by the other services. Sections of each platoon trained as stretcher bearers and learned how to lower the injured, strapped to a stretcher, from tall buildings, or how to carry them over great distances. In November 1941 Dr E Neil Reid, Medical Officer of Health for Stirlingshire, was appointed as Zone Medical Officer to the HG to ensure cooperation between the HG and ARP services.

The continuous practice, combined with military training exercises, undoubtedly sharpened the minds of the HG involved. An odd case from Bo'ness may be used to illustrate this. In April 1944 a three-year old toddler, Simon Wilson of East Castleloan, squeezed through the gap in a fence surrounding the large sunk static water tank immediately behind his home:

> He was floating a piece of wood when he toppled in. Some children who had been playing with him raised the alarm and soon a large crowd gathered. Four Castleloan men jumped in to rescue him, but their waterlogged clothes hampered their efforts and they too had difficulties in the 6ft of icy water. Sgt Alex Orr was returning from his HG duties when he heard the shouts. On arrival, he noticed that the lifebelt that is kept beside every tank was still in place on the board. He threw it to

the man nearest the drowning child and got them both ashore. He then helped the other three men to the side of the tank in the same way. The little boy was unconscious, but one of the rescuers, Mr Welsh of East Castleloan, started artificial respiration assisted by Mr Orr. After a short time the boy recovered.

(Bo'ness Journal 28th April 1944)

At the end of 1942 there was a smallpox scare in the Falkirk area. Bellsdyke Military Hospital was closed to new admissions for two months and all the local HG men had to receive inoculations. At Grangemouth they filed into the Red Cross building at the foot of Dock Brae.

CHAPTER EIGHT

The End

Stand Down

At the time of D-Day in June 1944 the HG was on a high status of alert. There was a possibility of an enemy counter-attack on the weakened British mainland to force the recall of troops. Even if such an attack was not mounted, there was an even greater probability that with high casualty figures during the Normandy landings the HG would be drawn into the south of England to help to supply and maintain the continental foothold. In the event, the war went well for the allies. In the following months absenteeism in the HG greatly increased until, on 16th September it was announced that parades would once more become voluntary. Attendances plummeted and it was not too much of a surprise when the 'Stand Down' order was released on 28th October.

Souvenir programme for the farewell social of the 1st Stg HG Bn at Stirling.

Over the following November and December the quartermasters recorded the return of HG equipment such as the weapons, gas masks and so on. Adverts were placed in local newspapers to recall this material and by 3rd September the 2nd Stg HG Bn had returned roughly 75% of it. It was only as a result of public protest that the men were allowed to keep their boots and battledress, both useful items for work at a time of continued rationing. The greatcoats, which were supposed to be returned, were in demand and many were dyed for civilian use. There were Stand Down dinners and functions at platoon, company and battalion level throughout the Falkirk district. The Airth HG, for example, celebrated in the Crown Hotel.

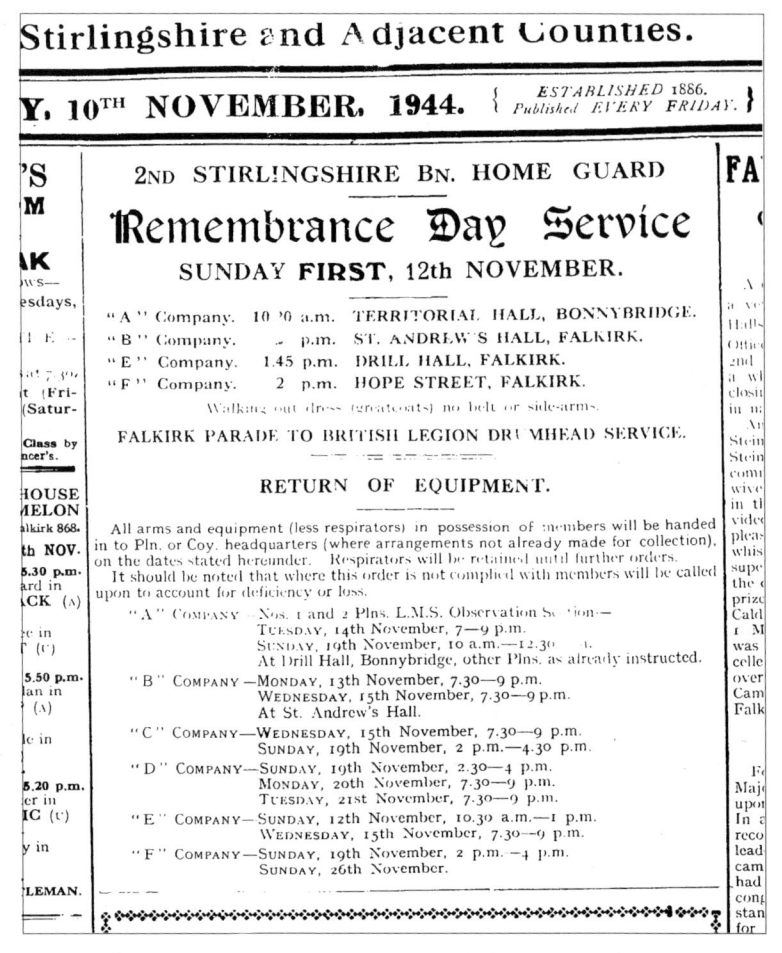

> **Stirlingshire and Adjacent Counties.**
>
> **Y. 10TH NOVEMBER, 1944.** { *ESTABLISHED* 1886. *Published* EVERY FRIDAY. }
>
> **2ND STIRLINGSHIRE BN. HOME GUARD**
>
> ### Remembrance Day Service
>
> SUNDAY FIRST, 12th NOVEMBER.
>
> "A" Company. 10.30 a.m. TERRITORIAL HALL, BONNYBRIDGE.
> "B" Company. ... p.m. ST. ANDREW'S HALL, FALKIRK.
> "E" Company. 1.45 p.m. DRILL HALL, FALKIRK.
> "F" Company. 2 p.m. HOPE STREET, FALKIRK.
>
> Walking out dress (greatcoats) no belt or side-arms.
>
> FALKIRK PARADE TO BRITISH LEGION DRUMHEAD SERVICE.
>
> **RETURN OF EQUIPMENT.**
>
> All arms and equipment (less respirators) in possession of members will be handed in to Pln. or Coy. headquarters (where arrangements not already made for collection), on the dates stated hereunder. Respirators will be retained until further orders.
> It should be noted that where this order is not complied with members will be called upon to account for deficiency or loss.
>
> "A" COMPANY—Nos. 1 and 2 Plns. L.M.S. Observation Section:—
>   TUESDAY, 14th November, 7—9 p.m.
>   SUNDAY, 19th November, 10 a.m.—12.30 p.m.
>   At Drill Hall, Bonnybridge, other Plns. as already instructed.
> "B" COMPANY—MONDAY, 13th November, 7.30—9 p.m.
>   WEDNESDAY, 15th November, 7.30—9 p.m.
>   At St. Andrew's Hall.
> "C" COMPANY—WEDNESDAY, 15th November, 7.30—9 p.m.
>   SUNDAY, 19th November, 2 p.m.—4.30 p.m.
> "D" COMPANY—SUNDAY, 19th November, 2.30—4 p.m.
>   MONDAY, 20th November, 7.30—9 p.m.
>   TUESDAY, 21st November, 7.30—9 p.m.
> "E" COMPANY—SUNDAY, 12th November, 10.30 a.m.—1 p.m.
>   WEDNESDAY, 15th November, 7.30—9 p.m.
> "F" COMPANY—SUNDAY, 19th November, 2 p.m.—4 p.m.
>   SUNDAY, 26th November.

Notice to the HG for Remembrance Day Services and the recall of equipment (Falkirk Mail 10th Nov 1944)

There was one slight problem with the disposal of the Small Arms Ammunition. Much of this had been obtained through unofficial channels and could not be 'returned'. At the end of November 1944 Robert Lyle, the Town Clerk for Falkirk, placed the following note in the Falkirk Herald:

> HOUSEHOLD REFUSE. It has been found that on several occasions recently 'LIVE' AMMUNITION, particularly cartridges, has been placed in bins containing household refuse. As household refuse is for the most part consigned to the incinerators at the Salvage Works, the inclusion of such ammunition or projectiles might lead to a very serious accident. Persons having ammunition of any description of which they desire to dispose should deposit same at any Police Office or communicate with the Police beforehand.

Stand Down

The final parades took place on Sunday 3rd December 1944. 400 men of the 2nd Stg HG Bn assembled at the Market Square in Falkirk and marched up Callendar Riggs to the High Street, then along to the West End and back along Newmarket Street to the Regal Cinema. The Bn CO, Lt-Col. Stein, took the salute from the steps of the Municipal Buildings witnessed by a large crowd. In the cinema the HG watched a film about the Allied preparations for the invasion called 'Eve of Battle' before having a singsong to the music of the Camelon Silver Band. Finally Lt-Col. Stein read congratulatory and appreciative messages from the King and from the Commander-in-Chief, Home Forces. He then added a few words of his own, quoting from the inscription on the Highland Division Memorial at Beaumont Hamel: "Friends are good on the day of battle." The proceedings terminated with the singing of 'Auld Lang Syne' and the National Anthem.

Notice for the recall of arms, Falkirk Herald 4 Nov 1944.

No. 3 Company of the 1st West Lothian HG Bn, 'Bo'ness' Own', took part in the farewell parade at Linlithgow that same day. At its peak it had numbered 280 officers and men and even at stand down this had only decreased to 240. Altogether there were 51 officers and 421 other ranks at Linlithgow that day to be inspected by the Marquess of Linlithgow. Company Order No. 108 had been issued the week before, on 27th November 1944, by Major G Dalyell of

---

BURGH OF FALKIRK CLEANSING DEPARTMENT.

WARNING

THE attention of the public is drawn to the increase in the quantities of "LIVE" AMMUNITION found in the household refuse. This is a most dangerous practice and liable to cause serious injury to the employees of the Department.

An appeal is made to all concerned to see that no such Ammunition is placed in the household refuse.

ALEXANDER G. FRENCH,
Cleansing Inspector.

Arnotdale,
Falkirk.

Advertisement from the Falkirk Herald concerning the disposal of ammunition, 24 November 1944.

the Binns. It read:

> The Home Guard are about to hold their final parade. To No. 3 Company has fallen that most difficult of all duties - training and waiting for a chance of active service. But let us all remember that the instant establishment of the Local Defence Volunteers at the most critical moment in our history, followed by the self-sacrifice and devotion to duty which transformed the Volunteers into a well-armed and efficient fighting force, was one of the major causes which deterred the German High Command from its aim of invading Great Britain. But for the Home Guard, our country, our homes and our families might have suffered the dreadful calamities which have befallen the occupied countries. Our endeavours have, under God's Providence, not only succeeded in their original purpose, but by freeing regular troops, have contributed directly to the great allied victories which are unfolding themselves day by day.
>
> Personally I am proud to have had the privilege of commanding No. 3 Company and thank all ranks most heartily for their keen and loyal co-operation in the magnificent task in which we have shared. May the best of fortune attend you all.

Notice for the final HG parade in Falkirk. (Falkirk Herald 24th November 1944)

One NCO of the Bo'ness HG, Sgt J C Smith, was chosen to represent the Battalion, along with four others, at that Sunday's farewell parade in London. He was also one of only 400 to attend a Mansion House dinner the day before. For the 2nd Stg HG Bn privates A Mckay (Polmont), R G Barr (Falkirk) and J Fulton (Falkirk) took part in the London parade. They left Falkirk on the Friday night and returned on Monday night. In London they were the guests of local HG units. A platoon from Falkirk was also present at the parade in Stirling, and in Edinburgh the local contingent of No. 1 Scottish HG Transport Column provided the motor coaches and motorcycle parade.

> Ye hae laid awa' yer rifle,
> Yer Bayonet, an' yer kit,
> 'Tho' at usin' them ye fairly had the knack;
> An' ye've dune yer bits o' trifles
> Wi' a thoroughness that stifles
> A' the cynics wad hae said ahint yer back,

> But altho' ye're no paradin'
> As ye did when Huns were raidin'
> Ye'll be ready still jist sort o' "hangin' round";
> An' if Britain e'er needs backin'
> Hame Gairds'll sune get crackin'
> An' there'll be nae courage lackin'
> In the men noo "staundin' doon"!
>
> Guidsakes d'ye mind the days
> When ye had nae airmy claes -
> Jist walkin sticks an' pikes, an' things like that?
> An' the stupid folk wid snigger
> As alang the street ye'd swagger
> In yer civvy suit an' bunnet or yer hat.
> Bit they ken mair noo about ye
> An' they're ready tae salute ye,
> Fur ye made wee Adolf's legions turn aroond;
> Noo they're back, near the Rhine,
> Among their shiverin Volkssturm swine,
> Wha'll ne'er staund up, like you
> That's staundin' doon!
>
> *J Moffat, Bonnybridge.*

In December 1944 Lt-Col Alan Stein, CO of the 2nd Stg HG Bn, was awarded the OBE for his HG service. Certificates of good service were given to the following members of his battalion: RSM J Fraser, CQMS J Rule, CSM J Russell, Sgt T Burns, Sgt W Elder, CSM W Sharpe, Sgt F Kierman, Sgt T Stannage, Cpl J Connall, Sgt J McNaughton, CQMS JA McArdle, Sgt D Nash.

For the 3rd Stg HG Bn Lt James Christine and Cpl James Fernie of 'D' Company (Grangemouth) were awarded certificates of Distinction. Sgt James Scott of Denny HG received the BEM. He lived at the Blaefaulds Filters, of which he had been in charge since their inauguration in 1936, and was one of the first to answer the call in May 1940. In the HG he specialised in signalling and transport.

No medals were awarded to the men of Bo'ness. Major HK Clarkson, OC of the Broxburn Company, was the only West Lothian officer to be honoured.

> **I**n the years when our Country
>
> was in mortal danger
>
> T. GARDNER
>
> who served from 9/7/40 to 31/12/44.
>
> gave generously of his time and
>
> powers to make himself ready
>
> for her defence by force of arms
>
> and with his life if need be.
>
> *George R.I.*
>
> ## THE HOME GUARD

Certificate of appreciation of service in the HG issued to Tom Gardner of Slamannan.

He had dutifully undertaken his HG work, despite having lost two sons in the RAF, with a third badly wounded.

Medals and certificates were mere decorations. The most lasting and tangible thing that the HG received for their devotion to duty they got from themselves – comradeship that was never lost. It was summed up in a letter by one of the officer's wives in Falkirk:

Way back at the beginning, we sewed on LDV armlets – and marvelled at the enthusiasm of the last-war veterans for this opportunity of service. As time went on, we were called upon to get together packets of food, nourishment for manoeuvres of a Sunday afternoon, then, as the movement developed, we began to forgive the postman for bringing only bundles of letters ominously marked OHMS. We knew then that the Home Guard meant business. Soon we got used to making supper at odd hours for guardsmen who came along to our house to consult and before long we knew something about other men's jobs and their families, and their experiences in 'the war', about which they never tired of reminiscing among themselves. And I remember one particularly happy Home Guard social gathering to which we went, en famille. The old-timers entertained while the younger guardsmen led the dancing. It is chiefly because of this quality of comradeship that I do not think the Home Guard will ever actually "disband", even when the official order to do so is given. (Falkirk Herald 8th December 1944)

Some officers, like Capt. William Miller of the Bo'ness HG continued in public life. He contested the East Ward seat in Bo'ness at the municipal elections as an independent in 1945. Most of the men returned to their former obscurity.

> Home Guard – Drill Hall
> No more to rustle down for chips
> While tea is drumming up;
> No more to pass on funny quips
> Or old jaw-warmers suck.
> No more to challenge who comes there
> 'Vance and be recognised;
> Can't get a shake-down anywhere,
> How often we've obliged.
> No more "good night, I'm up the stair
> And feeling rather drowsy."
> And in the morning for to swear
> The blankets are all lousy.
> No more to hear the 'phone go bur
> Or bellow "Guard, stand to,"
> Perhaps to hear a sleepy gurr,
> Or what the h—'s ado.
> No more to linger at the door
> List to receding feet,
> But while those things are now no more
> Their memories are sweet.
>
> JW.

Some of the men continued to meet in the rifle clubs that they had established, or in the halls of the British Legion. In small villages like Slamannan they were always together. On VE-Day the Slamannan HG paraded round the streets of the village with several pipers, but without weapons, which had been carefully retrieved by the government. Accompanied by the village youth they marched to Ham Row, the village boundary where they had spent many a cold night on patrol. The HG was finally disbanded in December 1945 and the men simply got on with their lives. In some ways it is that heroic quietness that echoes through the intervening years and the HG will never truly be forgotten. The Lion roared his defiance; the call came and was answered to the full — the Home Guard watched and waited.

Appendix 1

Structure of the local units

On the evening of 14th May 1940, when Anthony Eden made his broadcast calling for volunteers, plans for the force to be raised were still very much in their infancy. Just about the only practical arrangement that had been made on a local level was to ensure that the police would take the names of those coming forward. Sir Norman Orr-Ewing, the Lord-Lieutenant of the county of Stirling, agreed to push the organisation for Stirling and Clackmannan. Over the following week a register of names was compiled, which gave the Government time to formulate plans.

On 20th May instructions were received that LDVs were to be organised by the existing military areas, each to be divided into Zones formed of a number of Groups. The following day unpaid Area, Zone and Group organisers were appointed. The Group Organiser for Group 14 – Stirling and Clackmannan – was Col. D G Sandeman CIE, Khyber House, Bridge of Allan. The Group had three Areas (West, East and Centre) in Stirlingshire and one in Clackmannanshire. One company of three platoons was formed in each Area from 29th May 1940. The Rev J J S Thomson MC of Larbert Parish Church was called upon to raise a company of 160 men (equivalent to 53 per platoon) in East Stirlingshire, an area of roughly 140 square miles, from the Forth to Bonnybridge and from Bannockburn to Slamannan. He established the company HQ at Larbert (in the police station) due to its central location. His HQ staff was Capt. Logan, Capt. Powell adjutant, Major King and Capt McKinlay. The new company was called the "Stirling East Company" and the three platoon leaders appointed by Lt-Col. Thomson were Mr Graham for No. 1 Platoon, Capt. Teddie for No. 2 Platoon and Mr Farrell for No. 3. The "Stirling Centre Company" was commanded by Major G F Connal Rowan.

1940

Group: 14 (DG Sandeman)

Area/Company: Stirling East (JJS Thomson)

Platoon No. 1 (Graham) Larbert, Bonnybridge, Plean & Bannockburn
Platoon No. 2 (Teddie) Grangemouth, Polmont & Airth
Platoon No. 3 (J Farrell) Falkirk, Blackbraes & Slamannan

Area/Company: Stirling Centre (G F Connal Rowan)

Platoon No. 2 (J Paterson) Denny & hills to west

No. 2 Platoon (Denny) of the Stirling Centre Company was divided into two areas – an inner and an outer area. The inner area was to the east of the Stirling/Kilsyth Road from Auchenbowie to the road junction at Haggs and as far east as the skyline. The outer area consisted of the Carron Valley to the west end of the new reservoir, and to the water sheds on the north and south.

The clamour of the general population to help in the moment of crisis, combined with the enthusiasm and hard work of these appointed leaders, meant that they were able to raise not only the 160 volunteers proposed, but some 4,000 in just three weeks. The Government was overwhelmed by the level of response nationally and had to reconsider the force's structure. On 24th June it was announced that the volunteers would be formed into Sections of 25 men. Sections would be grouped into Platoons, Companies and Battalions on the general basis of four sections to a platoon, four platoons to a company and four companies to a battalion.

1940	section	platoon	company	battalion
no. of men	25	100	400	1600

Consequently the four existing companies of group 14 became battalions and the Denny/Kilsyth area was augmented and split into two, bringing the number up to five. From 9th July 1940 the reorganised Group took the following form:

'A' Battalion Stirling
'B' Battalion Denny Platoon (2 sections) Longcroft & Carronbridge Sections
'C' Battalion Clackmannan
'D' Battalion Kilsyth, etc
'E' Battalion East Company

Appendix 1

243

The local Territorial Army Associations agreed to help with the administration of these LDV units and they became affiliated with the local regiments. In the case of East Stirlingshire this meant the Argyll and Sutherland Highlanders (A & SH), and for West Lothian it was the Royal Scots. An odd coincidence occurred when a man who had joined the Royal Scots in 1914 with the serial number 2124, was given the same number when he joined the LDV at Bo'ness in 1940. The LNER had established numerous units of the LDV throughout its railway network in Scotland whose chief task was to protect railway property and these were incorporated into the new structure, though they retained a degree of independence and were affiliated with the Highland Light Infantry (HLI). It was the cap badges of these three regiments that were worn by the HG in the Falkirk district.

Further readjustments were made from time to time. On 3rd August 1940 part of Stirlingshire west of the line Stirling/Denny/Hollandbush (Glasgow Road excluded) became known as the Stirlingshire Sub-Sector of the Highland Area. LDV sub-units at Denny and Longcroft were transferred from 'B' Bn, West Stirling, to 'E' Bn, East Stirling, but the Carronbridge Section remained in 'B' Bn. Then, on 9th August the name of the whole force changed from LDV

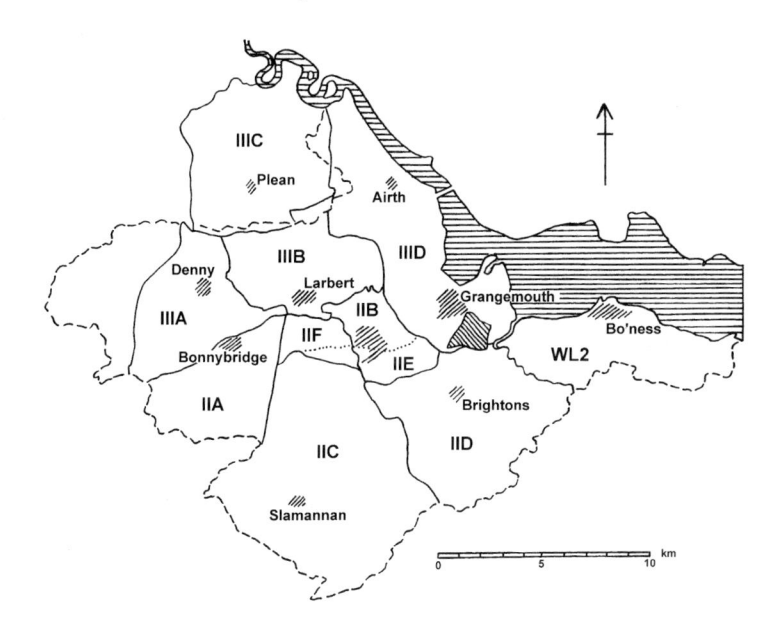

Map showing battalion and company areas. Battalions are shown as II for the 2nd Stg HG Bn, III for the 3rd Stg HG Bn and WL for the 2nd West Lothian HG Bn. The letters after the battalion names are the company designations.

to Home Guard. The East Stirlingshire Battalion LDV, already too unwieldy was split in two and renamed. The parent unit became the 3rd East Stirlingshire HG Battalion, still under the command of J J S Thomson, and the new unit was designated the 4th East Stirlingshire HG Battalion under Col. Alan Stein MC., TD. And as if that was not confusing enough, on 26th February 1941 the 'East' part of the name was dropped altogether, and the latter battalion was renamed the 2nd Stirlingshire HG Battalion. Commissioned rank had been granted to its officers on the first of that month. Alan Stein took the rank of Lt-Col. and continued in command of the 2nd Stg HG Bn from its inception until stand down – a period of four years and four months. Sadly, Lt-Col J J S Thomson died on 15 December 1943. His place was taken by Lt-Col. A R Bain MC., DL. who until that time had acted as Assistant Zone Commander.

> 3. (a) The Battalion Area is that part of Stirlingshire south of the Rivers Bonny and Carron as far east as the Ferry at Carronshore (395046), thence south of the line to Dalderse Mill Farm, Newlands farm, Beancross, to Jinkabout Mill (44016) on the River Avon. The part of Bonnybridge village lying north of the River Bonny is also included.
>
> Defence Scheme 12.1942.

Both of these battalions consisted of four companies. The 2nd Stg HG Bn was reorganised on a six company basis as a result of compulsory enrolment to the HG, which had occurred on 16th February that year. In December it was agreed that a seventh company would be temporarily formed from the others upon receipt of the warning signal "ACTION STATIONS", but only for the duration of the alert. It was specifically designed for the defence of RAF Grangemouth. This structure introduced a period of stability in which there were no more major changes and lasted until stand down in December 1944. A few months before stand down a movement had been initiated with a view to the 2nd Stg Bn taking under its aegis a troop of Light Anti-Aircraft, but this did not materialise.

Strength

Battalion	July 1940	Aug 1940	Jan 1941	Jan 1942	Jan 1943	Jan 1944	Dec 1944
2nd Stg	4,000	1843	1718	1973	1675	1418	1453
3rd Stg.	?	?	?	1475 +33	1486 +59	1444 +62	1522 +65

The numbers after the + sign are for officers.

Three days after Anthony Eden's appeal to the Nation to form the LDV, on 17th May 1940, Colonel PJ Blair OBE, DSO, TD, was appointed the Group Organiser for Edinburgh and the Lothians. He immediately held a meeting with the Lord Lieutenant of the Lothians and it was decided to appoint County Organisers. The names of the gentlemen concerned were agreed and in due course Major Lord Charles Hope took up this position for West Lothian. On the advice of the county officials he invited an ex-officer or NCO in each large centre of population to collect the names of recruits and to act as unofficial platoon commanders. In Bo'ness this role fell to W G Robson. Robson was the chairman of the Bo'ness Branch of the British Legion and he called a public meeting in Bo'ness Town Hall in the first week of June. With him was Major Anderson, and Hugh McVeigh agreed to act as the secretary, taking details of when volunteers would be available for duty.

In a remarkably short time over 3,000 men enrolled in the West Lothian Company, with 200 in Bo'ness. The sub-leaders (ie future platoon commanders) were chosen in many cases by the men themselves. George Murdoch, an agent of the Bank of Scotland, and William Broome were put forward for the two sections in Bo'ness. John Napier, manager of Thomas Ovens and Sons Ltd, acted as quartermaster sergeant. The rural nature of the county meant that overall the HG units were rather scattered.

In July/August 1940 the West Lothian Battalion was formed with eight companies. This number was increased to ten in November 1940 to help cover the ground, but even so the battalion area made it unwieldy. It was not found possible to split it in two until 1st August 1942. Lt-Col. Charles Hope remained as battalion commander of 1st West Lothian HG Bn, which included No. 3 Company at Bo'ness. Col HM Cadell OBE, who had recently retired from the Active List, was appointed to the command of the 2nd West Lothian HG Bn. The strength ceiling of the 1st West Lothian Bn was fixed at 1,520, composed of five companies. In July 1942 WG Robson resigned his commission to concentrate on his ARP work, and Major Gordon Dalyell of the Binns took over command of No. 3 Company.

On the ground the number of men in a platoon varied from about 40 to 100 depending upon the geographical area that the platoon represented. In isolated rural communities such as that at Avonbridge it was bound to be on the lower side. By the end of 1942 the rank accorded to a platoon commander was that of lieutenant. Normally his second-in-command would be a second-lieutenant, but for a small platoon it might be a sergeant. These two men found accommodation for the platoon, oversaw tactics, supplies and paperwork, as well as directing the training programme. In was the sergeant, the next

53 members of No. 1 Platoon, A Company, 3rd Stirlingshire Battalion HG. 1941. The platoon is in the field to the north of their hall in Kirkslap, Denny. The road in the background is Herbertshire Street. Front row: W Robertson CSM, James Mercer, ——, ——, Capt. Donald McIntyre, Alexander Hay, Major John Paterson, ——, ——, — Mochrie, George McArthur. 2nd row: Robert Storrie, W Wilson, ——, ——, ——, William Kerr, William Sibbald, John Scott, — Bradbury, John Duncan, Sandy Sneddon. 3rd row: Alex McDougall, James Retson, ——, ——, McCafferty, William Dyer, John Forsyth, Robert Sinclair, William Johnston, Donald Sinclair. 4th row: McCafferty, Alex Sawyers, Leslie Sinclair, ——, John McNally, ——, ——, ——, L/Cpl James Kerr, Hugh McNally, David Forsyth? Back row: ——, ——, ——, ——,

rank down, who implemented the training and put into practice the orders of the day. Any of the men, of whatever rank, who were found to be particularly good at one aspect of HG work often found themselves training the rest of the platoon in that subject, be it Morse code, map reading or bayonet practice. More and more specialities were introduced as the HG became better trained, but at the very minimum each platoon had someone in charge of signals and a clerk, usually with the rank of corporal. Those heading machine gun or sub-artillery sections became lance-corporals.

The platoons were bunched together to form companies in discrete topographical areas, such as the Slamannan Plateau or the Polmont Braes. Consequently the number of platoons in a company often deviated from the norm of four. 'C' Coy of the 2nd Stg HG Bn covered the Slamannan Plateau and possessed four platoons, whereas 'B' Coy represented the more densely built up area in the northern part of the town of Falkirk and had six platoons.

Appendix 1   247

It was essential for neighbouring platoons to co-operate so that they could coordinate their activities, and so exercises tended to be organised at company level. Priorities in the allocation of equipment and the siting of permanent road blocks, strong points, observation posts and so on, were also overseen by the company command. The senior officer of the company held the rank of major and his second-in-command that of captain, with the company sergeant major (CSM) to implement orders. To oversee the distribution of equipment and training the company HQ would also have a quartermaster, clerk, drill instructor and transport officer.

Officers of A Company, 3rd Stg HG Bn (Denny), 1942 in the field to the north of their hall in Kirkslap, Denny. The road in the background is Herbertshire Street. Those wearing Tam O' Shanters are the company commander, his second-in-command and senior company officers, along with the four platoon commanders. At least two of the men wearing field service caps can be seen to sport sergeant's stripes.

Bn	Bn HQ	Coy	Coy HQ
2nd Stg	Falkirk Drill Hall	A	Bonnybridge Drill Hall, Bridge St
		B	St Andrew's Church Hall, Falkirk
		C	Band Hall, Shieldhill?
		D	Brightons Church Hall, Main St
		E	Falkirk Power Station, High Station Rd
		F	Gothic Ironworks, Camelon
3rd Stg	Stenhousemuir Police Station then Larbert Parish Church Hall	A	Denny Drill Hall, Kirkslap
		B	Burgh Stables, Stenhousemuir
		C	Plean
		D	Grangemouth Drill Hall
1st WL	—	3	Old Burgh Court Room then Free Gardeners' Hall, Bo'ness

In October 1941 a decision was made to form an extra platoon in each company to consist of the specialists such as weapons officers, signallers, the CSM, and some of the fitter young men. These men were to be called out first in the event of a suspected alert, with the remainder of the company to follow if a situation developed. Banded together these platoons formed a mobile unit and were known as HQ platoons, or rather confusingly as HQ Company.

Further specialists occupied the battalion HQ. These included the Medical Officer (MO), Assistant Medical Officer, Permanent Staff Instructor (PSI) Quartermaster (QM), Signals Officer, Liaison Officer, Intelligence Officer, Gas Officer, Armourer/Ammunition Officer, Transport Officer, Adjutant, typist, Engineer and Guide. To protect the battalion HQ a number of men were first seconded from the companies and later transferred, so that the battalion HQ staff essentially became yet another platoon. At Larbert these men were augmented by the instrumentalists of the battalion pipe band. To look after them was an officer with the rank of Lt-Col. and his second-in-command with the rank of major. The officers at the Larbert HQ at the time of stand down in December 1944 are shown in the following table:

Appendix 1   249

Post	2nd Stg HG HQ Coy	3rd Stg HG HQ Coy
Commanding Officer	Lt-Col A Stein	Lt-Col AR Bain (JJS Thomson)
Second-in-command	Major Ross T Haddow	Major AW Wilson (RB Peddie, D Tough)
Medical Officer	Major DC McLachlan	Major H MacKenzie King
Assistant MO	Capt. J Fleming	
Commander HQ Coy		Major FG Griffiths (RB Peddie, D Tough)
Intelligence Officer	Lt J Hill (RT Haddow)	Capt D McKinlay
Ammo Officer	Lt C Palmer	Lt DB Campbell
Signals Officer	Lt R Harvey	Lt RM Peddie
Transport Officer	Lt W Mathieson	Lt JD Steven (WM Shanks)
Traffic Officer		Lt JD Steven (W Aitken)
Gas Officer	Lt RH Clowes	Lt AG Rees (C Shaw)
Liaison Officer	Lt A White	Lt W Shaw (W McBryde, DB Campbell)
Traffic Control/Guide	Lt RB Morrison	Lt W Aitken (GCH Boyd)
Engineer Officer	JK Thomson (JS Brown)	Lt J McDonald (D McIntyre, J Notman)
Platoon Commander		Lt W Reid
Platoon Officer		2nd Lt TIC Bevan
Adjutant	Capt A MacDonald	Capt BS Powell (H S Sanderson, D Tough)
Records		Sgt R Bailey (E Filby, R Turpie, VG Elmslie)
Armourer		Sgt R Bailey
		CSM Roberts
RSM	James Fraser	A Kemp (James Dowie)
RQSM		Sgt RS Jackson (D McLaren)
Admin Off (Adjutant Q)	Capt W Carmichael	Capt JM Logan (WW Kay)
Orderly Clerk		Sgt JW MacAra
Machine gun Officer		Capt W McBryde (AE Skipsey)
PSI	A/C S/M H Robbins	

The battalion HQ staff numbers built up slowly as the HG gathered experience. When, in May 1940, J J S Thomson established the East Stirling Company (later made into a battalion) HQ at Larbert he only had a small side room and two police cells in Stenhousemuir Police Station for the office, armoury and HQ. The office staff to establish the battalion were David Tough, an experienced soldier of the First World War, and WW Kay, an ex Scots Guardsman and retired colonial civil servant. Tough took on duties equivalent to those of an adjutant, while Kay assumed the role of Executive Officer on the 'Q' side. This skeleton staff, with the assistance of Police Superintendent Turpie, defined the area of the companies. WW Kay was later confirmed as the Administrative Officer and became the battalion's first paid member of staff. He was, however, forced to resign due to bad health, and in October 1940 JM Logan was appointed in his place. Before long larger accommodation was needed. A regular army unit billeted in Larbert offered part of Larbert Old Parish Church Hall and this was eagerly taken up. When that unit subsequently moved out, the HG was able to take over the whole building, enabling it to increase the battalion HQ staff.

When the East Stirlingshire Bn was divided into two in August 1940 the HQ at Larbert remained in use for the 3rd Stg HG Bn. The 2nd Stg HG Bn at Falkirk took over the Falkirk Drill Hall and Capt. W Carmichael became its administrative assistant. Along with the typist he was the only paid member of its staff. In March 1941 Sgt. H Robbins was appointed as Permanent Staff Instructor of this battalion and remained until stand down. A second PSI was not forthcoming until January 1943, and then in April 1943 Capt. A Macdonald was added as a whole-time adjutant.

The HG was in existence for four and a half years and so it is not surprising, given the constitution of the manpower, that the personnel changed on several occasions. If we take a closer look at the officers of the 3rd Stg HG Bn for example: Major R B Peddie resigned from second-in-command at the end of December 1942 owing to pressure of business and became the Liaison Officer for 'D' Coy with the rank of lieutenant. Major David Tough, who was the adjutant, was promoted to second-in-command in his place, leaving his position vacant. A full-time adjutant from the regular army was subsequently appointed in the person of Capt. H S Sanderson of the KOSB. He took up duty in March 1943 and was followed by Capt. B S Powell SWB in July 1944. In October 1943 Major Tough was compelled to resign on medical advice and Major Wilson, Officer Commanding 'B' Coy was promoted. Lt-Col. J J S Thomson died on 15th December and his post was taken by A R Bain.

Appendix 1

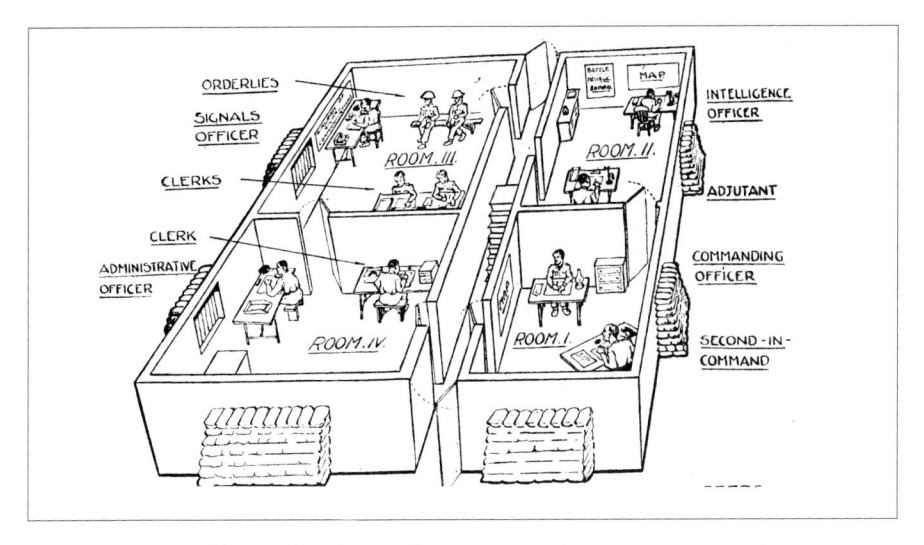

General layout of battalion HQ (from Home Guard Instruction, No. 51, 1943).

Many of the original officers had their own businesses to run and as the war progressed they had to spend longer looking after them. If their business was involved in war work they had to cope with overall increased work loads. In Bo'ness Lt. Napier Thomson was the managing director of Thomson & Balfour making Nissen huts, stretchers, boxes and even motor torpedo boats. This important work precluded his attention to the HG duties and he resigned to concentrate on it, though he later ran a Sea Cadet unit in Bo'ness. On the other hand, if their business was not directly involved in war work then their employees would be called up to serve in the armed forces. With attenuated staffs at work the HG officers were forced to restrict their HG activities to take up the slack themselves. This was the case for another platoon commander at Bo'ness, Lt. William Broome, and with his commanding officer Capt. G Murdoch. The hard working sergeants from the platoons were promoted to take their places – Sgt-Major J Smith and Sgt. R McPherson.

As well as losing personnel at the upper age limit due to enforced retirement at 65 years or to ill health, the HG had to surrender those at the lower end to the armed forces. This meant not only the teenagers who had turned military age, but also men who due to changes in the regulations were no longer exempt or who chose to join up. Thus the 3rd Stg HG Bn lost 410 men to the services, each company taking its share of the burden as follows:

A – 96   B – 153   C – 52   D – 103   RNAD (Throsk) – 6

Similarly No. 3 Coy (Bo'ness) of the 1st WL HG Bn discharged 91 men to the forces. The equivalent number for the 2nd Stg HG Bn was a little over 1,000, many of whom got rapid promotion as a result of their experience with the HG.

At 16 years of age William Sharp had joined the Falkirk Power Station LDV upon its formation. After two and a half years in the HG he went to Stirling for his service medical and was able to choose to join the Navy. His father had won the DSM at the Battle of Jutland in the First World War and he intended to maintain the family link with the senior service. This was just after the Navy had lost the Prince of Wales, Repulse and Hood, so they were happy to accept him. William's father was as pleased as Punch, though his mother was apprehensive, as she knew the trouble that she had getting letters in the earlier war. William went back to the Burgh Stables and handed in his Home Guard uniform. The officers there, including Major Farrell, asked him which regiment of the army he was to join and were horrified when he told them that he was going to the Navy. They felt that he had let the platoon down. They had intended to recommend that he be made straight into a sergeant. William, however, knew that the chances were high that he would have been put into the Argyll & Sutherland Highlanders, which made up part of the 51st Highland Division, and were always in the worst of the action. He never regretted his choice. The Home Guard had provided great comradeship. It was here that William learnt to share life with his fellow men. He was not to see his home for another two and a half years. Major White of Bonnybridge did write a strong letter of recommendation for one of his men by the name of Young. It was 1943 and the HG commander looked forward to seeing another of his able men join the A & SH as an officer. To his horror he served with the Scots Guards instead!

The result of all this coming and going was that, although the average strength of the 2nd Stg HG Bn over the years was 1680 men, a total of 4,407 had actually served in it – a remarkable record!

Appendix 2

HOME GUARD PLATOONS

The following is a list of guardsmen who have come to my notice as serving in the local HG units. They are listed by platoon within each company and then within each battalion. It is by no means an exhaustive list and we would always welcome further additions. Officers of each unit are given first according to rank, with the rank and file then listed in alphabetical order. (1) refers to the commanding officer and (2) to the second in command. Each platoon was designated a number within the battalion and those used here are from the period 1942-1944. For day to day purposes they were simply known from the area in which they operated and this is given in ordinary brackets followed by the location of the building from which they operated in square brackets (rather grandly called their HQ).

II Stirlingshire HG Battalion

HQ Rosehall House/Drill Hall, Falkirk

1. Col. Alan Stein
2. Major Ross T Haddow.

Battalion HQ Company (Falkirk)

Major DC McLachlan (MO), Sgt Major H Robbins (PSI), HC Davey, Capt J Fleming (Assistant MO), Capt A McDonald (Adj 4.1943-sd), Capt W Carmichael (Admin Ass QM), Lt JS Brown (Engineer), Lt R Harvey (signals), Lt J Hill (intelligence), Lt W Mathieson (transport), Lt RB Morrison (guide), Lt C Palmer (ammunition), Lt JK Thomson (engineer), Lt A White (liaison), R H Clowes (gas), RSM Watson, Lt Haig, Lt Stephen, Sgt Major CSM John Russell, Lt Thomas Aitken (Liaison), Lt A Dennison, RSM James Fraser, Sgt G Robertson, Sgt Jack Livingstone?

*Officers of "A" Company, 2nd Stirlingshire Battalion HG.
Presumably the six platoon commanders, with swagger sticks. Lt Alex McLaren on the left.*

'A' Company
(Bonnybridge)

Major James White, Capt Joseph F Curran

HQ Platoon (Bonnybridge)
McArdle (quartermaster)

No. 1 (Bonnybridge) Platoon [Nissen Hut, Bonnybridge Mill]
1. Lt JF Curran then Lt James Cairns
Sgt Mcnaught, Sgt Rankine,
James Brown, William Brown

No. 2 (Bonnybridge) Platoon [Guide Hall]
1. Lt Robert H Thomson
Sgt Thomas Burns, Sgt Ferguson, Cpl Milne
William Candish, J Irvine, Archibald Lees, W B Macpherson, Albert Maxwell, James Rankine, D Thomson

Appendix 2   255

No. 3 (Smith & Wellstood & Mitchell, Russel & Co, Works Section) Platoon [Drill Hall]
1. Lt Alex McLaren

Sgt Robert Bellingham, Sgt R Jordon, Sgt David Nimmo, Cpl A Bain, Cpl Alfred Holmes (No. 1 section), Cpl James Torrence

Thomas Aitken, Robert Blair, George Brown (oldest member), William Esplin, George Gibson, Jack Irvine, R McIntyre, J Morris, Victor Pacitti, Robert Sneddon, Tom Turnbull, William Turner

Bonnybridge Power Station Section
Sgt D Anderson, Sgt JD Thomson

Fallin, Hamilton, Fergus Liddle, McLeod, Milne, R Roy, Trafford,

No. 4 (Milnquarter Works) Platoon [St Helen's Church Hall]
1. Lt T Fraser then Lt Andrew Pettigrew

Sgt D Mathieson, Sgt A Rankine, Cpl Sutherland, L/Cpl J Logan, L/Cpl J Napier

Bill Ferguson, James Gray, Godson, Laird, McPherson, James Rankine

No. 5 (High Bonnybridge) Platoon [Railway Hall, Greenhill]
1. Lt R Bell then Lt J MacDonald Muir

Sgt William Godson, Sgt A Rankine, Cpl EwenMcPolland

Abel, H Hutchean, R Hutcheon, Kerr? McAllister, J McDonald, A Peat, D Totten

No. 6 (Castlecary Works) Platoon [Brickworks]
1. 2nd Lt William McEwan

Sgt Stewart Cunningham, Sgt Moffat, Cpl Alex Birse, L/Cpl Robert Stewart, L/Cpl Alex Miller

T Dalrymple, George Buchanan, Robert Lyons, James McAuley, A McEwan, James O'Neill, William Proffit, George Scobbie, Alfred Sludden, Thomas Valentine, Thomas West

Unknown Platoon (A Company)
Cpl GF Browning, Cpl J Finlay, Cpl Wilkins, Sgt G McLay, Sgt McNeilage, Cpl W Aitken, Cpl Bayne, Cpl J Dyet, Cpl James Milne, Cpl A Tottins, L/Cpl Birse, L/Cpl J Provan, L/Cpl Rankin, L/Cpl J Scott,

Willie Baron, Colquhoun, A Finlay, Adam Irons, T McBride, J Millan, G Smedley, JD Thomson

'B' Company
(Falkirk North)

Major Robert McNair, Capt William Rattray

HQ Platoon (Falkirk North)
CSM Robert McNair, CQMS John Rule, Sgt G Gladstone, Sgt William Gladstone, S/Sgt John Heath, Cpl J Carmichael, Cpl H Ronald, Cpl AR Paterson, L/Cpl James Forgie

James Clerk, William Henderson, William Holmes, John McGregor, Alex McIntosh, Charles McLean, R McMorland, A Mason, G Muir, William Scott, William Smith, James Stirling, R Stobbie, T Swan, Andrew Telfer, Robert Wilson, William Wilson.

No. 7 Platoon
1. Lt James Green

Sgt James McLeod, Cpl R Colquhoun, Cpl Peter McFarlane, Cpl Robert Monfries, Cpl J Paterson, Cpl Philip Thomson, Cpl Robert Wilson, L/Cpl J McFarlane, L/Cpl Harry Rule

William Adamson, Bartholomew, A Bell, Robert Bell, A Brown, Alexander Bryson, R Buchanan, D Calder, James Cheyne, Peter Cumming, H Deans, Hugh Ferry, J Gillespie, R Hastings, Frances Howden, Arthur Jones, Kenneth Lusted, Douglas McDonald, H McFarlane, Thomas McGregor, T McIntosh, William McLaren, C McLuckie, William McNeill, J Main, Robert Park, C Ramsay, J Richardson, John Riggs, William Roberts, A Ross, Pte William Scobbie, John Sinclair, AG Smith, Thomas Somerville, John Stevens, Samuel Stobbie, John Strathie, WF Sutton, David Todd, D Wardrope, T Watson

No. 8 Platoon [Falkirk Ironworks]
1. Lt William Rattray then Lt RA Morrison (15.9.43) then Lt RF Clark

Sgt Ian Cameron, Sgt John Fotheringham, Cpl James Benwell, Cpl John Connell, Cpl Robert Muir, Cpl J Parker, L/Cpl William Black, L/Cpl James Keith, L/Cpl P McNaughton, L/Cpl Peter Taylor

David Austin, Thomas Bartholomew, Alexander Beattie, R Bell, James Campbell, RF Clarke, J Conny, D Crawford, D Cruickshanks, George Darling, A Deans, William Deans, P Dick, J Fitzpatrick, J Graham, G Hill, Harry Laird, Henry Laird, M Leishman, Alpin McGregor, M McKay, R McLean, James McVey, Morris Meikle, Thomas Moffat, W Montgomery, James Morrison, Richard Parker, Peter Ramsay, Robert Ross, D Service, C Taylor, T Thomson, R Walker, David Veitch, John Walker, John Wilson, Albert Wright, H Young

Appendix 2   257

No. 9 Platoon
1. Lt Robert S Turnbull then Lt John M Millar

Sgt George Niven, Sgt C McKinnon, Sgt CS Taylor, Cpl HD Anderson, Cpl Thomas Erskine, Cpl John McKenzie, Cpl A Martin, L/Cpl Alex Fleming, L/Cpl H Forster, L/Cpl J Philp, L/Cpl James Ronald, L/Cpl John Sim

Tom Bremner, Alexander Brown, Robert Cockburn, WJ Coull, S Cowan, John Cummings, Alexander Cunningham, R Dunlop, AM Grant, James Hall, D Jenkins, E Kelly, William Kirkwood, J Leishman, AC McKenzie, WC McMahon, Fred Marchi, George Marshall, James Morrison, Peter Morrison, George Morton, James Muirhead, A Murchison, Andrew McNair, J Philp, C Sands, James Weir, G Wilson.

No. 10 (Randyford) Platoon
1. Sgt JD Hossack

Sgt A Nicol, Cpl D Cox, Cpl James McNeill, Cpl John Porteous (signals), Cpl Albert Snow, Cpl David Yuill, L/Cpl Andrew Nisbet

T Barclay, RG Barr, Alexander Brown, John Buchanan, John Crozier, G Donaldson, J Drummond, A Duncan, Thomas Fleming, A Gibson, G Jamieson, AM Kelly, W Lawrie, John Leishman, Thomas McCabe, W McCabe, RJ McIlroy, T McLeay, Alexander Meikle, Alex Morrison, C Nisbet, William Paterson, R Perrie, A Renton, James Spinks, John Stevens, FG Taylor, J Wighton, William Wilson

No. 11 (Grahamston) Platoon [Falkirk Ironworks]
1. Lt Robert Wilson then Lt Harry Wilson

Sgt Thomas Lindsay [d 11.44], Cpl Peter Gibson, Cpl John Laidlaw, Cpl William Potts, Cpl Duncan Rigg, Cpl William Smart, L/Cpl Robert Lindsay, L/Cpl James Middleton, L/Cpl Hugh Nicol, L/Cpl Andrew Rae, L/Cpl Norman Thomson, L/Cpl Harry Young

W Bennett, W Binning, William Bishop, F Bowie, Thomas Brown, Thomas Brown, Daniel Campbell, Alexander Christie, Michael Cleary, Joseph Cowan, James Dawson, Archibald Fairfowl, James Fish, James Frame, James Gardner, John Gibson, Ian Godson, T Grierson, James Handry, James Isdale, J Kane, John Laing, P Lamont, William Leishman, James Lindsay, Thomas Lindsay jnr, Alex Logan, Alexander Marshall, John McCulloch, C McFadden, David McGoff, John McIntosh, Douglas McIntosh, William McLachlan, Alexander McNiven, Peter Monro, James Napier, John Penman, William Reap, Harry Rodgers, Marcus Rodgers, Robert Sinclair, George Todd, William Walker, James Walls, George Webster

No. 12 Platoon [Falkirk Ironworks]
1. Lt Alex Lawson

Sgt Richard Sharpe, Int. Sgt John Steel, Cpl James Bell, Cpl Peter Bennie, Cpl William Hobson, Cpl Robert Muray, Cpl William McDonald, L/Cpl signals A Abercrombie, L/Cpl A McCulloch, L/Cpl Robert Mauchline, L/Cpl William Robb, L/Cpl Alex Waugh

William Balloch, William Campbell, William Cloughley, J Dinsmore, James Ferguson, John Ferguson, Robert Ferguson, J Finnie, William Fraser, William Gardner, J Graham, Alex Huskie, James Isdale, Timothy Lenathen, William Maltman, R McGregor, John McIlroy, JB Paterson, Thomas Robertson, Andrew Scott, RL Smith, William Sutherland, James Taylor, Robert Turpie, Charles Williamson

Millar Section [J M Millar Garage, Callendar Rd]
Sgt Robert Millar, Cpl James Mochrie, L/Cpl John Meikle

E Bain, Robert Buchanan, John Cameron, Hugh Christison, Peter Gibson, Alexander Gow, A Hunter, John McKenzie, David McPherson, A Morrison, John Ogilvie, John Strang, A Thomson, Wilfred Young, C Wilson.

Unknown Platoon (B Company)
Sgt G Robertson, J Stirling

Slamannan Home Guard behind the Miners' Welfare Hall. Front row: Tom Beattie, David Nimmo (petrol Station), Willie Miller, Will Fyfe (janitor - left of dog), ———, Willie Dunlop, Campbell, Robert Hay, Pete Macmillan or Stevenson, Alex Emery Middle row; Willie Fullar, ———, Sam McLintoll, Harry Kerr, —McCreary (farmer), Tam Menzies, Bill Menzies, Willie Abercrombie, Rudy Kerr, Johnny Miller. Back row: Duncan Wright, Danny Drysdale, Tom McRobbie, ———, Wilfred Berwick, James Stevenson, Andrew Tulloch, Robert McAlpine, Alex McNiven

Appendix 2

'C' Company
(Slamannan, Avonbridge, Blackbraes, Shieldhill)
1. Major John Farrell 2. Capt JS Brown

HQ Platoon (Braes)
Captain H Armstrong, Lt JM Millar, CSM John Russell, Sgt Leslie

No. 13 (Slamannan) Platoon [Welfare Hall]
1. Lt George T Ewen then Lt N McLean, Lt Tam Menzies [to 1.10.1942] then Lt GF Watt then Lt Robert G Kerr. 2. Thomas Menzies then R Kerr

Sgt David Nimmo, Sgt James Storrar, Sgt (Cpl) Wilfred Berwick, Cpl J Jamieson, Cpl William Millar, L/Cpl James Meek

Willie Abercrombie, Ian Arthur, Tom Beattie, Camel, A Chalmers, John Chalmers, G Connell, T Connell, Andrew Drysdale, G Drysdale, Willie Dunlop, Sandy Emery, Will Fife, Charles Finlay, Willie Fullar, William Fyfe, Alex Gardiner, J Gardner, Thomas Gardner, Robert Hay, Daniel Kerr, Harold Kerr, H Lambie, H Leggat, J Lynn, Robert McAlpine, McCreary, Tom McCrobie, Sam McLintock, Alex McNiven, Hector Maxwell, William Menzies, Alex Millar, John Miller, William Miller, John Murphy, David Nimmo, W Orr, A Penman, Barney Schoneville, A Scott, C Simpson, D Simpson, C Sneddon, Stevenson, Thomas Tripney, Andrew Tulloch, Thomas Whyte, Charles Whyte, David West, T Wilson, Willie Wright.

No. 14 (Avonbridge) Platoon [Wool Mill Hall]
1. AE Davies then Lt David Clark, Lt A Gibson

Cpl J Ferrier, L/Cpl Davies, L/Cpl J Easton,

No. 15 Blackbraes & California Platoon
[California School, Blackbraes Miner's Welfare Hall]
1. Lt J Boyd.

2. Sgt Macmillan, Sgt John Leadbetter, Sgt Macmillan, Sgt Alex Pryde, Cpl John Lockhart, Cpl T Smith, Cpl J White, L/Cpl G Brown, L/Cpl D Carson

Samuel Adam, David Anderson, Robert Anderson, George Drysdale, Joe Fergusson, Jim Heeps, John Heeps, Robert Heeps, William Heeps, Alex Liddle, Daniel Liddle, John Liddle, J M'Cowan, Tom McIntyre, John Munnoch, Simon Marshall, A Myles, Sandy Pryde, Sandy Ross, Bill Smith, Watson Smith, William Strang, George Thomson, William Walker, John White, William White, David Williamson

No. 16 Shieldhill Platoon [Miners' Welfare Hall]
1. Lt James FR McCowan then Lt APM McLuckie
2. Allanwood Neilson, Pn Sgt J Jamieson

Sgt James Leslie, Sgt Thomas Stannage, Sgt C Penman, Sgt (Cpl) Dan Penman, L/Cpl J Jamieson, L/Cpl Kyle, L/Cpl A Penman, Piper K Penman

John Alalrdyce, A Beattie, J Beattie, J Bennie, G Brown, Alex Bryce, Robert Cockburn, J Colson, English, J Gibb, R Gray, James Grierson, W Hay, James Higgins, Andrew Jamieson, John Jamieson, Edward Kellow, J Lindsay, C McLean, McLung, John Miller, C. Penman, Robert Penman, George Sneddon, J Spence, W Spence, Tom Tripney, H Webster

Unknown Platoon (C Company)
Sgt James Leslie,

'D' Company
(Polmont, Laurieston, Redding, Westquarter, Brightons, Maddiston & Whitecross)

1. Major AW Steven then Major A Sharp. 2. Capt A Ernest Thomson

HQ Platoon (Polmont)
Lt Alexander, Lt William Allison, Lt Grant, Lt Haig
Cpl Crosbie, Sgt Harper Orr. CSM Walter Sharp

No. 17 (Laurieston) Platoon [Laurieston School]
1. Lt M Douglas Haston

Sgt Adam G Keir,

Alison, Alistair Barclay, E Cruickshanks, Sandy Cunningham, Charlie Dunn, George Erskine, Ian Fleming, Charlie Finlay, Ian Grant, Charlie Hartley, Jimmy Hunter, John Lapsley, Peter or Alfie Liddle, McBride, Donald McGregor, Neil McLean, T McLeod, Douglas, Wilson? Jackie Morrison, Watt Morrison, Robert Stirling, Thomson Porteous, Archie Provan, Jim Rankine, Robertson, Jim Robinson, Sharpe, Alex Tidy, Webster, John West.

No. 18 (Redding & Westquarter) Platoon
1. Lt R McCowan

[*Redding Colliery Section* Sgt John Easton, Robert McNab, Joe McLeish]

Appendix 2   261

No. 19 (Brightons) Platoon
[Girl Guide hut in Whitesideloan; Brightons Parish Church Hall]
1. Lt John W Monfries 2. Sharp

Cpl Benson

Allison, Hugh Baird, John Bennie, Bremner.

No. 20 (Maddiston) Platoon
1. Lt RMcW Brown, 2. 2nd Lt W Stannard

Sgt David Donald, Sgt James D Heeps, Sgt Kerr, Cpl D Gardiner, Cpl R Jack, Cpl Jack Robertson, L/Cpl J Dougall

James Allardyce, George Wallace

No. 21 (Whitecross) Platoon [Manuel Brickworks]
1. James Rogers

James Blair, G Bryson, Danny Buchanan, Jock McCauley, William Milne, Jack Smith

(Polmont LNER) Platoon
[Railway carriage west of station]
1. Lt A Sharpe then Lt T Cockburn then Lt N McGilchrist then Lt J K Neill

Sgt Brown, Sgt William McGilchrist, Sgt J Nicholson, Sgt J Bryce, Sgt L Robertson, Sgt J S Gilray, Cpl T Anderson, Cpl Matthew Hoggan, Cpl A Robertson, Cpl J Sinclair

Henry Alexander, William Bennie. W Benvue, James Cockburn, William Dick, William Farquharson, Peter Henderson, Charles John, W Kelly [f-2.43] , Edward Malloy, Martin Preston, Andrew Robertson, Andrew Thomson

Charles John of the Polmont LNER HG

Unknown Platoon (D Company)
Lt D MacAlpine, Sgt J Grant,

G Cook, James Forrester, Greenhorn, E Low, A McKay, R Mackay, McNee, Sinclair, A Somerville, J White

'E' Company
(Falkirk South)

1. Major H Armstrong 2. Capt RS Turnbull

HQ Platoon (Falkirk South)

(Falkirk Post Office) Platoon
2. 2nd Lt J McKenzie

CSM A Macrae, Sgt AD Brown, Sgt Jack Livingston, Cpl W Smith, L/Cpl AK Kerr, L/Cpl David S McIntosh., L/Cpl W McKintosh.

Alexander Arthur, A C Couser, W Burns, W Downie, Wm Heggie, Andrew K Kerr, K Mackenzie, DA McPherson, Alexander MacRae, DE Marshall, Norrie Reid (?), Alex Ritchie, Norman Spowart, EC Sutherland, JA Winchester

(Falkirk LNER) Platoon [High Station]
JC Alexander, IG Gentles, Melville Grindlay, TC Hawkes, D Low, E Milroy, G Reid, J Scott, Spence,

[Dollar Park]
Lt Allanwood Neilson then Lt E Kimber

No. 28 Platoon [Drill Hall]
Jeffrey D Morris

Unknown Platoon (E Company)
Lt H Armstrong, Lt William Boyd, Lt Alexander Brown, Lt Clarkston, Lt JAF Dean, 2nd Lt J McKenzie

Sgt W Elder, Sgt Klernan, Sgt McLay, Sgt Nash, Sgt Ure, Cpl Burgoyne, L/Cpl Robert Boyd

Adamson, RG Barr, Crearer, Joe Duncan, J Fulton, Henderson, Howie, Lister, W McWhinnie, Madden, Robert Nelson, Penman, J Reid, J Sim, R Struthers.

Appendix 2

'F' Company
(Camelon)

1. Major HC Davie 2. Capt GW Wortley

HQ Platoon (Camelon)
CSM J Russell

No. 30 (R & A Main) Platoon [Gothic Foundry]
1. Lt GW Wortley then Lt HN Riddell then Lt David Cattanach

Sgt Morrison, Cpl Peter Cole, Cpl J Milne

James Allan, Andrew Auchterlonie, Campbell, David Cheape, John Cochrane, Duncan Cram, Alex Denison, Michael Dunn, Alex Harrison, Harrower, Hill, Robert Laidlaw, Leslie Hill, Jack, James Jardine, Walter Logan, McIntyre, Alex Maxwell, William Milton, Mungal, Larry O'Neil, John Orman, Orr, Powell, Ronald Walton, Jack Winchole, John Winchole, Harold Sales, Tom Spence, Thomson

No. 31 (Rosebank Distillery) Platoon [Rosebank Distillery]
Robert Laidlaw, James Strang

No. 32 (Forth & Clyde & Sunnyside Iron Co) Platoon [Foundry]
1. Lt AC Johnstone 2. 2nd Archibald Nicol

Sgt Thomas Arthur, Sgt W Craig, Sgt James Higgins, Cpl Mitchell, Cpl Smith, L/Cpl Harry Jones

A Annand, W Deans, A Duncan, F Hoggan, G Johnstone, Alex McLean, A Mitchell, D Simpson

No. 33 Platoon (Camelon) [Templer's Hall, Hedges]
1. Lt E J Boston

Sgt Donaldson, Sgt James Higgins, Cpl Laidlaw, Cpl Finlay, Cpl Fleming, Cpl Jones, Cpl Mitchell, L/Cpl Hamilton, L/Cpl Harry Jones

Cuthill, W Deans, A McFarlane, Alex McLean? A Watson

No. 34 (Scottish Tar Works) Platoon [Wallside Stables]
1. Lt HC Davie then ?

Andrew, Cyril Ashcroft

2nd Stg Bn unknown company or platoon
Lt H Barlow, Lt H Chalmers, Lt J Grierson, Lt N McLean, Lt J Pryde, Lt A Young.
Brown, KA Cossar, William Duncan, John Harley, Laurie, Larry O'Neil, James Strang

Officers of A Company, 3rd Stg HG Bn (Denny), 1942 in the field to the north of their hall in Kirkslap, Denny. The road in the background is Herbertshire Street. Those wearing Tam O' Shanters are the company commander, his second-in-command and senior company officers, along with the four platoon commanders. At least two of the men wearing field service caps can be seen to sport sergeant's stripes. Back row: ——, ——, ——, ——, ——, Poodle, ——, ——, Geordie McArthur Front row: Poodle, ——, ——, Paterson, ——, ——, ——, Jimmy Smith, ——, ——

Appendix 2

III Stirlingshire HG Battalion
HQ Stenhousemuir Burgh Stables.

1. Lt Col J J S Thomson {d. 15.12.43} then Lt Col AR Bain.
2. Major R Bruce Peddie {1941-31.12.42} then Major David Tough [11.10.43] then Major AW Wilson.

Battalion HQ Company (Larbert)

Major Mckenzie King (medical), Capt John Logan (adjutant), Capt W McBryde (liaison), Capt D McKinlay (intelligence),Capt D McIntyre (engineer), Capt HS Sanderson (adjutant), Capt BS Powell (adjutant), Lt W Aitken (guide), Lt GCH Boyd (guide), Lt DB Campbell (Ammunition), Lt J McDonald (engineer), Lt D McIntyre (engineer), Lt J Notman (engineer), Lt RM Peddie (signals), Lt AG Rees (gas), Lt WM Shanks (transport), Lt C Shaw (gas), Lt WMA Shaw (liaison), Lt AE Skipsey (training), Lt JD Steven (transport), Sgt J B Gilchrist, CSM JA Green (PSI), CSM T Cousins (PSI), Major David Tough, RSM James Dowie, Allan Rankine (pipe-major).

'A' Company (Denny/ Longcroft)

1. Major John Paterson.
2 Capt Walter McBryde (1.1.42) then Capt Donald M McIntyre.

HQ Platoon (Denny)
W M Shanks (transport), Lt J Thomson (deputy transport), G McArthur (quartermaster), TB Mochrie (clerk), A Hay (clerk), Sgt A Bar (drill inst), CSM William Roberts

No. 1 (Denny) Platoon [Drill Hall, Kirkslap]
1. Lt Donald McIntyre then Lt Alex Hay then 2/Lt R Busby.
2. Alex Hay then 2/Lt G Stanners then 2/Lt F O'Neill.

Sgt George Drummond, Sgt James Scott, Sgt James Baxter, Andrew Robertson, Cpl Nisbet, Cpl Smith, Cpl R Storie (clerk), Cpl Wilson, L/Cpl Kerr.

James Barr, Bateman, Bradbury, R Busby, Andy Comrie, Joe Duncan, William Dyer, David Forsyth, John Forsyth, W Gardiner, John Hannah, Kit Hannah, William Johnston, James Kerr, William Kerr, George McArthur, McCafferty, Alex McDougall, J McEwan, Hugh McNally, John McNally, Mochrie, Paterson, Poodle, Poodle, James Retson, H Robertson, Leslie Saucer, William Sibbald, Donald Sinclair, James Smith, Sandy Sneddon, L Stock, R Storrie, W Strang, James Buchanan Weaver, Alex Westwater, W Wilson

No. 2 (Dunipace) Platoon
1. Lt AJ Moodie then Lt John Bryson. 2. 2/Lt J Bryson then 2/Lt A Ferguson.

Sgt J Allan, Sgt W McEwan, Sgt Thomson, Sgt Wilson, Cpl G Allan, Cpl A Brown, Cpl G Forsyth, Cpl J McEwan, Cpl H Strachan.

R Blair, James Duncan, A Erskine, W Fleming, C Lawless, W Leishman, John Paterson, A Stocks.

No. 3 Platoon
1. J Smith then Lt J Nelson. 2. J Nelson then 2/Lt J Glenn.

Sgt Kirkwood

A Adams, W Gillespie, R Graham, R Loney, W Pryde, Robertson (clerk), Frank Simpson, G Smith, Ian Wright

No. 4 Platoon [Russell Hall, Haggs]
1. Lt J Galbraith then Lt C Abercrombie. 2. 2/Lt C Abercrombie then 2/Lt J Gibson then Lt J Thomson then 2nd Lt J Marshall then 2nd Lt GC Stanners.

Sgt A Barr, Sgt Marshall, Cpl Battison, Cpl Smith

W Henderson, R Kerr, J McKechnie, M Milligan, Daniel Thomson

Unknown Platoon
Sgt-Major J Mercer, Sgt W France, Sgt McLeod, L/Cpl G Dunford

J Allan, W Black, Richard Burns, A Dickson, C Duncan, W Duncan, D Henderson, Archie Hunter, R McPake, J Meechan, J Peebles, W Sinclair, James Sloggatt, J Sutherland, Thomson, Harry Madden, J McDougall

No 4 Platoon, A Company, 3rd Stg Bn HG (Haggs) in 1941. Daniel Thomson is 3rd from right in the second front row.

Appendix 2

'B' Company (Larbert, Stenhousemuir, Carronshore)

[HQ Co-op Hall then Larbert Parish Church Hall]

1. Major David Tough then Major Alex W Wilson (f-11.10.43) then Major TJ Malcolm.
2. SA Jardine (-10.40) then Capt BW Webb (4.10.40-15.2.42) then Capt J Johnstone

HQ Platoon (Larbert)

R Taylor (Observer Section), J Dobson (clerk), Sgt/Major Roberts (armourer),
R Rollo (armourer) JS Symon, Sgt-Major William Reid (drill inst).
Lt Boyd, the minister of the West Church in Larbert, (-Jan 43). Major D Tough, Major H McKenzie King (MO), Captain McBryde, Cpl J Brunton,
Captain Archibald McCallum, Captain McKinley, Lt R Smith, 2nd Lt JA Donaldson.
Sgt Aitken, Arthur Davis, Robert Milroy, Andrew Stewart, Peter Swan

No. 5 (Larbert) Platoon

[Hardie's Garage, then Shell Factory, Scottish Enamelling then Co-op Hall]
1. Lt Tom C Malcolm 2. 2nd Lt VG Elmslie

Sgt Robert Rollo, Sgt JB Gilchrist, Cpl D Cheape, Cpl G Dunford, Cpl Sidney R Jackson, L/Cpl G Binnie, L/Cpl John Spalding

A Dalgetty, John Hope, N McKenzie, Dan Niven, W Tough.

No. 6 (Carron) Platoon [hut, park]

1. Lt William Muir then Lt Wm Donaldson 2. 2/Lt John Johnston

Cpl McLaren

JA Bauchop, Jack Braidwood, Willie Ferguson, John Grady, Wm Hodge, C Liston,
J McArthur, J McFarlane, Bobby McGill, Thomas Rae, Colin Sharp, Charlie Smith.

No. 7 (Stenhousemuir) Platoon [Burgh Stables, Stenhousemuir]

1. Lt EO MacFarlane 2. AW Atkinson then J Watters
Sgt S Penn, Sgt J Simpson, A Duncan, Daniel Geichan, J Kelly, R Laird,
D McIntyre, J McKinlay, R Milroy, T Nisbet, J Smith, P Taylor, Johnny Watters, W Wilson, G Wright.

No. 8 (Carronshore) Platoon [Scout hut, Bothkennar Rd/North Main St]

1. Lt D Syme then Lt AW Atkinson then Lt James Dowie, 2. John A Green then Lt A Deans.

Sgt Boyd?, Sgt A Deans, Sgt Riddell, Sgt Peter Wright L/Cpl J Donaldson,
L/Cpl J Russell.

Baird, P Campbell, George Charleston R. Laing, R Leishman, J Marshall, W Marshall,
T Miller, W Rae, Joseph Russell, William Russell, D Stoddart, J Thornton, Livingstone Turnbull, Joe Webster, William Wilson, W Wright

A section of the Stenhousemuir HG. Daniel Geichan back row, 1st on left.

Officers and members of the Carronshore HG Platoon at the new school building at Carronshore in 1941. Lt James Dowie in the front centre.

Appendix 2

Unknown Platoon (B Company)

Sgt A McCallum, Sgt James McLaren, Sgt J Thomson, Cpl A Mills, Cpl R Taylor. W Anderson, A Dickson, W Donaldson, D Gold, W Hendry, J Hotchkiss, C McIntyre, J McLaren, R Reid, D Millar, J Millar, A Paterson, J Roughead, A Roy, J Roy, J Waugh, J Webster

---

'C' Company
(Bannockburn, Cowie, Plean, Fallin)

1. Major WM Edmond 2. Capt J McLaren & Capt FG Griffiths (-27.7.44)

HQ Platoon
Capt AFC Forrester (Admin)

No. 9 (Bannockburn) Platoon
1. Lt J Chalmers then Lt W Whitehead
2. 2nd Lt W Whitehead then 2nd Lt WJB Clark

No. 10 (Fallin) Platoon
1. Lt D McGill then Lt WN Sanderson then Lt Allan 2. 2nd Lt WN Sanderson

No. 11 (Cowie) Platoon
1. Lt John Hannigan then Lt John Robinson 2. 2nd Lt J Easton then 2nd Lt John H Robinson

No. 12 (Plean) Platoon
1. Lt A Watt then Lt J Balloch 2. 2nd Lt R Caruthers then 2nd Lt H Allan then 2nd Lt J Ramage then 2nd Lt SL Smith

Sgt A Wales, Sgt Wylie, Cpl W Rae, Cpl J Stillie, L/Cpl J Brooks

A. Fairlie, T Gibson, A Rae, D Stillie sen, D Stillie jnr, J Williamson

RNAD Company (Bandeath Platoon)
1. Lt KK Etchells then Capt D McGrouther then Capt WP Jones 2. 2/Lt J Polley then Lt WP Jones. Detachment officers: 2nd Lt RA Newton, 2nd Lt Niven, 2nd Lt D Sutherland, 2nd Lt JCH Young, Lt HW Oliver

'D' Company
(Grangemouth, Airth)

1. Lt Walter Bain [-6.40] then Major WJ Campbell [-8.40] then Major RB Peddie then Major JS Thompson (1941-sd). 2. Capt JS Thompson (1940) then Capt T Ifor Davies [1941-sd

HQ Platoon (Grangemouth)
J Reid (quartermaster), A Stewart (clerk), Lt RB Peddie (Liaison)

No. 13 (Airth) Platoon [Airth Castle]
1. Capt AFC Forester [-6.1944] then Lt John Ramage then Lt WE Evison. 2. A Watson then Lt Stewart Smith then 2/Lt W Graham

CSM Rae, Sgt Gavin Fraser, Sgt W D Miller, Sgt AR Steel,

Crab, Dowie, A Dunn, Fish, Sandy Govan, W Johnstone, G McGregor, McNaughton, Murray, William Sneddon, W Young

No. 14 (Grangemouth) Platoon [Police St./Town Hall/Drill Hall]
1. Lt Walter Bain then Lt James Anderson then Lt GM Cumming 2. FJP Craven then 2/Lt TW Stanners Sgt Alex Kemp, Sgt Wightman, Cpl James Fernie, Cpl D Marshall, L/Cpl JH Robison

T Barke, A Black, J Boyle, James Buckie, RSM Green, Hempreed, Joe Hunter, Kirk, Jim Laurie, J Lawson, James MacDonald, Mclean, W Marshall, T Otway, P Randalls, John Robinson, James Scott, AH Stanners, Jock Strathie, Wilson Galloway.

Men of the Grangemouth Home Guard, late 1940

Appendix 2

No. 15 (Scottish Dyes) Platoon [ICI Works]
1. Lt RS Brisbane then Lt WJ Campbell then Lt RP Chinn 2. J McArthur then TI Davies.
Sgt RP Chinn.
A Cornwall, HW Deans, Charles Donald, Alec Findlay, William Hamilton, D Kennard, Harry McPherson, T Mitchell, Ian Munn, J Paxton, R Pearson, AG Rees, Bob Roberts, A Silver JK Thomson. H Whitelaw.

No 16 (LMS) Platoon [Railway Club, Lumley St]
1. Lt P Liddell then Lt James Christine 2. 2/Lt J Christine
Cpl Ross (head of stretcher-bearer section)
T Barclay, D Dewar, Nixon, Philp, S. Roxburgh, James Scott.

No. 17 (Scottish Dyes) Platoon [ICI Works] – bomb disposal
1. Lt R Greig then Donald 2. 2/Lt JG Stewart
John Buchan

Members of the ICI HG platoon at the entrance to the Scottish Dyes Recreation Club. Back row: 1st from left Dr Charlie Donald of ICI. Front row, 3rd from left sawmill worker. 2nd from right Jim Cornwall, railway worker.

Unknown Platoon (D Company)
Baillie, William Burns, A Duncan, D Kincaid, Peter Moodie, P Randalls, Rees, M Thomson, Whitefoot

III Stirlingshire, unknown company or platoon
Cpl Brisbane,
W Denison, E Dewar, E Drake, Dumford, W Kay, D Lind, J McAra, D Moffat, A Smith, D Swan

II West Lothian HG Battalion
Colonel Lord Charles Hope then Colonel H M Cadell

No. 3 Company
(Bo'ness)

1. Major WG Robson then Major Gordon Dalyell of the Binns. 2. Capt G Murdoch then Capt JT Dewar then Capt William M Miller.

HQ Platoon (Bo'ness) [Gardeners' Hall, Hope St]
George Murdoch (quartermaster), Captain Shafto (medical officer),
Lt WG Findlay then D Cochrane (transport & traffic control officer),

Sgt-Major J Smith then Sgt-Major T McKinnon then Sgt-Major Andrew Rothnie, Pipe-Major D McIntosh, Lt Robert McPherson, Capt Donald Gair (adjutant), Sgt James F Foot (machine gun instructor then Bn armourer)

A platoon of the Bo'ness Home Guard on the steps on the north side of Bo'ness Town Hall., c1940. Back row: John Johnston? George Clelland (blacksmith), ——, John Robertson (chemical plumber), Emerson McNeish? Back but one row: Charlie Small (miner)   , Wullice Smith, Billy McGuck? John Miller, ——. Front row: Hamilton? Rendall Brodie, Tommy Beglin, Johnny Girvan, McIntosh, Baillie, —Simpson, George Burns. In front: Jim Foot, Bob Grant (patternmaker), Adam Burnett

Appendix 2

No. 11 Platoon (Bo'ness) [Drill Hall, Corbiehall]
1. Lt William W Broome then Lt James Johnston then Lt L Dickson then Lt Thomas McKinnon. 2. 2nd Lt Thomas McKinnon then 2nd Lt W W Broome then 2nd Lt George Sneddon then 2nd Lt John Smith then 2nd Lt R McPherson.

Sgt William Johnston, Sgt Thomas Martin, Sgt John Meechan, Sgt John Crawford Smith, Cpl John Rooney, Cpl Sam Sneddon, L/Cpl H Wright

Tommy Beglin, Jim Blair, J Boles, James Brown, Frickleton, Gilmour, Girvan, Glening, Grant, Gray, Henderson, Irvine, McCann, McGurk, R McPherson, R Morrison, Bernard Rooney, Sherrat, Simpson, Sinclair, Steward, Stirling, Walton, White

No. 12 Platoon (Bo'ness) [Foundry sec - Gardener's Hall, Hope St]
1. Lt William Miller then Lt J White. 2. 2nd Lt J White then 2nd Lt J Smith then 2nd Lt James Galbraith

Alex Furnam

No. 13 Platoon (Bo'ness) [Thomson & Balfour]
1. Lt JT Dewar then Lt W Napier Thomson then Lt George Murdoch then Lt Robert Grant. 2. 2nd Lt Robert Grant then 2nd Lt W Findlay then 2nd Lt Thomas McKinnon.
Sgt Tom Davidson, Sgt James Foot, Sgt Major Sam Martin, Sgt Major Andrew Rothnie, Sgt Robert Smith, Cpl J Buchanan, Sgt (L/Cpl) A Ritchie, Johnny Girvan, Billy McGuck, J McIntosh, John Miller, HL Pritchard, John Robertson, John Russell, Charles Small, Temporal.

Unknown Platoon (No. 3 Company)
Sgt W Martin, Sgt Alex Orr, Cpl W Forrester (Calgary Highlanders), Cpl McCorquodale, Cpl J Nimmo, L/Cpl R Bernard, L/Cpl James Black, L/Cpl (Vol) J Cleland, L/Cpl William Sneddon, L/Cpl H Wright

T Allan, Baillie, Archie Black, Tommy Beglin, Alex Bell, John Bernard, R Bernard, J Blair, Rendall Brodie, James Brown, J E Bruce, T Burnett, George Burns, Sandy Cameron, George Clelland, John Conlin, E Cook, J Cunningham, James Currie, T Denton, H L Dickson, James Duncan, James Forest, Robert Gilfinnan, W Gardner, C Grant, J Grant, W Grant, Cornelius Guthrie, Bernard Hampson, Thomas Hampson, Wilson Jackson, John Johnston, Robert Livingstone, J Martin, W McAlpine, J McGregor, Robert B McGregor, John Mackie, George MacKnight, John McFarlane, Alexander McGregor, Vol J McIntosh, Emerson McNeish, William Miller, R Moffat, Sam Montgomery, Peter Moodie, R Morrison, Charles M Neil, J Neil, P Nesbit, J Porteous, W Reid, Bernard Rooney, John Rooney, Scullion, W Seaton, Edward Sheehan, D Simpson, J Smith, JC Smith, Wallace Smith, James Stanners, W Stewart, C Pow, A Ure, Wood.

Transport Columns

No. 1 Scottish HG Transport Column 2162 Company [Brown St Depot, Camelon]
1. Capt R Bruce {1941-44} then Major T McMain (1944-sd), 2. Lt W Clark (1941-44) then Capt R Bruce (1944-sd).Platoon commanders: Lt David Bennie, Lt M McMain, Lt J Laidlaw, Capt W Clark (1944).

[Larbert Rd Depot]
Sgt Jim Campbell, Charles Anderson

No 2 Scottish HG Transport Column 2184 Company [Bowling]

'B' Platoon [Grangemouth]
Capt William A Mitchell (1943-sd).
Sgt George Ward

Appendix 3

SAS EXERCISE

31st May 1944:

"Enclosed are reports on this exercise held recently in the East of Stirlingshire by 'C' Squadron of the above Regiment which the latter asked us to forward to you. Excerpts which affect the HG have been taken and distributed to them."
General Staff, Stirling Sub-District.
The Castle, Stirling.

Exercise 'C' Squadron 11-15th May

Report on Home Guard co-operation in West Lothian and Stirlingshire areas.

1. It may have been due to the short notice of the exercise that was given, but in numerous cases it was found that the Home Guard units did not know that the exercise was taking place. Even when they were so informed by the police they did not seem over keen to take any action. In one case the men were very keen to try to round us up, but when the Company Commander applied for permission to take his men out that night he was refused, with the direct order that "no action would be taken". Would this be the same case in the event of an actual landing by enemy paratroops in the area?
2. Among other places, prompt, efficient, and sometimes spontaneous action was taken by the Home Guard at Mid Calder, West Calder, Livingston, Bathgate (south area), Avonbridge, Black Loch and Glenboig. Also we are very grateful to those members of the HG who turned out unofficially, in civilian clothes, to co-operate against us, in cases where their own units were not mobilised (eg. Torphichen).
3. It seemed usual for HG units to choose as their headquarters a farm. Farms are favourite targets for German mortars, and it is suggested that the open country would have made a less obvious and more mobile headquarters. Also the farms chosen were often out of contact with the scene of operations.

4. It was usually found that HG patrols warned parties of their approach by making considerable noise.
5. At Avonbridge a party successfully ambushed an attacking HG patrol, because they advanced along a road towards their objective.
6. Sentries should be taught that they should always, where possible, avoid standing up at night. Greater observation and less chance of being located is afforded from the lying position.
7. It seemed that HG units seldom took into account the fact that grenades might be used by the enemy with disastrous effect, when men are bunched together.
8. At West Calder, the interrogation of prisoners was poor. At the end of the interrogation period, our men knew a considerable amount about the location of HG headquarters, defences, etc, and names of sub unit commanders, while they themselves gave away no information.
9. Objectives such as railway bridges, river bridges were well guarded so far as number of men were concerned, but all the men were on the top of the bridge and parties found no difficulty in placing their charges beneath.
10. Many more parties would have been captured if HG patrols had been available to act at once on reports received by the local police through their excellent system of communications.
11. It is emphasised that speedy and silent action is essential when dealing with small groups of enemy troops in the area.

Appendix 3

Party Commander	Strength	Objective	Success	Times Captured	Time and Place of Capture	Remarks
L/Sgt Higham	5	road over river 558890 [Mid Calder]	No	1	0115 hrs Mid Calder 12/5	1 HG patrol, 1 officer and 3 ORs captured near objective
Sgt McDiarmid	3	railway over river 574865	Yes 2230hrs	nil		3 police blown up on objective 4 enemy captured crossroads 4887. Night 12/13.
Lt Richardson	3	crossroads 530843	No	1	537863 West Calder night 11/12	1 HG captured night 12/13 at 501842
L/Sgt Belsham	3	Livingston Station 522900	Yes 0145 hrs	1?		Heavy kit captured by HG at 523900. Comdr gave himself up to recover it.
Lt Rosborough	4	pylons over road 606902	Yes 0030hrs	nil		Railway line found to be very easy line of march. It was unguarded.
Lt Goddard	4	road junction	Yes 0015 hrs	1	By HG at 1730 14/5 at 362947 [Slamannan]	Attacked RAF guard at aerodrome near objective.
Cpl Kennedy	3	bridge over river 528876	No	2	a. By HG 1630 12/5 at 525848 b. Rydings farm 2591 by HG at 1000 14/5	Civilian co-operation with the police good.

Party Commander	Strength	Objective	Success	Times Captured	Time and Place of Capture	Remarks
Sgt Downes	4	railway over road 553849	Yes	nil		Not seen by the enemy throughout exercise.
Lt Close	4	railway junction 582879	Yes 0045 hrs	nil	Seen by civilians at 3189 but not reported.	Policeman and signalman captured on objective. They gave valuable information.
Sgt Storey	5	bridge 558985	No	4	a. Bdge 585974 0300 12/5 b. 568978 1700 12/5 c. bdge 582974 2300 12/5 d. road 543975 0045 13/5	Police did not give this party a chance to start from scratch after capture.
Reynolds	6	railway station 583925	No	2	a. wood 591914 2020 12/5 by police b. wood 449917 1230 13/5 by police.	Police strongly commended.
Sgt Mitchell	5	road over railway 545917	No	1	Armadale stn 234 12/5	Civilians suspicious but not hostile. Took no action.
Lt Iredale	5	track over railway 586975	No	2	a. wood 597977 1930 12/5 by police. b. bdge over river 453955 2359 13/5 [SE of Bowhouse]	Police commended.

Appendix 3

Party Commander	Strength	Objective	Success	Times Captured	Time and Place of Capture	Remarks
Sgt Robertson	5	railway over road 623970	Yes 2345 hrs	nil		Passed through police cordon as they were capturing party at 453955 [SE of Bowhouse]
Lt Mycock	5	railway over road 624938	Yes 2359 hrs	2	a. Lousmuir 3692 by HG at 0115 14/5 b. New Monkland 2489 by HG at 1615 14/5	HG gave ample warning of their approach at Lousmuir and could easily have been ambushed.
Cpl Jones	5	pylons over road 529957	Yes 0030 hrs	1?	13/5 1715hrs attacked by HG wood 406936. Enemy successfully ambushed. [Avonbridge]	White bedding betrayed position. Dogs and children troublesome.
Lt Bryce	4	bridge over canal 585947	No	1	2045 12/5 by police in wood 6096.	
L/Sgt Goldie	4	pylons over road 557943	No	3	a. by police 2040 12/5 in wood 5595 b. by HG 1200 13/5 402942 [Avonbridge] c. by police 1030 14/5 farm 247807.	Civilian co-operation with police was better than HG co-operation with police.

Lt Iredale: Police patrol of 3 caught whole party on the riverbank before crossing the bridge at 453955. They were hiding in the bushes.

Lt Goddard: Observation of objective not possible due to late start & RAF lamp occupying original lying up area made reaching observation point impossible. Started for objective 11.00. Waited at edge of wood for dark. Reached objective at 23.45, held till 0030. Not occupied by enemy. Captured 12 civilians returning from RAF dance. On withdrawal attacked RAF guard at 617870. Attack partially successful. Guards too alert, but not very confident. Party was not captured. Distance 10m on 322 to 583902 & on 303 to 510935. Arrived 05.30. Lying up in wood. Proceeded on 280 to railway at 436943 & as line not in use at night & later pulled up. Proceeded to Slamannan - distance 9.5 miles. Arrived at wood 05.30. Due to time lost avoiding civilians night 13/14 at daybreak 1.5 miles short of lying up area. Wood chosen was only one available. Found by children at 16.00 hrs HG learnt of presence through children, captured 17.30 by 2 STG Bn HG.

Cpl Jones: Woods 406936. 1715 hrs Sat 13th attacked by Home Guard. Took 1 officer 5 men prisoners, others put to flight. Lt Kerr 13 Plat "C" Coy 2 Stg; Cpl Fowler 14 Plat ditto; Pte Stein 14 ditto; Pte Anderson 14 ditto; Cpl White 15 ditto. Home Guard would never have found us if bedding had not been white. Also Home Guard rely on dogs and children to find enemy. We found them very troublesome.

Report on police co-operation in Mid Lothian, West Lothian and Stirlingshire areas.
1. All ranks were very impressed and, in fact, somewhat disturbed by the efficiency of the police in all areas, in tracking down parties, and reporting their movements. Every man of the police force who came into contact with our men, had entered into the spirit of the exercise with remarkable enthusiasm, to such an extent, that our men met with more than they had bargained for in almost every area, and were given a very hectic time throughout the exercise. This served to bring out many training points of great value to us.
2. The police were especially commended in the villages of Mid Calder, West Calder, Broxburn and Winchburgh. At Winchburgh in particular their wood search was excellent, and they seemed to know exactly the right placed to look for our men.

3. In the interests of the exercise, it was understood that once a party had been contacted by a member of the police force, their names could be taken, as it is not the job of unarmed policemen to round up armed men. It should be pointed out, however, that in practically every case, captures reported as such, would not have occurred, as two notebooks do not afford much protection against five automatics.
4. Liaison between civilians and police, was, on the whole, very good. Though between the Home Guard and the police it was rather poor. (This is probably explained by the fact that the Home Guard were not co-operating in the exercise as had been anticipated.)
5. It was considered that too little attention was paid to the watching of railway lines, against their use as a line of approach. The defences were situated solely by bridges and stations, etc, which were easily avoided.
6. It was noted that on a few occasions police reports were inaccurate, in that they portrayed the situation as being more favourable to them than in actual fact it was. Eg umpires, liaising with the police were reported as having given themselves up, and having given away valuable information. Another party, which forced its way into a HG HQ to recapture kit that had been discovered by the Home Guard was reported as having given itself up.
7. Once a party was 'captured', in some instances, it was not given a chance by the police to get properly on its way again, with the result that parties were being continually under observation, and were 'captured' as much as three times in one day.
8. The work of the police near Glenboig in Lanarkshire is especially commended. Acting on reports from the Home Guard they rounded up one of our parties, believing them to be either German parachutists or deserters from the army, since they had not been warned about the exercise. In fact their insistence on locking these men up was rather embarrassing, until the arrival of an umpire on the scene.
9. We wish to express out thanks to all ranks of the police force who took part in the exercise, for the really excellent way in which they all co-operated, and for the many useful lesson they taught us. We were glad we were not up against them as a real enemy.

Appendix 4

Home Guard Social Events

Smoking concerts

9 Nov 1940	No. 3, Denny	Denny Drill Hall
16 Nov 1940	'C' Coy, Falkirk	Mathieson's Restaurant, Falkirk
30 Nov 1940	Shieldhill	Band Hall
30 Nov 1940	No. 1, Denny	Denny Drill Hall
18 Jan 1940	Grangemouth LMS	
8 Feb 1940	Carronshore	
15 Feb 1940	Forth & Clyde & Sunnyside	Tudor House, Falkirk
22 Feb 1940	No. 5, Larbert	Co-op Hall, Larbert
15 Mar 1941	'A' Coy, Denny	Drill Hall, Denny
5 April 1941	No. 6, Larbert	Co-op Hall, Larbert
14 June 1941	No. 8, 'B' Coy, Carronshore	
22 Nov 1941	No. 1, Denny	Drill Hall, Denny
14 Feb 1942	'D' Coy, Grangemouth	
10 Dec 1943	Bo'ness – pie & pint	Free Gardeners' Hall, Bo'ness
17 Nov 1944	Bo'ness	Free Gardeners' Hall, Bo'ness
29 Dec 1944	'B' Coy II Stg	Falkirk Ironworks canteen

Social evenings

1940

15 Nov 1940	Polmont – dance (Mitchell's Band, Grangemouth)	Brightons Masonic Hall
Dec 1940	'A' Coy, Denny (series of Sunday concerts)	Denny Drill Hall
13 Dec 1940	Camelon (whist drive, concert & dance)	HG Social Club
20 Dec 1940	Bonnybridge – whist drive & dance (Ladies Committee)	Bonnybridge Drill Hall
21 Dec 1940	LNER, Falkirk	Temperance Café, Falkirk

1941

3 Jan 1941	Brightons – Christmas party	Brightons Masonic Hall
11 Jan 1941	Shieldhill	Shieldhill Welfare Hall
11 Jan 1941	Bonnybridge	
17 Jan 1941	Bo'ness – social	Free Gardeners' Hall, Bo'ness
25 Jan 1941	Denny (St Alexander's Concert Party)	Denny Drill Hall

25 Jan 1941   Bonnybridge – Burns' supper
31 Jan 1941   Bo'ness   Star Theatre, Bo'ness
(Burns' supper with special constables, bully beef instead of steak pies)
1 Feb 1941   Shieldhill – Burns' night

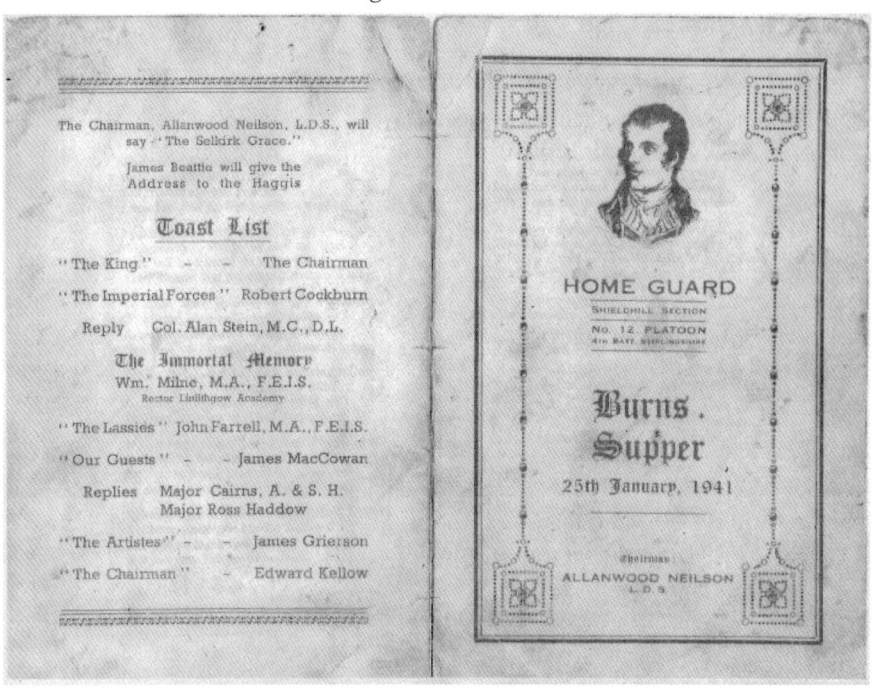

15 Feb 1941   Nos. 9 & 10, Falkirk   Mathieson's Rooms, Falkirk
23 Mar 1941   Falkirk Ironworks Pl   Mathieson's Rooms, Falkirk
12 Apr 1941   No. 6, Larbert   Plough Hotel
7 June 1941   Denny HG v Camelon 1st Aid Post – table tennis
18 Oct 1941   No. 12, 'C' Coy, Plean (cabaret dance)   Plean Public Hall
18 Oct 1941   Denny HG v AA Battery – darts, draughts, dominoes
1 Nov 1941   officers 'B' Coy II Stg Bn   Falkirk Town Hall
               (entertain NCOs with concert)
8 Nov 1941   Cowie – social
21 Nov 1941   Bo'ness – services dance   Bo'ness Town Hall
               (RAF Grangemouth Band)
22 Nov 1941   Slamannan – dance (Connelly's Band)
28 Nov 1941   Bonnybridge whist drive & dance   Bonnybridge Drill Hall
               (F Graham & his Band)
29 Nov 1941   Slamannan – dance (Connelly's Band)   Slamannan Masonic Hall
29 Nov 1941   Allandale – annual whist drive   Allandale Bowling Club
12 Dec 1941   Bonnybridge – social & dance   Bonnybridge Church Hall
19 Dec 1941   Redding – social & dance   Redding Co-op Hall
               (McCabe's Band)

Appendix 4

1942

19 Jan 1942	Bonnybridge – dance	Russell Hall
24 Jan 1942	III Stg Bn – dinner for officers	Denny Drill Hall
24 Jan 1942	No. 16, Grangemouth LMS	Ambulance Hall
30 Jan 1942	Bo'ness – Burns' supper – 2nd social event	
21 Feb 1942	'D' Coy – annual dance (Henderson's Band)	Brightons Masonic Hall
28 Feb 1942	No. 14 Grangemouth – social	Imperial Hall
28 Feb 1942	LNER – whist drive & dance	Brightons Masonic Hall
28 Feb 1942	Airth with Civil Defence – dance	Airth Welfare Hall
11 April 1942	No. 16 – dance (Bryce's Band)	Maddiston School Hall
9 May 1942	'A' Coy III Stg – social	Denny Drill Hall
6 June 1942	No. 2 section of No. 6, 'B' Coy – swear box (collected 10s for the Falkirk Herald Relief Fund)	
8 Aug 1942	No. 2, 'B' Coy III Stg – late dance in aid of battalion pipe band (Mayfair Dance Band)	Carronshore Co-op Hall
5 Sep 1942	Carronshore – social (Mayfair Dance Band)	Carronshore Co-op Hall
19 Sep 1942	No. 2, Denny (Bobby Drummond's Bohemian Band)	Denny Drill Hall
20 Nov 1942	Bo'ness – WG Robson's leaving do	Bo'ness Masonic Temple
28 Nov 1942	Blackbraes – supper & dance	California School Hall
5 Dec 1942	No. 2, Denny – social (CO retired)	Albert Hall, Dunipace
5 Dec 1942	Carronshore – whist drive & dance	Carronshore Co-op Hall
5 Dec 1942	'D' Coy II Stg – whist drive & dance (Cooper's Band)	Brightons Masonic Hall

1943

5 Feb 1943	Polmont LNER – 2nd annual social/ dance	Brightons Masonic Hall
26 Feb 1943	No. 3 Bonnybridge – dinner & dance (V Pacitti's Collegian Dance Band)	New canteen, Broomhill Rd
6 March 1943	'E' Coy II Stg – whist drive & dance (Smith's Elite orchestra)	Falkirk Technical School
18 Mar 1943	Nos. 9 & 10 'B' Coy – dance / tea (George Burt & his Falkirk Technical School Bunk House Boys)	Lea Park Tearooms, Falkirk
12 Nov 1943	Bonnybridge – 2nd annual social (Kilsyth Concert Party & Mansfield Singers)	Bonnybridge Masonic

1944

14 Jan 1944	No. 32 Camelon – dance	Camelon School
29 Jan 1944	Polmont LNER – 3rd annual whist / dance	Brightons Masonic Hall
25 Feb 1944	No. 32 Camelon – encore dance (for ex-Forces)	Camelon School

An open-air concert held under the auspices of Denny & District Branch of the British Legion in the grounds of Herbertshire Castle on a Sunday. It was attended by members of the Legion, Red Cross nurses, Home Guard, special police, AFS and ARP services. (Falkirk Herald 4 Sep 1940.)

3 March 1944	No. 13 Slamannan – whist drive / dance	St Lawrence Church Hall
19 May 1944	Bo'ness – social	Free Gardeners' Hall
26 May 1944	Bo'ness – first dance in new HQ 100 couples (Sam McLean's 8 Merry Men)	Free Gardeners' Hall
28 Oct 1944	'D' Coy II Stg – film show & dance	Brightons Masonic Hall
3 Nov 1944	High Bonnybridge – social & dance (Imperial Band)	St Helen's Church Hall
10 Nov 1944	'B' Coy II Stg – whist drive & dance (Burt's Dance Orchestra)	Union Halls, Grahamston
24 Nov 1944	'D' Coy, Polmont – social	
8 Dec 1944	'C' Coy – social & dance (Connerton's Dance Band)	Shieldhill Welfare Hall
8 Dec 1944	III Stg Bn officers	Larbert Masonic Hall
15 Dec 1944	No. 13, Slamannan – social & dance	St Lawrence Church Hall
15 Dec 1944	'E' Coy II Stg – social & dance (Doak's Orchestra)	Falkirk Technical School

1945

19 Jan 1945	'A' Coy II Stg – social & dance	Bonnybridge Public Hall
26 Jan 1945	Polmont LNER – Burns' supper	Brightons Masonic Hall
16 Feb 1945	No 16 Grangemouth – social	Imperial Hall

Appendix 4

Grangemouth HG marching past Grange School. Three pipers are followed by a lone drummer – all in civvies – then the CO with his 2nd in command in uniform and carrying swagger sticks. The CO has a pistol in a holster. The men are carrying rifles. The kerbstones are painted white to help people to find their way in the black-out.

Parades

16 Nov 1940	Shieldhill & California	Blackbraes Church/war memorial
16 Nov 1940	Carronshore (40 men)	Bothkennar Parish Church
23 Nov 1940	Airth, Bannockburn, Denny, Grangemouth, Larbert & Stenhousemuir	
		Larbert Old Parish Church
30 Nov 1940	Falkirk	Citadel, Bank St
6 Dec 1940	Bo'ness – march round town	Bo'ness Old Kirk
12 Feb 1941	Polmont (with ARP) – War Weapons Week	
22 Feb 1941	'B' Coy III Stg Bn	Larbert Parish Church
29 March 1941	——	Larbert West Church
5 April 1941	——	Falkirk Town Mission
19 April 1941	Denny	Dunipace Old Parish Church
25 April 1941	Bo'ness with Civil Defence	
3 May 1941	Dennyloanhead (with Haggs Pipe Band)	Dennyloanhead Church
27 June 1941	Bainsford with Civil Defence	Bainsford parish Church
27 June 1941	Larbert – recruiting march	
29 June 1941	Grangemouth – march past (Provost took salute)	Zetland Park, Grangemouth
28 June 1941	'B' Coy – march (Bellsdyke Rd to Carronshore)	Central School playing fields
5 July 1941	Grangemouth	Zetland Park
23 Aug 1941	II Stg Bn – 800 men	Erskine Church
12 Sep 1941	Bonnybridge (Lt R Thomson read the lesson)	St Helen's Church, Bonnybridge
13 Sep 1941	Shieldhill & Blackbraes (led by Piper Penman)	Blackbraes Church

One of the Grangemouth HG platoons photographed outside Kerse Church in Abbots Road. C1942. Adam Deans middle row 5th from left.

Appendix 4

A Grangemouth HG platoon salutes the dignitaries on the podium in front of Grangemouth Municipal Chambers. The event was probably one of the many fundraising campaigns, such as 'Salute the Soldier'. C1943.

26 Sep 1941	III Stg Bn with Civil Defence	Ochilview Park, Stenhousemuir
	(Inspected by Thomas Johnston, Secretary of State for Scotland)	
15 Nov 1941	'C' Coy – Remembrance Day	Erskine Church
15 Nov 1941	other HG units	various war memorials
20 Mar 1942	Bo'ness	
4 April 1942	'B' Coy, Falkirk (c300 men)	Hope St Car Park
4 April 1942	California & Shieldhill	Blackbraes Parish Church
4 April 1942	'B' Coy III Stg	Larbert East Church
	(Lt Wm Muir played the organ)	
25 April 1942	'A' Coy – usual company parade on 1st Sunday	
15 May 1942	Bonnybridge	Bonnybridge Drill Hall
30 May 1942	'B' Coy	Ochilview Park
	(with Polish Army & artillery, Sir Pat Dollan and 200 public)	
7 Nov 1942	Blackbraes & California	Blackbraes Church
14 Nov 1942	Shieldhill	Shieldhill Church/war memorial
14 Nov 1942	Bonnybridge	War memorial
23 Jan 1943	Denny	Dunipace Old Parish Church
30 Jan 1943	Denny HG Pipe Band with ATC	Denny Baptist Church
30 April 1943	Bo'ness – 3rd Anniversary, march round town, Glebe Park, Bo'ness	
7 May 1943	Bonnybridge with B & District Band – 3rd Anniversary	
14 May 1943	II Stg Bn – display, demonstration & parade, Brockville Park, Falkirk	
21 May 1943	III Stg Bn – display with commentary, Ochilview Park, Stenhousemuir	
9 July 1943	Denny	Dunipace North Church
9 June 1944	Bo'ness – Salute the Soldier	Bo'ness Town Hall
28 Oct 1944	'B' Coy II Stg – ceremonial parade (Camelon Brass Band)	

Sports events

18 Oct 1940	Bo'ness v RAF Leuchars at football	Newtown Park
20 Dec 1940	Bo'ness v RAF	Newtown Park
7 June 1941	Denny v Camelon ARP at table tennis	
14 June 1941	Slamannan v Avonbridge at football	
18 July 1941	Grangemouth Coy – sports day	Earl's Road football pitch

An HG officer receive a trophy shield on one of their sports days.

9 Aug 1941	'A' Coy sports day	Carronbank Park, Denny
15 Aug 1941	III Stg Bn sports day	Ochilview Park, Stenhousemuir
10 July 1942	Bo'ness v Civil Defence at football	Newtown Park
11 July 1942	Denny – race	
8 Aug 1942	Carronshore v Services XI at Football	Gairdoch Park, Carronshore
5 Sep 1942	Denny – Saturday sports meeting	Brightons
10 Oct 1942	Carronshore v Carron Works team	Gairdoch Park, Carronshore

Index

Absenteeism 54-55
Airth Platoon 160,198
Allandale 38,75,*137*,159,160
 (see Castlecary Brickworks Platoon)
Ammunition 10,11,12,14,44-45,58,61-82, *69*,120,140-142,153,*160*,188,219,234
Anti-aircraft guns 160
Anti-tank mine 57,137-138
Antonine Wall *114*,121,159
ARP, Stirling & Clacks. Joint Authority 3,27,97,103,164
Armband 16,*21,22*,25
Armouries 62,67,73-74,135,158
Arnotdale House, Dollar Park *10*,11,89,90
Auchengean School *149,150*
Auxiliary units 45-46
Avon Bridge *197*,198
Avon Viaduct, Linlithgow Bridge *91*
Avonbridge platoon 45,82,189,206-207
Avonside, Grangemouth 94,112

Bagpipes 24,*143*
Bainsford Bridge 62,94-95,195
Bainsford Church 71
Bainsford Platoon 74,97
Bandeath RNA Depot 160
Barbed wire 210
Barrwood 175,*176,177*
Bayonet 66,81,82,104,175,185
Beancross 46,*47*,184,*184*
Bells; church 40,47-50,51
Bellsmeadow, Falkirk 130
Black Watch 112
Blackbraes & California platoon 144
Blacker Bombard see spigot mortar
Boer War 3,6
Bombs 31,215-217
Bo'ness Docks *62,63*,93-94,108
Bo'ness Drill Hall 14
Bo'ness Parish Church 47-50,*49*
Bo'ness platoons 9,13,14,17,18,20,28,31, 47-51,58,60,62-63,74,86,90,108,110,123-124, 132,150,157,167,168, 172-173,175,187
Bo'ness Police Station 3,28

Bonnybridge Drill Hall 15,71
Bonnybridge platoons 10,15,29,36,41,45, 70,*72*,82,87,111,113
Bonnybridge Power Station 29
Bonnybridge Toll 35,*36*
Boys anti-tank rifle *159*,226
Bren gun 147,*148*
Brightons Masonic Hall 4
Brightons Platoon 4,45,73,130,133, 182-183,187
British Legion 3,4,9,71,245
Brockville Park, Falkirk 158
Browning Automatic Rifle 57
Browning machine gun 143-144,*145*
Bus 34,36,223-225

Cadets 72,*179*,190
Caldercruix 75
Callendar House & Park 69,75
Camelon 203-204
 (see R & A Main platoon; Three Bridges)
Camelon Bridge 122,195,196
Camouflage 168
Canada Row 31,*32*
Carhowden House 206
Carron Bridge 158,192,197,210
Carron Platoon 23,*24*,77,118,159,188
Carron Reservoir *101*
Carronbank House 161
Carronshore Platoon 24,*35*,229
Cars 10,34-37,220-222
Castlecary Brickworks 52,*138*
Castlecary Brickworks Platoon 7,38,51,75, 92,137,159,160
Causewayend munitions depot, Muiravonside 108
Children 190,191,192,195,204,210,215,219
Cinder Hill, Bainsford 74
Cinema 22,174
Clay pigeon 12,19,58
Clergy 4,8,9,24
Clydebank Blitz 223-224
Columbian Stove Works, Bonnybridge *122, 123* (see Smith & Wellstood Platoon)

Commandos 189-190
Compulsory service 53-56
Craigieburn, Falkirk 80,82,83,149-*150*,155, 164,175
'Cromwell' 43-47

Dales Bridge, Denny 74,185
Dean, Rev JAF 8,24,74
Denny 4,11
Denny Drill Hall 4,11,71,160
Denny Muir 155,156
Denny platoons 11,*12*16*,*25,28,30,74,132, 157,185,186,195,210,*246,247*
Denovan 12
Dock Pit, Bo'ness 14,62-63
Dollar Park 10,11
Dreghorn Barracks 69,74,161,162,169
Drill 14,15,89
Dunkirk 8,9
Dunipace Church 28,*29*
Dykeneuk 74

Elf Hill, Bonnybridge 121
Explosives 160-162,188,217

Falkirk & District Co-op 97
Falkirk & District Royal Infirmary 81,219
Falkirk Burgh Stables/Power Station Platoon 8,33,47,80,100,105-107,131,136,158, 163,185
Falkirk Bus Station 16,*17*
Falkirk Drill Hall 71,*73*,131,250
Falkirk Ironworks 95
Falkirk Ironworks Platoon 8,*59*,62,65,67,68,94-95*117*-118,132,141, 150,155,184,192
Falkirk Museum 10
Falkirk Police Station 3,10
Falkirk Post Office platoon 100,102,130
Falkirk Power Station *107*
Falkirk Rifle Club 71
Falkirk Women's Rifle Club 74
Films 173-174
First aid 187,231
Flame barrel 83-87,*85*,121
Football 19
Forth & Clyde & Sunnyside Platoon 122

Forth and Clyde Canal 184,195,196
Forth Conservancy Board 74
Foundry Loan, Larbert *118*,119

Gas *126*,162-*164*,*163*,231
Glenbervie Golf Course 77
Grahamston Bridge 202,*204*
Grangemouth Airfield 25,45,94,112-116, *113,114*,160,180-182,200,225,244
Grangemouth Docks 25,43,92-93
Grangemouth Drill Hall 71,79,156,157,162, 226,*227*
Grangemouth platoons 15,18,*20*,22,26,37, 40-43,68,*81*,112-116,155,156,157,158,162, 180-185,*213*
Grangemouth Police Station 67
Grangemouth Railway Station 183,*185*,227
Grangemouth Refinery decoy 109-110
Greenhill Range 69,76-77,*78*,80,130,136, 140,141,144,159,225
Grenade; hand see hand grenade
  Grenade No. 68 82,*134,135,136*
  Grenade No. 69 135
  Grenade No. 73 136
  Grenade No. 74 136-137
  Grenade No. 75 137-138
  Grenade No. 76 138-140,*139*,151-152

Haggs Church 72
Haggs Platoon 37
Haining Wood 168
Hand grenade 57,82-83,129-135,*130,132, 133,134*,170-*171*,225
Hedge hopper 83-84 (see flame barrel)
Holidays at Home 214,215

ICI *26*,98,125
ICI Platoon *41*,67,125-126,218
ICI Recreation Club 40,41,*42*
Identity card 28,213-215
Incendiary grenade 138-140,151-152
International Brigade 13,60,158
Invasion alerts 40-52

Kerse Bridge *114*, see Pay Brig
Kerse House, Grangemouth 161,218
Kincardine Bridge 89,198,*199,200*

Index

King's Hundred 78
Kinnaird House, Larbert 83,151,161,*169*-171
Kinneil Estate 58
Kinneil petrol can factory (Satellite Can Factory S1) 108,*109,110,114*
Knobkerrie 9

Land mine 42,217-218
Larbert 4
Larbert Platoon 92,111
Larbert Station *170*
Larbert Viaduct 18,92,111,189,*207*
Laurieston Platoon 45,66,*76,130,141*
Laurieston School 66
Leapark Tearooms, Callendar Rd 213
Lewis machine gun 30,57,140-142,*141*,217
Lochgreen Road, Falkirk *32*,33,84-*85*,201
Lochgreen Road Ordnance Depot *85*, 104-107,*105*,147
LMS 43
LNER platoon *92,93*
Lord Roberts Miniature Rifle Club 11,70,71, 73,78

McKillop's Buildings, Thornbridge 135,143
MacLellan, P & W 72
McNellie, Mrs 77,80
Machine guns 121
Maddiston Platoon 33
Manuel Brickworks *44*
Manuel Brickworks Platoon 6,22,44,68,91, 108,162,168
Messengers (boy) 137,186,218,230
Midget submarine *123*
Mills Bomb see hand grenade
Mobile units 168-169
Molotov cocktails 13,60,138
Mortar 13,158-159
Motorbike 181-182,219,227-230
Mumrills 29,45,183

Northover Projector 151-*152*

Observation posts 28-30
Ochilview Park, Stenhousemuir 19
Operational base 46

Parades 167
Paratroops 1-2,32,41-43
Patrols 28,30-32
Pay Brig, Grangemouth 97-98,*196*-197
Pend, Bonnybridge *86*,121
Petrol pumps 98,99
Physical exercise 18-20,168
Pill box 33
Pike 9,15,57,153
Planes 43,111-112,128
Police 1,3,6,15,27,36,37,52,67,89,93,96-97, 98,186,217,218,234,241
Policy Pit, Falkirk 68
Polish army 69,116,149,187
Polmont Churchyard *115,116*
POW 25
Protected areas 211-215,*212*

R & A Main Platoon 44-45,73,83,111,122, *124*,144,203-204,*207*
Railways 45,51,91-92,108,111,170
Range; firing 74-83,112 (see Greenhill Range)
Range; grenade 130-132
Redding Platoon 37,131,183
Report centres 89,*90*,102,184
Revolver 10,17,62,83,*84*,94,228
Rifle 13,*15*,16,37,42,44-45,51,57,61-82, *65,66,68*,106,186,188,225
Rifle; Browning automatic 82
Rifle; EY 57,82-83,135
Rifle; smooth bore 1,11,58,69,70,71,74,75, 78,*79*,227
Road blocks 27,32-40,94-98,195-196,198, 200-203,213,214
Rosehall House, Falkirk *202,228*
Royal train 111

St Francis RC School 1,3
Salterhill, Slamannan 74
Scottish HG Transport Column 25,223-227
Scottish Tar Distillery *125*
Scouts *4*,8,175,179,230
Shieldhill Platoon 18,24,80,103,*143*,156,207
Shot guns 10,11,12,17,58,60,107
Signalling 102,230-231
Slamannan 4,*155*,206,*207,209*

Slamannan Miners' Welfare Hall 4,*6*,17,67, 72,128,133,207
Slamannan Platoon 4,*7*,15,17,18,30,31,32, 34,37,*60*,61,67,74,76,80,81,127,128,130,141, *148*,156,164,190-*191*,198,207,216-217,219
Slamannan Road, Falkirk *203*
Smith gun 57,156-*158*,*157*,203,207, *209*
Smith & Wellstood platoon 67,*72*,82, 120-122,*121*
Spigot mortar 57,153-156,*154*
Sports days 19,129
Stand down 233-240
Station Hotel, Larbert *120*
Stein, Alan 4,6,7,235,244
Sten sub-machine gun 57,145-147,*146*,*148*
Stenhousemuir Platoon 9,40,151,181-182
Stenhousemuir Police Station 3,67
Sticky bomb 136-137
Stirling Castle 147,161,169,187
Stirling County Constabulary see police
Stop line 195-197
Sword 12

Tanks 136,137,138,155,158,178,202-203
Thief's Road, Bo'ness 86
Thomson, Rev JJ *4*,8,9,25,241,244
Three Bridges, Camelon 87,111,144,205,*207*
Thunderflashes 162,186,192
Tommy gun 57,140,143,144,*145*

Torphichen Bridge 133
Torwood 11,28,*29*,131,136,161,176
Transport 5,76,77,91-101,113,133,192, 218-230,*224*
Truncheon 57,153

Umpire *181*,186,187,188
Uniform 9,16,21-26,233

Vickers machine gun 11,140,142

Walter Alexander's Platoon 25,37,76,92,192, 223-225
Walton, Bo'ness 39
Water supply 101
Weapon pit 156
Weedingshall House 131
Weekend camps 175-177
West Lothian Battalion 9,14,32,38,61,63, 69,91,162
Westerglen BBC transmitter station 15, *103*-104,*150*
Westquarter Valley 206
Westquarter Works 124
Windsor Road, Falkirk 202,*205*
Women auxiliaries 230
Woodend Farm, Falkirk 185,201

Zetland Park, Grangemouth 13,*14*

Abbreviations

A & SH	Argyll & Sutherland Highlanders	NCO	Non-commissioned Officer
AA	anti-aircraft	NFS	National Fire Service
ARP	Air Raid Precautions	OP	observation post
BAR	Browning Automatic Rifle	OSB	ordnance smooth-bore
Bn	battalion	PIAT	Projector infantry anti-tank
CO	commanding officer	POW	prisoner of war
Coy	Company	PSI	permanent staff instructor
CSM	company sergeant major	RAF	Royal Air Force
GHQ	General Headquarters	RASC	Royal Army Service Corps
HE	high explosive	RNA	Royal Navy Auxiliary
HG	Home Guard	RSNI	Royal Scottish National Institute
HLI	Highland Light Infantry	SAA	small arms ammunition
HQ	headquarters	SAS	Special Air Service
ICI	Imperial Chemical Industries	SEC	Scottish Enamelling Company
ID cards	identity cards	SIP	Self Igniting Phosphorus [grenade]
IO	intelligence officer	Stg	Stirlingshire
LCV	load carrying vehicle	TA	Territorial Army
LDV	Local Defence Volunteers	VP	vulnerable point
LMS	London & Midland ScottishRailways	WL	West Lothian
LO	liaison officer		

FALKIRK LOCAL HISTORY SOCIETY

Falkirk Local History Society was formed in 1981 to provide a forum for those interested in the history of east Stirlingshire, that is the present Falkirk Council area. There are now over 200 members involved a wide range of activities including regular meetings, research and publication, guided walks in the Falkirk area, field trips, talks to interested groups and heritage related campaigns.

The meetings are held on the third Wednesday of each month from September to May at 7.30pm in the hall of Falkirk Old and St Modan's Parish Church in the town centre. Visitors are very welcome. During the Summer there are a series of guided historical walks within the Falkirk area.

The Society publishes a regular Journal called *Calatria* containing articles on the history of the area. Each issue is over 100 pages with maps, photographs and drawings. The next issue, number 25 will be published in early 2009. The Society's website was set up in 2006 and contains many illustrated articles on the Falkirk area as well as many photographs. You can find it at www.falkirklocalhistorysociety.co.uk

Anyone interested in further information should contact Ian Scott on 01324 627692 or email him at ianqscott@blueyonder.co.uk